UITGAVEN VAN HET
NEDERLANDS INSTITUUT VOOR HET NABIJE OOSTEN TE LEIDEN

voorheen Publications de l'Institut historique-archéologique néerlandais de Stamboul
sous la direction de
J.G. DERCKSEN, J.J. ROODENBERG, K. van der TOORN et K.R. VEENHOF

CVIII

THE RULING FAMILY OF UR III UMMA

A Prosopographical Analysis of an Elite Family in Southern Iraq 4000 Years Ago

THE RULING FAMILY OF UR III UMMA

A Prosopographical Analysis of an Elite Family in Southern Iraq 4000 Years Ago

by

Jacob L. DAHL

NEDERLANDS INSTITUUT VOOR HET NABIJE OOSTEN
2007

Nederlands Instituut voor het Nabije Oosten
Witte Singel 25
Postbus 9515
2300 RA Leiden, Nederland
ninopublications@let.leidenuniv.nl
www.nino-leiden.nl

Jacob L. Dahl

The Ruling Family of Ur III Umma: A Prosopographical Analysis of an Elite Family in Southern Iraq 4000 Years Ago
Uitgave: Nederlands Instituut voor het Nabije Oosten
(*voorheen* Uitgave van het Nederlands Historisch-Archeologisch Instituut te Istanbul. ISSN 0926-9568;108)

ISBN 90-6258-319-9

Printed in Belgium

Genesis of a work:
1. Draw strictly from nature, possibly using a telescope.
2. Turn No. 1 upside down and emphasize the main lines according to your feeling.
3. Return the drawing paper to its initial position and bring 1 = nature and 2 = picture into harmony.

Paul Klee, 1908

PREFACE

This book is the result of a long process, stretching not only over many years but also across several borders. My work on the ruling elite of the ancient city of Umma began with my MA studies in Denmark, continued throughout my doctoral years in the USA, and has finally come to a sort of conclusion with the publication of this revised version of my PhD dissertation. In the last three years the manuscript and indeed the work has traveled with me to France, and most recently to Germany.

As is presumably often the case, both student and advisor have certain expectations of a PhD dissertation: these do not always conform to what is acceptable for the later publication. In the course of editing I have removed about a third of my original manuscript which dealt exclusively with the reading and understanding of Neo-Sumerian administrative documents. This chapter will appear in a revised form as the introduction to an edition of ca. 250 Ur III texts I am currently preparing for publication. I have not systematically incorporated all the material that has been made available since the conclusion of my dissertation (May 2003) and the final editing of this book (August 2006 – January 2007), many unpublished texts which have since been published were made available to me through the CDLI before the conclusion of my dissertation in 2003. I have collated substantial numbers of texts during the last three years, in most cases verifying my suspicions as to the actual content of the tablets. As a result most arguments in this book are based on a range of evidence rather than just single texts.

I would like to thank the following persons for their direct or indirect help in producing this book (in alphabetical order): Bendt Alster, Elizabeth Carter, Sasha M. Dahl, Peter Damerow, Lindy Divarci, Robert K. Englund, Cale Johnson, Natasha Koslova, Bertrand Lafont, Remco de Maajer, Rudi Mayr, Manuel Molina, Jürgen Renn, Marcel Sigrist, Nicolas Vanderroost, and Magnus Widell.

I would furthermore like to thank the Danish Research Academy, Forskerakademiet (now Forskeruddannelsesrådet), for their financial support. In equal measures I would like to thank the University of California, Office of the President, for awarding me the Chancellors Dissertation-Year Fellowship.

Finally, it is necessary for me to mention that this study would not have been possible without the framework of the Cuneiform Digital Library Initiative (CDLI), and without the support of the Max Planck Institute for the History of Science, Berlin. All the associates of the CDLI who have contributed over the years with data and work shall here be cordially thanked.

Berlin, January 2007.

TABLE OF CONTENTS

LIST OF FIGURES

ABBREVIATIONS

A list of the text identifications used in this book can be found online at the CDLI project at: <http://cdli.ucla.edu/wiki/index.php/abbreviations_for_Assyriology>.

This book is appended with a list of cited texts. As far as it has been deemed necessary museum numbers have been added to the text IDs for clarification. The following additional abbreviations are used in this study:

AbZ	R. Borger, *Assyrisch-babylonische Zeichenliste* (= AOAT 33-33A; Neukirchen-Vluyn 1981)
AhW	W. von Soden, *Akkadisches Handwörterbuch* (Wiesbaden 1959 - 1981)
CAD	*The Assyrian Dictionary of the University of Chicago* (Chicago 1956 ff.)
CDLI	Cuneiform Digital Library Initiative (joint project of the University of California, Los Angeles, and the Max Planck Institute for the History of Science, Berlin, see http://cdli.ucla.edu)
Ellermeier	F. Ellermeier, *Sumerisches Glossar 1/1/1-2* (Nörten-Hardenberg 1979-1980)
Lagaš I	First dynasty of Lagaš (pre-Sargonic Lagash)
Lagaš II	Second Dynasty of Lagaš (the dynasty of Gudea, also called the dynasty of Ur-Ba'u)
RAI	Rencontre Assyriologique Internationale
SKL	Sumerian King-List
USKL	Ur III recension of the Sumerian King-List
Ur III	Third Dynasty of Ur

CONVENTIONS

Dates, mostly the terminal date of an administrative document, are given in the following format: 1) abbreviated ruler-name (Š = Šulgi, AS = Amar-Suen, ŠS = Šū-Suen, IS = Ibbi-Suen) followed by 2) a year-count (in Arabic numbers), 3) the month number (in lower-case Roman numerals) and 4) the day number (in Arabic numbers).

Examples:

AS 5 v 12	= Amar-Suen, year 5, month 5, day 12.
ŠS 9	= Šū-Suen, year 9, no month or day information.
X iv	= Unknown ruler, month 6.

Question marks and comments are added when necessary.

Transliterations follow AbZ, and Ellermeier. Akkadian and Sumerian is transliterated with the same font and type. Signs with unknown readings are transliterated in capitals. The sign-name is given in parenthesis when a new reading is proposed. Index numbers are always given with numerals. Broken signs are indicated with half-brackets. Breaks are indicated by square brackets: square brackets are never placed inside a sign. If it is useful to indicate in the transliteration which part of a sign is broken this is done in the notes to the texts. Standard Assyriological fonts are used in both transliterations and transcriptions. However, sade (ṣ), tet (ṭ), and nasalized g (ŋ) are not rendered in the transliterations, for example. the sign *ze*$_2$ is presumably to be read *ṣe*, *ga*$_2$ is always used for *ŋa*, etc.

All names are transcribed in this book. Akkadian and Sumerian names are transcribed with the same font and type. Names are capitalized in the transcriptions but not in the transliterations. Akkadian names have been transcribed as closely as possible to the standard conventions of Akkadian (see, for example, Soden 1952: 8–9 (§6c–d)). Sumerian names are transcribed in a reader-friendly way that does not attempt to render any phonetic qualities of the names. All personal names presumably had a meaning to their owners, whether we understand it or not. The system of transcribing names in this book aims at rendering these in a way that illustrates the meaning of the name, however, I will not attempt to translate any names, many of which were abbreviated. The name *lu*$_2$*-kal-la* has thus been transcribed Lu-kala, since the double writing of the final "l" is understood as a result of scribal conventions rather than expressing the phonetic values of the signs. *ur-e*$_{11}$*-e* has been transcribed Ur-E'e, since E'e is a divine name (a god in the local pantheon of Umma). The apostrophe does not relate to pronunciation, it is added only to indicate that the name is spelled with two signs, each transliterated "e". *lugal-e*$_2$*-mah-e* is transcribed as Lugal-Emah(e), since Emah is a proper noun (the main temple of Šara in Umma), and since the name apparently can be written with or without the final "e". *šeš-kal-la* has been transcribed Šeš-kala, since this name consists of a noun and a nominalized verb. A name such as gu-du-du has simply been transcribed Gududu, since we are unable to isolate the meaning carrying components of such names. Names which unknown reading have not been transcribed. Examples are the city of KI.AN^{ki} and the personal name GIRI$_3$.NI, etc. First references to these names are always accompanied by notes to the orthography and if possible comments about the probable reading.

Sumerian words have been translated throughout this study, whenever possible . The Sumerian form, and any necessary discussion, is to be found either in the notes or between brackets in the main text (not in repeated instances). Certain words such as *sukkalmah* (*sukkal-mah*, a high-ranking title in the imperial administration), or *nam-šatam* (*ša$_3$-tam*, a certain administrative function discussed throughout this study) have been left untranslated, but pseudo-transcribed, for the sake of convention.

Numerical notations are transliterated using current CDLI standards (digits or fractions followed by a qualifier between brackets).

When texts or text excerpts are transliterated in the footnotes, they are as a rule given in a running format, using / as a line separator, and // as a surface separator (for example, obverse line 1 / obverse line 2 // reverse line 1 / reverse line 2 // seal line 1, etc.). Note that if the full text is quoted, line IDs are omitted. Texts transliterated in the main text follow standards in Assyriology. Whenever possiblle all text samples have been translated into English.

Sumerian and Akkadian words and sentences within the running text have been italizised to facilitate reading.

CHAPTER 1. INTRODUCTION

Tens of thousands of administrative documents have survived from the time of the Third Dynasty of Ur (ca. 2112-2004 BC), making it one of the best documented periods in the early history of man. In brief, the Ur III empire underwent four stages of development: consolidation, expansion, stability, and decline. During the consolidation period, the local ruler of Ur managed to unite the city-states of Sumer and to conquer the Akkadian area. Subsequently, during the expansion period, the king was able, by way of political alliances and military raids, to subjugate neighboring areas to the east and northeast. The empire flourished for a few years, during which the administrative machinery produced thousands and thousands of records. Shortly after the empire had reached its zenith, it collapsed, and, following a period of territorial losses, the capital city, Ur, was taken by invading troops from the neighboring, former vassal, Elam.[1]

In spite of the extraordinarily rich documentation describing in detail many aspects of the social history of the period, sources are not clear on the issue of succession. Consequently, it has been impossible to establish, beyond doubt, a genealogy of the royal family, the clan of Ur-Nammu. Succession within the elite families in the provincial centers such as Umma—the topic of the current study—is far better documented.

The aim of this study is to reconstruct the genealogy, and the line of succession for the important offices of Umma, using the administrative records. The majority of these offices were in the hands of one family, the so-called ruling family of Ur III Umma. This study therefore naturally focuses on the members of that family. The results of this study are then, in turn, used to propose a model for understanding other Ur III elite families, for which comparable rich data is lacking. In particular the question of royal succession during the Ur III period is investigated. The starting point of this study is the prevailing understanding in the field that restricted primogeniture was by far the most successful pattern of succession in ancient Mesopotamia.[2] Since this has never been systematically questioned it has become something of a dogma in the field. This study seeks to challenge that dogma.[3] Since the analysis presented here is the first detailed description of patterns of succession in

---

1 I divide the period as follows: The reign of Ur-Nammu and the first twenty years of Šulgi's rule until his deification are considered a period of consolidation. Šulgi's expansions, recorded in the year-dates from his twentieth till around his fortieth year, and the construction of the administrative center Drehem, characterize the expansion. The final years of Šulgi and the reign of Amar-Suen, with numerous administrative records, but fewer military achievements, were the apex of the Ur III Empire, and can be considered a period of stability. From the middle of Šū-Suen's reign and during the early years of Ibbi-Suen we find the first signs of weakness, while the last twenty years of Ibbi-Suen's reign are considered a period of decline.

2 See, for example, A. L. Oppenheim 1964: 77 and 79. See also D. Henige 1986, and in particular the section "Father-Son Successions" pp. 60-61, where the view that patrilineal succession was not particularly widespread in Mesopotamia is presented.

3 The only study which to my knowledge mentions the possibility of fratrilineal succession in non-royal

ancient Mesopotamia, references to previous studies of the same topic are therefore few.

Let us first turn to the issue of royal succession. The founder of the dynasty, Ur-Nammu, ruled for eighteen years, his son and successor Šulgi for forty-eight years; Šulgi was followed first by Amar-Suen who ruled nine years, then by Šū-Suen who likewise ruled nine years, and lastly by Ibbi-Suen who ruled twenty-four years. The latter three rulers were all, perhaps, sons of Šulgi.

According to the now contested middle chronology[4] the first year of Ur-Nammu fell around 2112 BC, and the last year of Ibbi-Suen around 2004 BC. In total the dynasty lasted only one hundred-and-eight years. The extent of overlap between the Ur III period and the preceding period, the Second Lagaš Dynasty (the dynasty of Ur-Baba), is unclear at best. The two dynasties are believed, however, to have overlapped considerably.[5] Chronological correlation between the Ur III period and the following Isin-Larsa period is, on the other hand, relatively clear: the Isin dynasty was founded by Išbi-Erra, a former ally of Ur, already in the eighth year of Ibbi-Suen.[6]

Early in the Ur III period, the formerly independent city-states of Sumer were subjugated and made provinces of the Ur III Empire. Military presence ensured permanent control over these areas. Some indication that supporters of the crown were awarded estates outside the old cities has come to light in recent years;[7] within the city proper, however, the local elite families remained the chief administrators.[8] The political center of the Ur III state was the city of Ur, presumably the main

---

circles during the Ur III period is P. Steinkeller 1987b: 73–115. Steinkeller did not discuss the sociographical implications of this, and the issue has remained almost entirely untouched. Since it has long been suggested that Amar-Suen and Šū-Suen were brothers following each other on the throne, some studies have described this as fratrilineal succession; however, there has never been any discussion of the consequences of having one system of succession for the royal family and another for the rest of society, if this was in fact the case. Edzard briefly mentioned but ultimately discarded the theories of fratrilineal succession in ancient Mesopotamia (see fn. 34 on page 27 in this study). That same sentiment was captured by D. Snell 1997: 20. See also N. Postgate 1992: 148 and 270, and N. Postgate 1995: 397: "...strict primogeniture is not universal: Sumerian rulers were sometimes succeeded by their brothers, and among sons it was not always the eldest."

4 J. Reade 2001: 1–29. See also P. Huber 1999/2000: 50–79.

5 See fn. 43 on p. 14.

6 D. Charpin 2004: 60.

7 New evidence suggests that Garšana, a location in Sumer, was indeed a (semi)-private estate (D. Owen 2001a).

8 We only know of one Ur III governor who was relocated, the governor of Assur, Zariqum. He is speculated to have been identical to Zariqum, the later governor of Susa. First discussed by W. Hallo in 1956 (W. Hallo 1956: 220–225.); for a more recent treatment, see B. Foster 1993: 28 and fn. 27, and P. Steinkeller 1987a: 32, citing the same literature as B. Foster. It is likely that the case of Zariqum was both unique and indicative of the state of affairs in the periphery, and that the ruling families of the old Sumerian cities, in most cases, were very capable of adapting to changes, and thus remained in office even during difficult times. The old elite family of Nippur may have been ousted by Amar-Suen as part of a succession-struggle during his reign; however, that family was perhaps reinstated by Šū-Suen, this was suggested already by W. Hallo 1972: 94.

residence of the court and a religious center as well, but Nippur retained a great deal of its former influence as the religious capital of Sumer and Akkad. During the reign of Šulgi an administrative center was constructed close to Nippur, known to us by its modern name Drehem, and its ancient name Puzriš-Dagan. It is uncertain whether there were more such administrative centers. The peripheral areas, which were conquered by the military, were subject to tribute, presumably organized through the military presence.[9] The core provinces contributed to the state through a system called "*bala*."[10] In addition to military control, the king of Ur spun a web of political alliances that covered the entire Syro-Mesopotamian area and reached well into Iran. Numerous references to the presence of foreign envoys in the Sumerian heartlands, coupled with the extensive use of dynastic or political marriages, suggest that a developed diplomatic machinery existed. The king of Ur also bestowed titles on his semi-independent vassals; as is not uncommon in history, such a title could later become the title of royalty after that vassal-state had regained its independence. Subsequently, the independent ruler of Susa, following the decline of Ur III, became know as the *sukkalmah*, whereas petty kings in northern Mesopotamia adopted the title *šakanakku*. It is important here to note that according to our understanding of the Ur III empire, the eastern provinces were under the control of the *sukkalmah* (*sukkal-mah*, sometimes referred to as the *grand vizir*), whereas northern Mesopotamia may have been under the control of the military, and subsequently the generals (*šagina*) of the Ur III empire.

The reconstruction of the social history of the Ur III period relies heavily on an analysis of the administrative documents. Historical inscriptions from the period contain very little useful information for a reconstruction of the organization and administration of the realm. The historical inscriptions are found on buildings (or rather on building materials such as bricks and door sockets, etc.), on commemorative objects (including stelae, statues, etc.), and on objects dedicated to the rulers, primarily seal inscriptions and miscellaneous cult objects.[11] The literary texts as well as the majority of the pseudo-historical inscriptions can only be used with great caution to investigate the social history of the third millennium BC due to their obvious political or literary biases.[12] The year names used by administrators to date the economic records, however, are a useful source for the

9 P. Steinkeller 1987a: 25–26.

10 Classically, *bala* is translated as a term of office, and this might also be an acceptable interpretation in this case. Each province was said to be in the period of the *bala* every year for a specific period of time (*ša$_3$ bala-a*). Presumably this meant being responsible for the maintenance of the collective fund of the state through deliveries to Drehem and other administrative centers for later redistribution. The periphery paid what was called *gun mada*, "tribute of the land," a kind of tribute or tax delivered by the military stationed there, undoubtedly calculated on a basis of how much they could collect from the land they controlled. See P. Steinkeller 1987a, which deals extensively with the system of redistribution and taxation in the periphery during Ur III.

11 For the historical inscriptions of the Ur III period, see D. Frayne 1997.

12 For the pseudo-historical inscriptions, or the intertextuality between historical inscriptions and the literary texts, see W. Hallo 1969: 117–122.

history of the period. The years were named according to important events, and these year formulae were used to date the administrative records. Early Assyriologists placed great hope in the Sumerian King List (SKL)—an Isin-Larsa pseudo-historical account of all previous kings of Sumer—as a source of the history of the Ancient Near East.[13] In later times scholars often discarded the text entirely, deeming it a fictitious political manifesto of the Isin rulers.[14] However, since the information given by the SKL regarding the last hundred years of the third millennium BC is basically correct, we must interrogate the sources available to the Isin scribe who composed this list.

The SKL recounts the Third Dynasty of Ur as follows:[15]

unug^{ki} ^{geš}tukul ba-an-sag$_3$	Uruk was slain with weapons,
nam-lugal-bi ⸢uri$_2$⸣ [ki-še$_3$] ba-DU	and its kingship was carried to Ur;
uri$_2$^{ki}-ma ur -[^{d}nammu] lugal	in Ur, Ur-Nammu was king,
mu 1(u) 8(diš) [i$_3$-ak]	(he) ruled 18 years.
^{d}šul-gi dumu ^{d}ur-nammu-ke$_4$	Šulgi, the son of Ur-Nammu,
mu 4(u) 8(diš) i$_3$-⸢ak⸣	ruled 48[16] years.
^{d}amar-^{d}suen dumu ^{d}šul-gi-ke$_4$	Amar-Suen the son of Šulgi,
mu 9(diš) i$_3$-ak	ruled nine years.
šu-^{d}suen dumu ^{d}amar-^{d}suen	Šū-Suen, the son of Amar-Suen,
mu 9(diš) i$_3$-ak	ruled nine years.
i-bi$_2$-^{d}suen dumu šu-^{d}suen-ke$_4$	Ibbi-Suen, the son of Šū-Suen,
mu 2(u) 4(diš) i$_3$-ak	ruled 24 years.
5(diš)[17] lugal	(They were) five kings
mu-bi 1(geš2) 4(u) 8(diš) ib$_2$-ak	who ruled 108 years.
uri$_2$^{ki}-ma ^{geš}tukul ba-an-sag$_3$	Ur was slain with weapons,
nam-lugal-bi i$_3$-si-in^{ki}-še$_3$ ba-DU	and its kingship was carried to Isin.
i$_3$-si-in^{ki}-na iš-bi-er$_3$-ra lugal	In Isin, Išbi-Erra was king.

The accuracy of this excerpt suggests that the Isin-scribe who wrote the SKL had access to lists

13 The 1939 edition by Th. Jacobsen remains the standard Assyriological work of reference (published as AS 11). Among later significant studies are C. Wilcke 1988: 113–140, and P. Michalowski 1983: 237–248. See F. Hrozny 1912: 1–20, for an introduction to the early debate on the use of the SKL. See also A. Schneider 1920: 3.

14 See, for example, P. Michalowski 1983: 237–248 and C. Wilcke 1989: 557–571.

15 Col. viii 7–23 following Th. Jacobsen 1939, and the addendum by C.-A. Vincente 1995: 234–270.

16 See C.-A. Vincente: 266.

17 See C.-A. Vincente: 266.

of year-formulae—some such lists have been recovered.[18]

It is likely that the author of the SKL, knowingly or unknowingly replaced the original Sumerian hereditary system of seniority and lateral succession with a system of primogeniture and lineal succession that the rulers of his own time and culture aimed at implementing, resulting in a simple, repetitive, pattern, PN son of PN son of PN, in SKL.[19] This interpretation is supported by the fact that the recently recovered Ur III recension of the SKL, the USKL,[20] is almost entirely free of kinship terminology (see pp. 9–10 below).

Some historical as well as quasi-historical sources are available for the study of the ruling family of Ur, but no sources other than the administrative corpus exist that document the lives, careers and offices of the members of the rural elite.

The relations between provincial elite families and the royal clan are poorly understood. The original thesis of this study, that the ruling family in Umma imitated the royal family, and that its members perhaps belonged to an old elite family centered for generations at Umma, is only partly supported by the data. Certain features of the succession to the highest offices of the Umma administration suggest an entirely different scenario, namely one in which Šulgi may have instrumented a "take-over" by a powerful clan of imperial administrators in his thirty-third year, or a favored group from within Umma, other than the ruling elite family known from the later sources.

In the following we shall first look more generally at systems of succession, followed by a discussion of the royal family of Ur, before we begin our investigation of the ruling family of Umma.

---

18 MS 1915, a list of year names, starts with Amar-Suen's first year and lists in an abbreviated form the next eight years. Then follows Šu-Suen's nine year names, and finally Ibbi-Suen's first three years. The forms of the year names used in this text seem to be the most widely used abbreviation found in the daily administrative records. It is thus very different in form and scope from the SKL. If MS 1915 is from Umma, it is almost ominous to see this text ending with Ibbi-Suen year 3, knowing that Umma records ceased to be written some time the following year. MS 1915 is being published by the author. Perhaps the commemorative stelae preserved at Nippur, copied and compiled into literary compositions, served as the sources for the SKL (W. Hallo 1969: 118ff.). See also P. Michalowski 1975: 716.

19 For a critique of the historicity of the SKL, see C. Wilcke 1971/75: 180 and fn. 66. See also E. Sollberger 1954–1956: 10–48.

20 Steinkeller 2003.

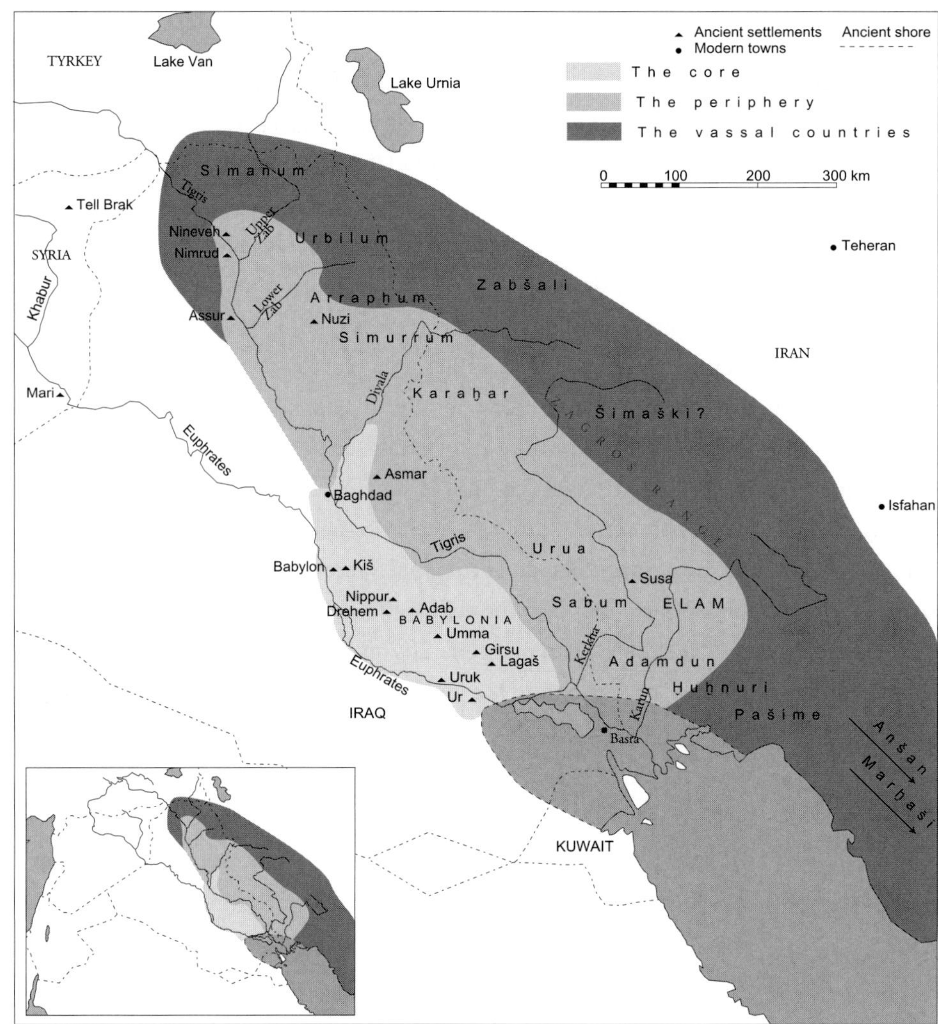

Figure 1: The extent of the Ur III Empire (based in part on P. Steinkeller 1987: 38 figure 6)

CHAPTER 2. PATTERNS OF SUCCESSSION

Mesopotamian systems of succession have never been dealt with systematically. It has become a dogmatic statement that strictly enforced patrilineal primogeniture was the prevailing Mesopotamian system of succession. This is apparent in the way in which the succession pattern described in the Sumerian King List has been readily adopted by Assyriologists. The obvious problem, posed by the fact that we have no written evidence of any rule of succession formulated by the ancients, paired with the fact that, for example, the sequence of the Ur III rulers cannot easily be established using the extant administrative records, should rouse our attention. As soon as an investigation concerning succession patterns is broadened to cover not only the royal family of Ur III, it becomes apparent that no obvious pattern exists. In this chapter, I will present a theory of succession applicable for the ruling family of Ur as well as for the provincial elite family in Umma, which presumably imitated the royal court. As an excursus, a study of the royal family of Saudi Arabia has been appended to this study.

In hereditary succession, power passes from one ruler to another according to a specific set of rules within the social group. Hereditary succession can be lineal or non-lineal, that is, it can pass from generation to generation or it can stay within the same generation and skip generations more or less randomly.[21] Lineal succession can be either matrilineal or patrilineal. In a matrilineal system, it is not necessarily the women that rule; rather, power passes through the matrilineal line. Patrilineal succession, which is by far the most common system, can find its expression either in primogeniture or seniority. Primogeniture is when the oldest son, by virtue of being the oldest son, succeeds his father. Seniority on the other hand is a system in which senior (male) members of the ruling clan (group) feel that they have a place in the line of succession. Whether they eventually will be asked to rule is another issue. Seniority is not always equal to lateral succession, since the latter implies that succession will stay within one generation as long as possible, whereas seniority only implies that the oldest descendant has a quasi-legal claim to succession.

If a ruler nominates an heir, he naturally propagates rivals as well. This problem is inherent in any system of succession and can be observed in most cultures.[22] There have been as many attempts to deal with this schism as there have been cultures adhering to hereditary succession. How can the ruler secure succession if he cannot trust his nominated successor?

The aging ruler can approach this problem from three angles. He can choose to wait and nominate his heir at the last minute, or even make it a posthumous decision, that is, to have the decision sealed until his death. Delayed appointment has the disadvantage of complicating succession, since the claim of the heir is more likely to be contested, and he lacks the relations that years as "heir apparent"

---

21 Lineal succession is by far the most successful of the two, securing a smooth transfer of power.

22 The following owes much to theoretical work of R. Burling 1974.

would secure.[23] Another possibility is to indoctrinate the offspring to such a degree that they become completely enervated—this method is also referred to as "caging the heirs"; the disadvantages of this system are obvious: it leaves the successor at the whim of courtiers and palace staff. Yet another option is to transfer the responsibilities for the election of the heir to either a particular group within the ruling house or a group outside of the ruling family. Delegating power to groups other than the innermost circles of the ruling family is, of course, very dangerous, since it easily becomes a catalyst for usurpation.[24] As we shall see below, at each succession power is necessarily delegated away from the ruler and those closest to him.

Clearly, fraternal rivalries have the strength to promote "succession of the fittest" (J. Kechichian 2001: 11), whereas strictly enforced primogeniture runs danger of bringing utterly incompetent persons to the throne. The designated heir himself has many choices to make before he can sit calmly on the throne. Will he have to kill all his brothers, or can he get around this quandary by confining them to life imprisonment? Can his brothers keep their positions in the hierarchy? Can they be bypassed in succession? Even more distant relatives such as uncles, cousins, and widows can become powerful adversaries that have to be reckoned with when securing succession.[25]

It is likely that the empire-builder, the strong man who accumulates almost divine status by virtue of his own dynamism on the battle field and at court can enforce his choice for succession by means of his charisma alone, and that his wishes will be adhered to for some time after his death. Such powers are not likely to be inherited, however, and the subsequent generations will have to deal with the problems of succession on their own.[26]

---

23 The choice of an heir could be issued as a will, sealed and only opened after the death of the ruler. In the Saudi system where seniority prevails, the exact age of a contestant for the throne is often surrounded with secrecy.

24 Hobbes discussed this problem in his typology of the different forms of common-wealth—the term Hobbes used for a society. Hobbes claimed that the ruler who did not control succession was not sovereign, but that the person or institution who controlled succession was also the real sovereign of that society. (See Th. Hobbes 1957: 125–129).

25 Although men have restricted the privileges of rulership for themselves in the majority of cultures, women have sometimes been able to rule through their juvenile sons, essentially bidding for power by promoting their own offspring.

26 M. Weber wrote extensively on the topic of charisma and control (see M. Weber 1968 for an introduction to Weber's writings on the topic). Weber wrote much less on succession, and remarkably little on hereditary succession; see pp. 54–57 in M. Weber 1968 (= M. Weber, "The Routinization of Charisma" from *Theory of Social and Economic Organization*), where his views are summarized. Following Weber, it would be possible to argue that the nature of the rule of Šulgi or even that of the first king of Saudi Arabia, Ibn Saud, was neither charismatic nor bureaucratic, since both rulers forged their "empires" from a tribal (or in the case of Ur III, clan-like) composition. However, it is precisely the fact that they were able to rise above petty tribal issues and create a social unit larger than their own tribe or clan, by means of their own personality and virility, that is in good agreement with the system of Weber. M. Weber described charisma as "a certain quality of an individual

Since no Mesopotamian text concerning rules of succession has ever been recovered,[27] and whereas it only appears, although this has never been proven, as if primogeniture was the rule, I suggest that the ancient Mesopotamian ruling families adhered to a system of seniority when dealing with succession.[28]

It is very likely that the ruler and his clan would project back in time the system of succession they favored in order to add legitimacy to their claim to the throne. Thus the SKL may be nothing more than a piece of political rhetoric; although fraternal succession is not altogether eliminated from this text, it tends to suggest an eternity of patrilineal succession.[29]

It is rewarding, in this regard, to consult the recently discovered Ur III recension of SKL (USKL), which is almost entirely free of kinship terminology. The USKL, however, does not record the familial

---

personality by virtue of which he is set apart from ordinary men and treated as endowed with supernatural, superhuman, or at least specifically exceptional powers or qualities." (p. 48 in M. Weber 1968, originally from p. 329 of M. Weber, *Theory of Social and Economic Organization*). The "routinization" of charisma, and the subsequent vesting of power in the head of the clan rather than in a single charismatic person as described by Weber, see, e.g., p. 50 and pp. 194–197 in M. Weber 1968, applies to our data-set as well. There is nothing to suggest that the Ur III state ever evolved into a true bureaucratic state, as has been formulated by Weber (pp. 66–69 in M. Weber 1968). For more on this particular problem, see Chapter 4 below. See also p. 11 in J. Kechichian 2001, and R. Burling 1974: 87–88.

27 The ancient Indian Hindu text *Arthashastra* (attributed to the fourth century BC, although the oldest extant copy dates to c. 150 AD) can be viewed as such a theoretic work, although it is mostly concerned with the techniques of rulership, and less with the problems of succession. Much later are Machiavelli's *The Prince*, and *Discourses*, both devoted primarily to instructing a ruler in the techniques of rulership, and only to a lesser degree with succession. Machiavelli pointed out in great detail the dangers of hereditary succession and the possibility of bringing an incompetent heir to the throne.

28 P. Moorey, while working on the Kish excavation reports (P. Moorey 1978: 165), suggested, in line with I. Gelb 1960: 265–67, that regional differences between the Akkadian North and the Sumerian South existed. Moorey went further than Gelb and suggested that the "the precocious emergence there [in the North] of a powerful secular kingship may have derived more immediately from the exploitation of a tribal system by singularly forceful individuals in the ruling family or group; a political pattern familiar in more recent Arab history." P. Steinkeller 1993: 121, and fn. 37, later quoted P. Moorey, although he disagreed with Moorey's statement on the "immediate" tribal background of the rulers of Kish, and suggested a city-based oligarchy as the source of Kishite kingship.

29 Compare with J. Le Patourel 1971: 225–250, and in particular 226, and fn. 1, where Le Patourel discusses a quote from Orderic (*Ecclesiatical History*, iii. 242.), which has been taken as a proof of the existence of primogeniture at the time of William, Duke of Normandy. Le Patourel argues "that Orderic is very apt to explain events of the eleventh century according to ideas of the twelfth, particularly in matters of inheritance." See also p. 230, J. Le Patourel suggests that the Norman Duke was not bound by any tradition, or popular "law of inheritance," and further, that it is very difficult, due to the absence of written contemporary sources to find any such rules. See, however, R. H. C. Davis 1980: 597–606, especially p. 599 for an assessment that Orderic's account of the same events can actually be used to unravel the facts.

relations of the rulers of the Third Dynasty of Ur, and the hereditary pattern of that dynasty remains debated: some argue that succession was strictly patrilineal,[30] as recorded in the SKL, and others that fratrilineal succession prevailed.[31]

The debate has circled around the following three questions: 1) Were Utu-hegal and Ur-Nammu brothers? 2) Was Abī-simtī the wife of Šulgi or Amar-Suen? 3) Who was the father of Ibbi-Sin? The most appropriate answers seem at present to be:

1. Only one historical inscription (= Utu-hegal 6) hints at the familial relationship of Utu-hegal (founder and sole member of the Fourth Dynasty of Uruk), and Ur-Nammu (founder of the third Ur Dynasty). C. Wilcke (1974: 180 and fn. 67) argued for a reconstruction of the last line of that text to read: ⌜*šeš*⌝*-[a-ne$_2$]*, indicating that Utu-hegal and Ur-Nammu were brothers. The fact that Ur-Nammu was Utu-hegal's army-commander (*šagina*) stationed in Ur does not prove their familial relationship, since later Ur III generals were recruited from both within the royal family and from among important allies.

2. No conclusive evidence exists favoring either Šulgi or Amar-Suen as the husband of Abī-simtī. She is called queen (*nin*) in a text dating to the final year of the reign of Amar-Suen (UTI 3, 2003 [AS 9]) as well as in texts from the reign of Šū-Suen (e.g., MVN 16, 713 [ŠS 4], and MVN 16, 916 [ŠS 3]), whereas she is not mentioned during Šulgi's reign. Abī-simtī is not the only person with the title "queen" during Šū-Suen's reign, she is mentioned together with Kubatum (the wife of Šū-Suen) in two texts (MVN 9, 165 [ŠS 5], and MVN 16, 960 [ŠS 3]), in which both women are called "queen" (*nin*). However "queen" (*nin*) is perhaps used as an honorary title: "queen-dowager," when referring to Abī-simtī. It is gratifying to note that P. Michalowski suggested a somewhat similar scenario in a recent article (Michalowski 2004: 232). She is mentioned without title during the reign of Amar-Suen, save for the single text cited above. D. Frayne 1997: 285–286 claimed that Abī-simtī was the wife of Amar-Suen, based in part on an Old Babylonian copy of the seal of Babati the brother of Abī-simtī (= RIME 3/2.1.4.33). The original Ur III inscription of that same seal (= RIME 3/2.1.4.32) can be used only to prove that Abī-simtī was the mother of Šū-Suen (see the seal rolled on PDT 2, 1200 [ŠS 7/i–7/iii] which fills the lacuna in the first line of RIME 3/2.1.4.32). The Old Babylonian copy, which substitutes mother (*ama*) with wife (*dam*), also names Šū-Suen as the benefactor of the dedication. Thus the original Ur III inscription can not be used to determine whose wife she was. Recently, D. Owen published a text with the interesting personal name Šū-Suen-walid-Šulgi ("Šū-Suen born of Šulgi"), which he argues might be the full name of Šū-Suen (D. Owen 2001b)). No other contemporary evidence links Šū-Suen with either Šulgi or Amar-Suen (the name of the son of Šulgi in the seal inscription on BRM 3, 52 reads *šu-^{d}EN.[...]*, not necessarily Šū-Suen, but just as likely Šū-Enlil, who was another known son of Šulgi).[32] Abī-simtī may still have been Šulgi's wife

30 See, most recently, J. Boese and W. Sallaberger 1996, with literature.

31 See, most recently, D. Owen 2001b. This viewpoint ultimately dates back to A. Falkenstein (1947): 45. See D. Frayne 1997: 285–286 for references to the debate.

32 See J. Boese and W. Sallaberger 1996: 36–37.

but perhaps not the mother of Amar-Suen.

3. Nothing is known about the father of Ibbi-Suen.

Although treaties from first millennium BC Mesopotamia concerning succession exist (e.g., the so-called Vassal Treaties of Esarhaddon[33]), nowhere is it stated that succession was limited to the oldest son, rather the choice of an heir seems to have been somewhat ad hoc. The pattern of succession in the dynasty immediately prior to that of Ur III, the Second Dynasty of Lagaš, is very difficult to understand, and its use as a comparative source must be excluded.[34] The dynasties following the fall of Ur III all seem to favor lineal succession with restricted primogeniture, which might be a peculiarity adopted from the specific Amorite tribe making up the ruling elites of those dynasties. However, throughout the third millennium, the brothers of the ruler seem to have had a bid at succession, verifying my suspicion that the prevailing system of succession indeed can be classified as seniority.[35]

The problem of any prosopographical analysis rests on the degree to which we trust the data contained in the sources. Whereas early Assyriological scholarship readily accepted any information written on a cuneiform tablet, modern studies have, advisedly, improved their historiography and learned the dangers of relying on court poetry as sources of history. Whether the administrative records are truly reliable historical documents seems to be the present-day controversy within Assyriology.

---

33 See S. Parpola and K. Watanabe 1988, with publication history. See M. Liverani 1995: 57-62, for an alternate view on the nature and purpose of the treaties; the author suggested that the main purpose of the treaties was to serve as a loyalty oath of the Median mercenaries at the court of Essarhaddon. The Assyrian title for an heir to the throne was *mār šār rabû ša bit redūti*, which translates as "the great son of the king, the one of the house of succession."

34 Lateral succession might also have preveiled in Girsu during the days of the second Lagaš Dynasty; see especially J. Renger 1976: 367–369, and in particular fn. 17, with reference to D. Edzard 1960: 255 and fn. 107. Edzard believed fraternal succession to be subordinated primogeniture, however, without eliminating an element of fraternal succession ("Fratriarchat") from the history of Sumerian hereditary systems altogether.

35 The founder of the the Old Akkadian Empire, Sargon, was succeeded by two sons; first Rimuš, then Maništusu. It is possible that the two struggled against each other for the throne (see Aa. Westenholz 1999: 41). Eventually, Maništusu was able to name his own son as successor (i.e. favor his own line), and lineal succession prevailed in the last generations of the Old Akkadian Empire (note that the SKL agrees on this point, column 6, lines 39–41; ma-ni-iš-ti-iš-šu / šeš gal ri$_2$-mu-⌜<<uš>>⌝-uš / dumu šar-ru-ki-in, "Maništusu, big-brother of Rimuš, son of Sargon"). The predominant succession pattern in Old Sumerian Lagaš was not primogeniture, but rather, again, seniority. Ur-Nanše, the founder of the First Dynasty of Lagash was followed by his son Akurgal, who again was followed by his son, Eanatum, who was succeeded by his own brother, En-anatum (I). En-anatum (I) was followed by a son, En-metena, who in turn was followed by a son, En-anatum (II). The next ruler, En-entarzid, was perhaps a brother of En-anatum (II). The dynasty ended with En-entarzid; his successor, Lugalanda, was presumably not related to Ur-Nanše (see J. Bauer 1998 for the most recent treatment of Old Sumerian history). For the few pre-Lagash I examples of fraternal succession known to us see D. Edzard 1960: 255 and fn. 107; these are in Kiš: Melamkiši and BAR-SAL-NUN-NA, and in Ur: A'annepada and Meskianganunna.

Are we capable of uncovering fictitious transactions in the documents? Can we trust our data?

It seems clear that the basic prosopographical information such as familial relationships as expressed in the seal-inscriptions can be trusted.[36] The perception that the term *dumu* (Sumerian for child, but in an Ur III context almost exclusively meaning son) can refer to a business associate is borrowed from later Assyrian and Babylonian sources,[37] whereas all third millennium BC Sumerian sources point to this being a genealogical term for son. Although adhering to such basic rules, Ur III prosopography remains complex due to the restricted information provided by the sources. Only the information necessary for the identification of a person was ever recorded in the administrative documents of the Ur III bureaucracy. It is therefore always necessary to keep the familial as well as the official standing of any person in sight when disentangling the many references to his activities. The use of personal names was not restricted on the basis of social standing or grouping—static social groups based on ethnicity or self-perceived or imposed tribal/clan affiliation, such as those known from, for example, India, did not exist as far as we can see in late third millennium BC Mesopotamia. Obviously Akkadian persons bore Akkadian names, and so forth, but this was apparently without relevance for their hierarchical standing. Some personal names were used very frequently, requiring increased use of titles and familial affiliation as identifiers in the administrative documents. When fewer people had the same name, and no two persons with the same name were active at the same administrative level, titles and patronymics were rarely used. This enigma permeates the identifications suggested below in Chapter 4. Certain particularly instructive examples are given there (e.g., Lu-kala the shepherd vs. Lu-kala the chief household administrator of the governor pp. 103 ff.).

36 Basic familial relations frequently expressed in the Ur III administrative record are *dumu* ("son," although *dumu* is gender neutral and has the meaning "child," it is in Ur III administrative documents normally contrasted to *dumu munus* "female child"), *šeš* ("brother"), *nin*$_9$ ("sister"), *ama* ("mother"), and *dumu munus* ("daughter"). Of these only the first two are attested with very high frequency. Father (*ad-da*, *ab-ba*, a or *a-a*, presumably vocalized */aya/*) was rarely used to describe a familial relation, as was the case with the more exotic terms such as *e-gi*$_4$*-a*, "daughter in law," etc.

37 M. Larsen 1976: 92–102, seems to be of the opinion that familial affiliation was of paramount importance to the Old Assyrian trading companies, allowing for the interpretation of kinship terms as both familial and official.

CHAPTER 3. THE HOUSE OF UR-NAMMU

The Ur III dynasty lasted three, perhaps four, generations, with five rulers: Ur-Nammu and his son Šulgi belonged to the first and second generation, respectively. In this study it is hypothesized that the remaining three rulers all belonged to the same generation. These three sons of Šulgi were Amar-Suen, Šū-Suen, and Ibbi-Suen.[38]

3.1. Ur-Nammu

Ur-Nammu,[39] founder of the Ur III dynasty, is little known since few administrative documents from his time have survived. The primary sources for his reign are so scarce that even the sequence of his year-dates remains to be finalized.[40] According to the Sumerian King List, Ur-Nammu reigned 18 years. Six years are still unaccounted for in the administrative record, and it remains impossible to place two known year-formulae within the sequence. The year-name formulae record peaceful activities only, such as the digging of canals.

Supported by both indirect as well as direct evidence, Ur-Nammu is considered a member of the ruling family of Uruk. This seems confirmed by the fact that Ur-Nammu served as a commander in the Urukite army. The exact nature of his familial ties with the ruling family of Uruk, and its paterfamilias, Utu-hegal, is unfortunately uncertain.[41] Ur-Nammu brought with him the royal ideology of the kings of Uruk when he founded his dynasty in Ur. The rulers of Ur would claim to have roles in

---

38 Whereas it is likely that Amar-Suen and Šū-Suen were brothers, we have no contemporary information about the ancestry of Ibbi-Suen. The almost purely hypothetical statement that Ibbi-Suen too was a son of Šulgi is spun on a theoretical framework generated, in part, from anthropological and sociological evidence, and supported by comparative evidence from the Ur III provincial elite families (described below). New evidence from the Garšana archive (D. Owen 2001a) seems to prove this theory.

39 For the reading of the theophoric element of Ur-Nammu's name see D. Frayne 1997: 9, with references to the literature suggesting a reading *namma* instead of *nammu*. See also E. Flückiger-Hawker 1999: 8–9, for a recent discussion of the reading *namma*. However, following D. Frayne 1997, *nammu* is retained in this study for the sake of convention.

40 See D. Frayne 1997: 9.

41 One fragmentary historical inscription records the familial relationship between Utu-hegal and Ur-Nammu: that text, Utu-hegal 6, can be used as evidence that the two were brothers (see C. Wilcke 1971/75: 180 and fn. 67). However, M. Sigrist 1992: 4 suggests that Ur-Nammu was the son of Utu-hegal of Uruk. Although several Ur III princes may have served in the army as military commanders (*šagina*), this cannot be documented for more than a few. The kings for whom evidence is at hand (Šulgi and Amar-Suen), seem to have installed "foreigners" as commanders of the army just as frequently as their sons held these powerful positions. Whether this was out of fear of the creation of powerful factions within the royal family is unknown. Ur-Nammu's relation to the royal house of Uruk can therefore not be proven by his involvement with the military of that city. He could have been a blood relative as well as a favored ally married into the royal house of Uruk.

the classical Gilgameš mythology by being siblings of Gilgameš and, to some extent, by taking over his role altogether. During the formative period of the empire, the clan of Ur-Nammu, legitimized through both pseudo-historical as well as theological claims of supremacy, managed to monopolize power and exclude all other families and cadet branches from succession. A cadet branch is defined as a distinct branch of the ruling family, related by marriage or through an uncle to the ruling line. We see the result of this policy in the later years of the empire when one family alone held all the important offices in the imperial administration, co-opting all other important clans in their own rule (see, e.g., the discussion about the *sukkalmah* below, pp. 22 ff.).

The historical sources pertaining to the reign of Ur-Nammu mostly refer to his building activities and to his refurbishing of the canal system. The sources are, on the other hand, silent concerning any military activities.[42] It is possible that Ur-Nammu only ruled a small territorial state in the southwestern part of Sumer. Furthermore, it is likely that his rule was contemporary with the Second Dynasty of Lagaš.[43]

Ur-Nammu was well remembered in later literary tradition. Two very famous texts have come down to us, "The Coronation of Ur-Nammu" and "The Death of Ur-Nammu." The latter suggests that Ur-Nammu died on the battlefield and that his corpse was not recovered.[44]

---

42 See W. Sallaberger 1999: 135–136 for a summary of the canal constructions of Ur-Nammu, and 137–139 for a summary of his building activities. See also E. Flückiger-Hawker 1999: 28–40 for a survey of the activities of Ur-Nammu and the sources pertaining to his reign. Old Babylonian copies of Ur-Nammu's historical inscriptions record military campaigns against the Elamites and the Gutians (see, for example, RIME 3/2 1.1.28 and 29).

43 So far no study has conclusively sorted out the chronology of late third millennium BC. The second Lagash dynasty, also called The Dynasty of Ur-Baba, has traditionally been considered an intermediate period between the Old Akkadian dynasty and Ur III, but it is now commonly believed to overlap with Ur III. Our understanding of the internal chronology of Lagaš II is limited because we have failed even to establish beyond doubt the sequence of rulers. The external chronology of Lagaš II is not well understood either, since the foreign relations of the Girsu court are known only from the royal inscriptions. The expressions of Gudea: "He opened the road from the upper to the lower sea," are standardized epithets at most, see Gudea Statue B, column v, lines 25–27, and compare to examples from literature, for example, *A song of Inanna and Dumuzid*, line 44 (Dumuzid-Inanna D1, see http://www-etcsl.orient.ox.ac.uk/section4/c40830.htm). For a recent discussion of the Lagash II chronology see, C. Suter 2000: 15–28, and E. Flückiger-Hawker 1999: 2–5, with references to the debate.

44 The theological implications of a burial without a corpse are thought to have been sinister, however, they lie beyond the scope of the present study and will not be dealt with here, see D. Frayne 1997: 20, with references. Note that E. Flückiger-Hawker 1999, see for example, 7, and 94, understands the text differently; according to her, Ur-Nammu is brought back to Ur where he was burried.

3.2. Šulgi

Whereas Ur-Nammu was the founder of the Ur III dynasty it was his son, Šulgi, who built the Ur III Empire.[45] He ruled forty-eight years and was the most important Ur III ruler. He was succeeded on the throne by two or possibly three of his sons. As seen throughout history, a powerful, long-lived founder of an empire would often be ascribed super-human powers.[46] Šulgi was no exception. He was deified by the middle of his reign and there is nothing to suggest that anyone dared contest his rule or his plans for succession while he was alive.[47] We do not know the names of any siblings of Šulgi. If there were any, they had been successfully excluded from the line of succession.

With the elevation in Š 18 of Liwwir-Mittašu, his daughter, to queenship of Marhaši, a political entity to the east of Mesopotamia,[48] the expansionist policy of Šulgi had begun. This policy, which from around Š 20 included military campaigns, coincided with the first attestation of the divine title used by Šulgi.[49] During Šulgi's twenty-first year, certain social reforms were formulated which seem to have eased the conversion of the population at large into a state of dependence on the crown. It is from that point in time that we, with reason, can call Ur III a well-functioning administrative machine. Thus, the beginning of the bureaucratic age of Ur III is introduced by the following year-formula:

> mu ^{d}nin-urta ensi$_2$-gal ^{d}en-lil$_2$-la$_2$-ke$_4$ e$_2$ ^{d}en-lil$_2$ ^{d}nin-lil$_2$-la$_2$-ke$_4$ eš-bar-kin ba-an-du$_{11}$-ga ^{d}šul-gi lugal uri$_5$^{ki}-ma- ke$_4$ GAN$_2$ nig$_2$-ka$_9$ ša$_3$ e$_2$ ^{d}en-lil$_2$ ^{d}nin-lil$_2$-la$_2$-ke$_4$ si bi$_2$-sa$_2$-a
> Year: "Ninurta, the *ensi$_2$-gal* of Enlil, having taken an omen for the house of Enlil and Ninlil, Šulgi, the king of Ur, set straight the fields and the accounts for the house of Enlil and Ninlil."[50]

The exact nature of the so-called "Reforms of Šulgi," to which this year-name is often attributed, is not well understood.[51] There exists no conclusive evidence that Šulgi ever wrote a set of social reforms; rather it seems plausible that Šulgi, by virtue of his unparalleled reign, was able to usurp

---

45 Šulgi's early years might have been contemporary with at least the latter part of the semi-independent Lagaš II dynasty. See fn. 43 above, and P. Steinkeller 1988: 51–52.

46 Note that the majority, if not all, third millennium Mesopotamian rulers were deified post mortem, but only a handful during their lifetime.

47 The smooth transfer of power between Šulgi and Amar-Suen suggests that Šulgi had appointed Amar-Suen "heir apparent" at some point.

48 See P. Michalowski 1975: 716–719.

49 D. Frayne 1997: 91.

50 See also K. Maekawa 1999: 66 and 68. Th. Jacobsen translates: "Year when Ninurta, ensi-gal of Enlil ordered an audit for the temples of Enlil and Ninlil, and Šulgi, king of Ur, straightened out the fields (forming) the core of the accounting for the temples of Enlil and Ninlil." Th. Jacobsen 1991: 115 (see also fn. 16).

51 See, for example, M. Sigrist 1992: 9, W. Sallaberger 1999: 148, and K. Maekawa 1999: 66–68.

a large portion of the power and possessions previously held by temple households and local elite families. Bookkeeping in the years following Š 21 seems to have aimed increasingly at embracing all aspects of society; whether ownership of the entire state had been transferred to Šulgi is not clear, but possible.

During the second half of Šulgi's reign, numerous military campaigns were directed towards the eastern and north-eastern regions bordering the Mesopotamian plain. The lands to the north and north-west are likely to have been kept under control more through alliances than through war.[52]

In Šulgi's thirty-ninth year a building of some significance was constructed at Puzriš-Dagan. The building was so important that the year was named after this event:[53]

mu ^{d}šul-gi lugal uri$_{5}$^{ki}-ma-ke$_{4}$ lugal dub-da limmu$_{2}$-ba-ke$_{4}$ e$_{2}$ puzur$_{4}$^{iš}-^{d}da-gan^{ki} mu-du$_{3}$
Year: "Šulgi, the King of Ur, King of the four corners, built the house at Puzriš-Dagan."[54]

Whether that building activity alluded to the whole city of Puzriš-Dagan or only to a particular temple or building within it is unknown. Drehem (Puzriš-Dagan's modern Arabic name is Drehem, a name which for the sake of convention will be used in the following) has been termed the great animal-pen of the Ur III Empire,[55] suggesting its redistributive character, but its exact function is still not entirely clear.

The officials in the local administrations of the Ur III provinces had their seal-inscriptions altered some time after the year when the "House at Puzriš-Dagan " was built, suggesting that the power of the king was being strengthened. Instead of carrying a dedication to the local governor, the seal-inscriptions now contained either a dedication to the king, or nothing but the title and perhaps the patronymic of the seal-owner. The exact date of this change is difficult to pinpoint, but it seems to coincide with the establishment of Drehem.[56]

---

52 See W. Sallaberger 1999: 156–161.

53 The thirty-ninth year of Šulgi was also called the "Year after the year after the wall of the land was built" (*mu-us$_{2}$-sa bad$_{3}$ ma-da ba-du$_{3}$ mu-us$_{2}$-sa-bi*). M. Sigrist wrote that the house of Drehem was constructed in Š 38, so that the next year (Š 39) could be named after the event (M. Sigrist 1992: 13). I doubt this interpretation and suggest that the years were named only some months after the New-Year when an important event had taken place, as is implied by the fact that many years had two names, one "the year after" and one "new." Chronological evidence from the data set corroborates this hypothesis to some extent. Texts dated with the year-formula *mu e$_{2}$ puzur$_{4}$-^{d}dagan ba-du$_{3}$* occur only from month 4 (except for some Umma texts with the month name *iti šeKINku*, a possible Drehem date in Umma documents?), whereas texts dated according to the year-formula *mu-us$_{2}$-sa BAD$_{3}$ ba-du$_{3}$ mu-us$_{2}$-sa-a-bi* are attested only from the three first months of the year, suggesting a naming of the year Š 39 to have taken place at the end of month 3.

54 See also D. Edzard 1973: 202

55 F. Thureau-Dangin 1910: 186.

56 See, for example, the peculiar history of the seal of Gudea, the son of Ur-nigar, chief livestock

Šulgi had at least one, but possibly as many as three wives and several concubines (*lukur*).[57] The kings of Ur used dynastic marriages extensively as a political tool, by sending their daughters off to foreign places and also by marrying daughters from neighboring chiefdoms and states. The clan of Ur-Nammu secured its supremacy by marrying daughters of the kings to high-ranking officials of the empire, co-opting these important families in the reign of the kings of Ur.[58] However, none of the wives of the governors of Umma were members of the royal family. The majority of the known royal women of the Ur III period had Akkadian names.

It is possible that Abī-simtī was the wife of Šulgi rather than the wife of Amar-Suen (see p. 10 above). She was from northern Mesopotamia as indicated by the seal-inscription of her brother Babati. A fragmentary genealogy of the family of Babati is presented below where it has been included among the cadet branches of the royal family of Ur (see Figure 2). Based in part on Old Babylonian sources, it has been suggested that Šulgi married Taram-Uram, a daughter of the ruler of Mari, Apil-Kin.[59] However, Amat-Suen, also read *GEME$_2$-Suen*, is the only person we can say for certain was a wife (*dam*) of Šulgi.[60] The names of Šulgi's concubines were Ea-niša,[61] Simat-Ea, Šuqurtum, Ninkala (written *nin$_9$-kal-la* or *nin-kal-la*), Geme-Ninlila, and Šulgi-simti. Šulgi-simti was perhaps

---

administrator (*šuš$_3$*). The same seal which prior to Š 43 had had a dedication to Ur-Lisi, the governor of Umma, was recarved to conform with the simple format of a patronymic inscription in fashion after Š 40 +/- 2. See also the seal of Lugal-inimgina, the scribe, son of Lugal-nesag'e, which had a destiny similar to the seal of Gudea. See the unpublished dissertation of R. Mayr 1997, and pp. 54 ff. below.

57 The Old-Babylonian Proto-LU (MSL 12) gives three Akkadian readings of *lukur* (*SAL.ME*): lines 263 –265 (p. 42): ^{lukur}*na-di-tum*, ^{lukur}*qa$_2$-di-iš-tum*, ^{lukur}*ba-tu-ul-tum*. The second of these, *qadištum*, translates as a woman of special status; it is also written *ereš-dingir*. *batultu* is an adolescent girl, also written *ki-sikil* in Sumerian. The more traditional Akkadian translation of *lukur*, *naditu*, is also of little help in understanding the Sumerian title; we read in the CAD (N1 p. 63) that a *naditu* is "a woman dedicated to a god, usually unmarried, not allowed to have children, usually living in a *gagû*," a translation contrary to the Ur III meaning of the term. See also Excursus 2.

58 In the end, the Ur III kings had perhaps become ensnared in a web of familial ties which facilitated the fall of the dynasty. The case of Išbi-Erra, a general of the Ur III army, and a possible blood relative of the ruling family of Ur who aided the downfall of the Ur empire, exemplifies the dangers of extensive use of political marriages.

59 J. Boese and W. Sallaberger 1996: 24–39.

60 See RIME 3/2 1.2.67. See also RIME 3/2 1.2.68, which has the unusual spelling *a-ma-at* instead of *GEME$_2$*.

61 A person called *i-TI-e$_2$-a* (presumably to be normalized *iddin-ea*) is mentioned as a brother of Ea-niša, see RA 73, 191, (AAICAB 1, 1971-351) (Š 48 viii) rev. 4, and OIP 115, 199 (A 2949) (Š 46 iii 19) obv. 5. A person by the same name is also mentioned as a man of Šulgi (*lu$_2$ ^{d}šul-gi*) in RA 59, 111 S 1 (month iv 2) obv. 5, as a chief administrator (*šabra*), in JEOL 33, 114 5 (Š 47 xi 4) obv. 5, and TCND 400 (Š 48 vii) obv. 4, and as chief livestock administrator (*šuš$_3$*) in PDT 1, 550 (month viii) obv. 8. He is also mentioned as the father of Šū-Ea in JCS 32, 171 1 (Š 47 viii) rev. 2. Note that all references are from the reign of Šulgi.

elevated to queenship around Š 30.[62] Ninkala is also called queen (*nin*) in a few texts.[63]

All of these women, except Taram-Uram and Abī-simtī, were recorded with their personal relationship to Šulgi in various inscriptions on seals and votive objects. Ea-niša, for example, is called "his concubine" (*lukur-ra-ni*), "beloved concubine" (*lukur ki-ag*$_2$*-a*), "beloved concubine of the king" (*lukur ki-ag*$_2$*-lugal*), "his travel companion" (*lukur kaskal-la-ka-ni*), and "campaign consort, his beloved concubine" (lukur kaskal-la lukur ki-ag$_2$-ga$_2$-ni).[64] Geme-Ninlila is called "his beloved" (*ki-ag*$_2$*-ga*$_2$*-ni*).[65] Ninkala is called "his beloved citizen of Nippur" (*dumu nibruki ki-ag*$_2$*-ga*$_2$*-ni*).[66] Šuqurtum is called "his beloved concubine" (*lukur ki-ag*$_2$*-ga*$_2$*-ni*).[67] It is unknown at present whether these "titles" were of any consequence for the standing of the concubine; we would expect the king to favor some women over others, allowing the formation of factions within the harem.[68] The nature of Ur III concubinage however, is not altogether clear. It was not limited to the king. The governor of Umma, the *sukkalmah* and governor of Girsu, as well as several generals, all may have cohabited with one or more concubines alongside their wife/wives.

---

62 See MVN 8, 97 (Š 32 v), rev. 2; NYPL 235 (Š 38 vii), rev. 4; MVN 3, 162 (Š 39 iii), obv. 4; AUCT 1, 952 (Š 39 iv 6), rev. 2; Princeton 1, 55 (Š 35 xii), rev. 2; RT 37, 129 ab. 1 (Š 35 ix), obv. 3; TCND 24 (Š 47 iv), rev. 1; and TCND 28 (Š 37 ii), rev. 2, all imply a relationship between Šulgi-simti and Tezen-mama (*te-ze*$_2$*-en*$_6$*-ma-ma*), who according to D. Frayne 1997: 267, was counted among the daughters of Amar-Suen. The texts cited here could perhaps aid future studies targeted at disentangling the maternal descent of the princes and princesses: Tezen-mama is never mentioned together with another royal spouse; she was perhaps the daughter of Šulgi-simti.

63 See ASJ 11, 129 59 (= BM 29874) (Š 48), rev. 10. CT 7, 27 (= BM 18376) (Š 42), rev. 16, and MVN 17, 8 (= BM 12237 = ASJ 2, 31 87) (Š 42), rev. 8, suggest that Ninkala held the city Urua (^{u2}*urua*$^{a\ ki}$ (or ^{u2}*urua*$_x$*(URUxGU)*^{ki} also read *šakir*) as her private estate (see also the house of Simat-Ištaran documented in the Garšana archive). The three texts all have the similar colophon *nig*$_2$*-ka*$_9$*-ak še* ^{u2}*urua*$^{a\ ki}$ / *nin*$_9$*-kal-la nin* (account of the grain of GN, Ninkala the queen). Only the latter text has been collated; it is the only one of the two to give Ninkala the title queen (*nin*). For the fields of various high-ranking members of the Ur elite, including Ninkala, see also ASJ 9, 126 57 (= BM 29860) (no date), and TIM 6, 3 (AS 1). In TMHC NF 1/2, 204 (ŠS 1 iv), Ninkala received 5 minas of wool; the tablet was sealed with the servant seal of Ummī-ṭāb, the slave-woman of Šāt-[Suen], the daughter of the king. Šāt-Suen is known as a daughter of Šulgi, but her relationship to Šulgi's concubine Ninkala is unknown.

64 See RIME 3/2 1.2.71 to 1.2.81 for the titles of Ea-niša.

65 See RIME 3/2 1.2.82 for the title of Geme-Ninlila.

66 See RIME 3/2 1.2.83 to 84 for the title of Ninkala.

67 See RIME 3/2 1.2.85 for the title of Šuqurtum.

68 It is also possible that the king divorced the women over the years, or that they perished, leaving Šulgi with only one wife at a time. Harem is used here strictly to refer to the group of women with some sort of marital tie to the king, and includes concubines as well as wives. It is unknown whether these women dwelled in the same house, or whether they otherwise can be said to constitute what can be compared to the classical Ottoman harem.

The consorts of Šulgi were involved in the economy, to which the Drehem administration testifies.[69] Contemporary evidence from the provincial capital of Umma, where the wife of the governor seems to have had her own resources, suggests that the queen may also have been in charge of a household of her own.[70]

Šulgi had more than twenty children, some of whom held important positions in the civil administration or the military.[71] No information has survived as to who the mothers of the different children of Šulgi were, but we may hope that future prosopographical work will give some clues as to the possible existence of royal factions based on maternal lineage.

Due to the particular nature of the sources—naming royal progeny "son of the king" (*dumu lugal*) rather than "son of PN the king," and often providing no title at all—it is not possible to specify a title for more than a few of Šulgi's sons. A handful served in the military, others were only mentioned a few times in the texts from Drehem. The most important sons of Šulgi were: Amar-Suen (the future king, see below); Šū-Suen (the future king, see below); possibly Ibbi-Suen (the future king, see below); Eštar-ilšu, perhaps the same as the general (*šagina*) mentioned in SAT 3, 2143 (no date); Lu-duga, who seems to have been active in the Umma province; Lu-Sunzida, who, although never mentioned by title, figures among high-ranking officials of the empire; Lu-Nanna, the general of Nagsu and Zimudar,[72] whose son Ennam-Šulgi is also known; Puzur-Eštar, another general; Šū-Enlil, who served as general of Uruk and BAD_3.AN^{ki};[73] Ur-Suen, who served as general of Uruk[74] and of BAD_3.AN^{ki}; and Ur-nigar, who also served as general of Uruk. One could point to the pattern that several royal sons held the position of governor of Uruk as an important discovery relating to both the self-understanding of the royal family of Ur, and the mechanics of succession. However, the sources are too meager to further advance this theory.[75] Several of Šulgi's daughters are also

69 W. Sallaberger 1999: 253–260.

70 The references to a chief administrator of Ea-niša (*šabra* e_2*-a-ni-ša*) corroborate this. See, for example, CT 32, 36 (= BM103403) (ŠS 2 to 3) (tenure of Šulgi-bani), PDT 1, 99 (Š 47 iii 4), and SACT 1, 131 (Š 46 xii 13) (tenure of Lu-duga). For references to a household of Šulgi-simti, see, for example, Orient 16, 107 174 (Š 43), and M. Sigirist, Drehem (1992) 222–246. The newly discovered archive of the household of Simat-Ištaran from Garšana supports this hypothesis. The archive includes references to the chief household administrator (*šabra* e_2) and the scribe of the chief household administrator.

71 See figure 4 below for a complete list of the members of the royal family, in parts adapted from D. Frayne (1997); for Šulgi see pp. 166–170; for Amar-Suen see pp. 266–268; for Šū-Suen see pp. 336–337; for Ibbi-Suen see pp. 375–376. Figure 2 (below) represents an attempt to sort out some of the cadet branches of the House of Ur-Nammu.

72 UET 3, 75 (ŠS 1 i).

73 See p. 10 above.

74 For example, RIME 3/2 1.2.96 (= NBC 1934), and RA 13, 21 7 (Š 48).

75 The possibility of Uruk as an Ur III Dauphinage was discussed by P. Michalowski in his article "Durum and Uruk during the Ur III Period," P. Michalowski 1977a: 83–96.

known. They were, among others, En-nirzi-ana, Nin-TUR.TUR-mu, En-uburzi-ana, Peš$_2$-TUR.TUR, Dadagu (?), Taram-Šulgi, and Liwwir-Mittašu, who became queen of Marharši in Š 18. Apart from Liwwir-Mittašu, it is not know if any of these princesses were married to high-ranking officials of the empire.[76]

Šulgi died on the first or the second day of the eleventh month of his forty-eighth regnal year.[77] He was well remembered in the literary tradition, with more than twenty hymns composed in his honor, some of them even said to be self-laudatory.[78]

3.3. Amar-Suen

Amar-Suen became king after his father, and ruled for nine years. All the year-dates of Amar-Suen are known. Whether or not Amar-Suen was the oldest son or his father's favorite is unknown. Some form of administrative training is believed to have been a prerequisite for any royal heir prior to his elevation to kingship; surprisingly Amar-Suen is never mentioned in the extant text corpus before his ascension to the throne. There are three possible answers to this peculiar problem: 1) Amar-Suen never held any important office before he became king. A very unlikely scenario, unless if he was too young to have had the vital training an administrative or military position would have given him. 2) The name Amar-Suen is only a throne-name. Throne names are only rarely attested during the third millennium, but they are not unknown. 3) Amar-Suen served his father outside Sumer, and references to his office remain in the royal archives of Ur, still to be unearthed. In all three cases, we are looking for a scenario that would present Amar-Suen with the ability to build a power base that would ensure his place in succession.

Amar-Suen is described in the historical tradition as a weak ruler. Perhaps this is done only to create a literary antithesis to the strong ruler Šulgi.[79] According to the historical sources, Amar-Suen's

---

76 Note that D. Owen recently suggested Simat-Ištaran was a daughter of Šulgi, and married to Šū-Kabta, a high-ranking official of the empire (D. Owen 2001a). Note also the unnamed daughter of Šulgi who was married to the ruler of Anšan in Š 30. Šulgi destroyed this city in Š 34.

77 See D. Frayne 1997: 110, for a summary of the evidence, with references to previous literature.

78 There exists, to date, no conclusive evidence that any of the Šulgi hymns were composed during the time of Šulgi. That some of the neo-Sumerian royal hymns contain an "historical kernel" is no evidence for their historicity (so W. Hallo 1966: 135–139, followed by J. Klein 1981: 58 and fn. 139). Whether the literary texts contained an historical kernel or not is of no consequence for their possible use in reconstructing the history of Ur III. Such an historical kernel can be found among all the legends, myths, and other incorporated folkloristic material, after the historical events have been reconstructed using the primary sources. The royal hymns are therefore not historical sources; they are primarily literary texts collected by scribes for use within the cult and schools of the Old Babylonian cities. The majority of the Ur III royal hymns were presumably composed long after the fall of Ur to the Elamites, and are perhaps based on Akkadian proto-types translated into Sumerian.

79 P. Michalowski 1977b: 155-157.

rule was a period of few conflicts, a condition that can be seen as both a weakening and a strengthening of the empire.

Following the example of his father, Amar-Suen had several concubines (*lukur*), including [x]-natum, ZagaANbi, Udad-zenat, and Puzur-uša. It is possible, but not certain, that Abī-simtī was the wife of Amar-Suen.[80] The brother of Abī-simtī, Babati, was an important figure from Northern Mesopotamia. Judging from the impressive array of titles listed in his seal-inscription, it seems justified to claim that Babati and his "gens" were an influential clan, whom the rulers of Ur co-opted during their reign.[81] Like his father, Amar-Suen had many children. Establishing a genealogy of the Ur III royal family is hampered by the administrative preference for referring to the title rather than to the name of a person. For the royal family in particular, reference to royal descent is almost exclusively expressed in impersonal terms: very few texts name a royal father. Rather, the expression "son of the king" (*dumu lugal*) was used. This has resulted in difficulties when attempting to connect an individual prince with either Amar-Suen or Šulgi; the family tree of the royal family presented at the end of this chapter is drawn primarily from the information in D. Frayne 1997, joined with the new evidence suggesting that Amar-Suen, Šū-Suen and Ibbi-Suen with some likelihood were brothers.[82] Amar-Suen's sons, like the majority of his brothers, are each known only from a few references in the Drehem corpus. Most of the generals known from Ur III sources were not direct descendants of the royal house of Ur; some of them had married into the royal family, and most of them had non-Sumerian names.[83] Akkadian names dominate among the generals (*šagina*) of the Ur III Empire, but it is important to note the shift in naming-practice that took place within the royal court itself and not to exclude any persons with an Akkadian name from the potential list of members of the royal family. A few of the generals had names that are neither Sumerian nor Akkadian, such as Hašib-Atal (presumably a Hurrian name), and Hun-Šulgi.

Among Amar-Suen's sons were Dada, the general of Zabala, a city in the eastern province of Umma,[84] and Šū-Šulgi (perhaps a captain, *nu-banda*$_3$).[85] Several other sons are known only by

80 It is paramount to the whole question of neo-Sumerian royal succession to establish whether Abī-simtī was the wife of Amar-Suen or Šulgi. See p. 10 above. D. Owen has suggested that Simat-Ištaran, amply attested in the Garšana archive was a daughter of Šulgi (D. Owen 2001a). This has implications for the genealogy of the royal house, since she claims to be the sister (*nin*$_9$) of Šū-Suen and later Ibbi-Suen (after he followed Šū-Suen on the throne). T. Gomi 1976: 1–14, rules out the possibility that Abī-simtī was the same person as Šulgi-simti, an otherwise attractive solution to the problem.

81 See RIME 3/2 1.4.32. See also R. Whiting 1976: 173–182.

82 New evidence can be found in the Garšana archive (kindly made available to me by D. Owen (through the CDLI project), see also D. Owen 2001a.

83 See, however, P. Steinkeller 1987a: 25–26.

84 See, for example, AUCT 1, 26 (AS 3 viii to xii).

85 See RA 49, 86 2 (ŠS 2 x), a text from Drehem, where Šū-Šulgi is mentioned together with other members of the royal family, and MVN 5, 116 (AS 7 iii), another Drehem text, where Šū-Šulgi is mentioned

name and affiliation with the royal clan.[86] Among his daughters we find Taddin-Eštar, Ninlil-tukulti, Geme-Nanna, Pakinana, Šāt-Mami, Nin-hedu, Geme-Eana, Tezen-mama,[87] the unnamed wife of Lugal-magure, Simat-Ištaran,[88] the unnamed wife of Šarrum-bani, and the unnamed wife of Lu-Nanna, the son of Ur-nigar.[89] Several of his daughters were married to high-ranking officials of the empire, a practice begun by his father Šulgi.[90]

3.4. The *Sukkalmah*

The highest official of the empire, second to the king, was the *sukkalmah*; his responsibilities were closely associated with the eastern provinces of the empire. During the tenure of ARAD$_2$(-Nanna/mu), the office of the *sukkalmah* was conjoined with the office of the governor (*ensi$_2$*) of Girsu. In this brief survey, I will concentrate only on this latter best known *sukkalmah*.

ARAD$_2$(-Nanna/mu), whose name was sometimes written ARAD$_2$, sometimes, ARAD$_2$-^{d}nanna, and sometimes ARAD$_2$-mu, held the office of *sukkalmah* from the time of Amar-Suen through

---

as a son of the king.

86 Ibbi-Ištaran, for example SAT 2, 774 (NBC 11644) (AS 4 ix). Ur-Ištaran, for example SACT 1, 153 (AS 4 viii). Ur-Ninsuna, for example ITT 3, 5001 (AS 8 iii). Taddin-Eštar (*da-din-eš$_4$-tar*) is mentioned together with Ur-Ištaran and Abī-simtī in DAS 51 (AS 8); see also the parallel text DAS 53 (AS 8). Amir-Šulgi, for example OrSP 47-49, 23 (AS 3 i), and AUCT 1, 418 (AS 2). Ur-Baba, for example MVN 3, 232 (AS 6), which mentions the dowry of Ur-Baba, to be entered into the house of Lu-Ninšubur, the chief administrator of An. Ahuni, for example TCS 336 (= Aegyptus 10, 274 37) (AS 2 iv), which mentions the dowry (*nig$_2$-munus-us$_2$-sa*) of Ahuni, to be entered into the *e$_2$ zabar-dab$_5$*, and UET 3, 1369 (IS 1), which mentions the *e$_2$-du$_6$-la* of Ahuni. Inim-Nanna, for example, TCL 2, 5563 (AS 1 i), which mentions the dowry of Inim-Nanna, to be entered into the *e$_2$ hu-ba-⌜a⌝* (House of Hubaya?), and MVN 5, 122 (ŠS 1 ix), which records the delivery of animals to Inim-Nanna, as well as to the throne of Ur-Nammu, Šulgi, and Amar-Suen. Lu-Šulgi, for example, TCL 2, 5508 (AS 4 i), and TLB 3, 98 (AS 4 iv). Nabi-Šulgi, for example STA 8 (AS 5 ii to x), and Zinbun 18, 102 7 (= BM 20262 = MTBM 81) (no year). Šulgi-rama, for example TrDr 88 (AS 7 iv). References to Mansum and Nanna-manba are very scarce. Mansum, HLC 75 (pl. 36) (AS 1), rev. 2 (according to RIME 3/2 268). Nanna-manba, see JANES 9, 21 3 (AS 5 ii 17), obv. 4 (according to RIME 3/2 268).

87 See fn. 62 above. Tezen-mama was perhaps a daughter of Šulgi rather than Amar-Suen.

88 See fn. 76 above.

89 Such is the order of daughters of the king as they are listed in CTMMA I, 17 (AS 4 vii), a text recording regular deliveries for the cult. The first entry records a delivery for the throne of Šulgi, the following entries recorded the deliveries to the daughters of the king, followed by the deliveries to the two wet-nurses (*ummeda*) of the king, and a number of persons called *mar-tu* (i.e. Amorite), and finally, a number of high-ranking officials from the north. We know the names of other daughters of the king mentioned during the reign of Amar-Suen; these were Ninlilemanag, see, for example, AUCT 2, 367 (AS 6 i), Šelepputum, see J. Klein 1990: 20-39, and En-mahgalanna, known from the formula of Amar-Suen's fourth year.

90 Hulibar the general (*šagina*) of Umma (?) was married to a daughter (called *dumu lugal*) of the king (see MVN 13, 735 [no date], from Girsu).

the early years of Ibbi-Suen. He was married to a daughter of Amar-Suen, Šāt-Mami.[91] One of his sons was married to another daughter of Amar-Suen, Geme-Eana. It is uncertain how many wives $ARAD_2$(-Nanna/mu) had, and whether he himself was a descendant of the House of Ur-Nammu.[92] This is in part due to the fact that references were often made to the office rather than the person in the administrative records of the Ur III empire, making identifications rather difficult. Several women besides Šāt-Mami were called wife of the *sukkalmah* (*dam sukkal-mah*). Šuba-dua is called wife of the *sukkalmah* (⸢*dam*⸣ *sukkal-mah*) in ITT 5, 6997 (AS 9 x), a text that carries the seal of a person called Ur-Lamma the son of $ARAD_2$-mu, perhaps identical with the son of $ARAD_2$(-Nanna/mu) the *sukkalmah*. In a text mentioning Ninkala as queen (*nin*), we find a woman called Nin-hedu as the wife of the *sukkalmah* (*dam sukkal mah*).[93] Baba-Ea is mentioned as both wife of the *sukkalmah* and wife of the governor (of Girsu). A semi-precious stone bears the sole reference to Aman-ili, wife of $ARAD_2$(-Nanna/mu), the governor of Lagaš.[94] Of all these women, Baba-Ea is perhaps the most important, and perhaps $ARAD_2$(-Nanna/mu)'s wife in his capacity as the governor of Girsu. Baba-Ea is also referred to as a *ereš-dingir* priestess.[95]

Several seal-impressions testify that $ARAD_2$(-Nanna/mu) was the son of Ur-Šulpa'e, who himself held the office of *sukkalmah* prior to $ARAD_2$(-Nanna/mu).[96] Several persons were called son of the *sukkalmah*, these were Ur-Nanna, Ahuni (also called brother of the *sukkalmah* (*šeš sukkal-mah*)),[97] Šū-Šulgi, Šū-ili (also called brother of the *sukkalmah* (*šeš sukkal-mah*)),[98] Nanna-mansum, and Ur-Baba.[99] It is not always possible to tell whose son they were. In figure 2, I have reconstructed a genealogy of the family of the *sukkalmah*, describing it as one of the cadet branches of the House of Ur-Nammu.

---

91 For reference to the dowry (*nig_2-munus-us_2-sa*) of Šāt-Mami see, for example, MVN 11, 192 (=MCS 3 (1953) 25) (AS 2).

92 According to D. Frayne 1997: 268, Amar-Suen had a son called $ARAD_2$-^{d}nanna, who he suggests is identical with $ARAD_2$(-Nanna/mu) the *sukkalmah*. The only reference cited in D. Frayne 1997 is AnOr 1, 111 (dated to AS 7, however the abbreviated date formula in that text, *mu bi_2-tum*, is ambiguous).

93 See ASJ 9, 126 57 (= BM 29860).

94 See RIME 3/2 1.5.2004.

95 See fn. 57.

96 Seal of Ur-Šulpa'e see, for example, NFT p.185 (=AO 4198) (=DynChal 16 V) (no date), and NATN 388 (no date). See also ITT 5, 8220 (=TCS 1, 183) (ŠS 6).

97 See TCTI 2, 3711 (no year).

98 See TCTI 2, 4161 (no year).

99 Lu-Šara is called brother (*šeš*) of the *sukkalmah* in MVN 17, 12; he is otherwise unknown. Ahuni and Šū-ili could have been brothers of $ARAD_2$(-Nanna/mu), or his uncles. It is unknown whether $ARAD_2$(-Nanna/mu)'s son inherited his office. The last *sukkalmah* was Libur-Suen. His familial relations are unknown to me (UET 3, 826 [IS 22 vi]).

Unlike Umma and Nippur where the same families seems to have remained in power throughout the years of the Ur III kings,[100] the seat of the governor of the most important province, Lagaš, appears to have been controlled more centrally. Eventually, ARAD$_2$(-Nanna/mu) who was married into the royal family and presumably a close ally of the clan of Ur-Nammu, was able to add governorship of the province of Lagaš to his impressive array of titles.[101] Ur-Lamma, the first well attested Ur III governor of Girsu (the main city in the province of Lagaš during the neo-Sumerian period),[102] ruled from as early as Š 41 to AS 3, when Nanna-zišagal succeeded him. Nanna-zišagal governed Lagaš for only two years; he was succeeded by Šarakam, who governed Lagaš from AS 4 (perhaps contemporary with Nanna-zišagal) to AS 6. Following the four years when Lagaš was ruled by Nanna-zišagal and Šarakam, the *sukkalmah* ARAD$_2$(-Nanna/mu) added governor of the province of Lagaš to his titles.[103] He governed Lagaš until the end of Ur domination over Lagaš in Ibbi-Suen's sixth year.

The family of the *sukkalmah* seems to be the most important among the cadet-branches of the clan of Ur-Nammu. A cadet branch, as mentioned above, is defined as a distinct family with only secondary familial ties to the ruling clan, which excludes them from the line of succession but places them close to the center of power. It is likely, but impossible to prove, that the ruling house of Mari was even more closely related to the House of Ur than the family of the *sukkalmah*.[104] Due to the lack of contemporary sources the Mari ruling family has not been included in this study.

---

100 Except, perhaps, for the brief intermediate period of Amar-Suen's reign when the old elite family of Nippur was perhaps replaced by bureaucrats from Drehem, see also below, pp. 25–26 and figure 3.

101 See RIME 3/2 1.4.13, ARAD$_2$(-Nanna/mu) is here mentioned as *sukkalmah*, governor of Lagaš, sanga priest of Enki, general of Ušar-Garšana, general of Ašime, governor of Sabum and the land of Gutebum, general of Dimat-Enlila, governor of Al-Šū-Suen ("The City of Šū-Suen"), governor of Hamzi and Karahar, general of NI.HI, and general of Šimaški and the land of Karda, in that order.

102 The title "governor of Lagaš" is only used in ARAD$_2$(-Nanna/mu)'s official seal-inscription (see above). The commonly used title of the governor of the province of Lagaš was "governor of Girsu."

103 According to K. Maekawa 1996a: 121–122, the sequence of Girsu governors following Ur-Lamma exemplifies the social unrest erupting in AS 2, and ultimately culminating with the elimination of the line of Ur-Lamma, and the positioning of two ad-hoc administrators from the central bureaucracy as governor until a more durable solution to the problem could be reached: the appointment of ARAD$_2$(-Nanna/mu) as governor of that province in AS 6.

104 Any reconstruction of the ties between the Mari ruling family and the clan of Ur-Nammu is based largely on quasi-historical documents.

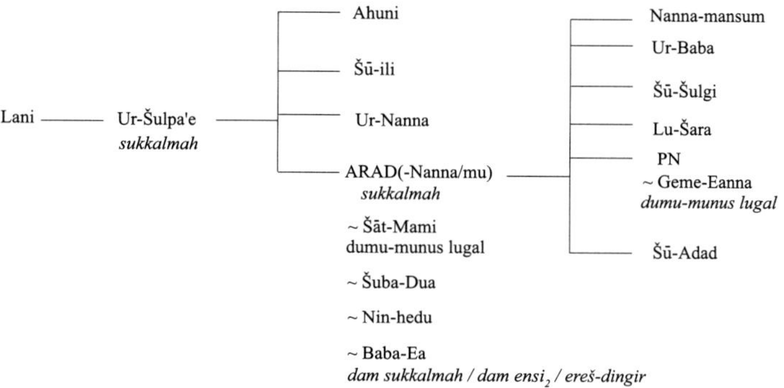

The family of the *sukkalmah*

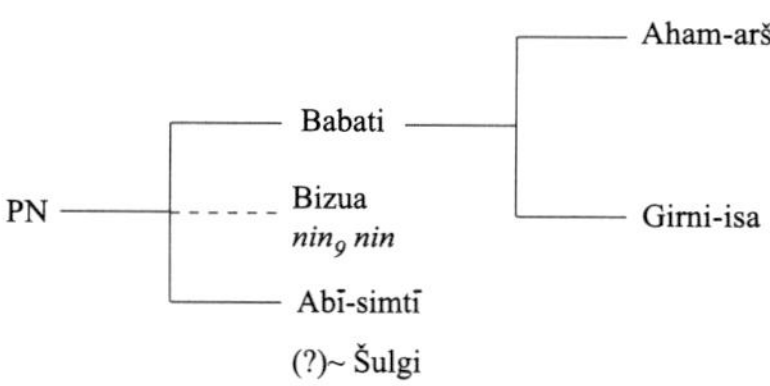

The family of Abi-Simti

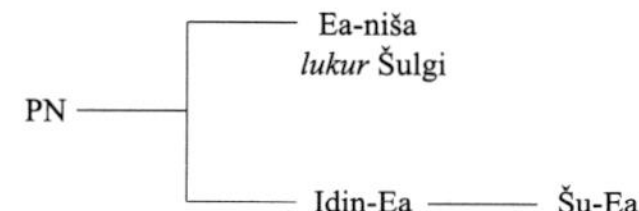

The family of Ea-niša

Figure 2: The cadet branches of the royal family of Ur

It is likely that Šulgi's two sons and successors, Amar-Suen and Šū-Suen, struggled for the throne. This is deduced from information from the provinces, since documentation from the capital is lacking. For instance, texts from Nippur are instructive. A provisional survey of the terms of office for three of the highest officials in the Nippur administration, the "foreman of the household of Inanna" (*ugula* e_2 *^{d}inanna*), the "chief administrator of Inanna" (*šabra ^{d}inanna*), and the "governor of Nippur" (*ensi$_2$ nibru^{ki}*), suggests that all three offices were controlled by the family of Ur-Meme (perhaps an old Nippur family, tracing its origins back to the time before the Ur III empire),[105] until the reign of Amar-Suen. During the reign of Amar-Suen the three offices were in the hands of persons not related to the old elite family of Nippur (perhaps members of the central (Drehem based?) bureaucracy). However, following the death of Amar-Suen, and the ascension of Šū-Suen, the offices were once again in the hands of the family of Ur-Meme.[106] This change might have taken place while Amar-Suen

105 R. Zettler 1987: 113–114.

106 W. Hallo 1972: 87-95. Hallo established a genealogy of the ruling family of Nippur, and discussed

was still, at least nominally, in charge at Ur.

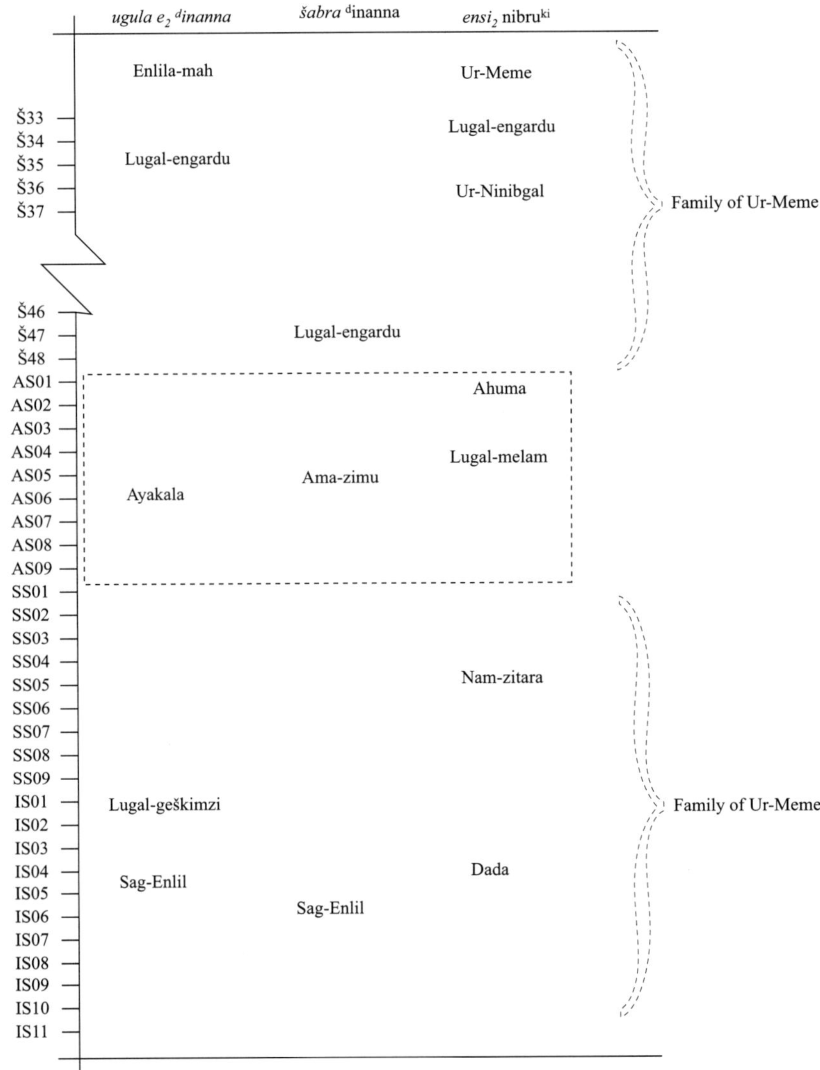

Figure 3: Succession of office in Nippur (preliminary survey)

Another important piece of evidence comes from Umma where we have additional evidence suggesting succession troubles at the royal court. From the sixth year of Amar-Suen, certain officials in the Umma province already began to use a seal with a dedicatory inscription naming Šū-Suen as

to some extebt the inheritance of office. He suggested that the clan of Ur-Meme lost its influence with the ascension of Amar-Suen (p. 94) but found no evidence of their re-installation by Šū-Suen. Another possible reason for the change in the line of succession may be connected to the legal suit brought against each other by members of this family during the reign of Amar-Suen; see, for example, R. Zettler 1987: 128 – 130.

the king of Ur. Nothing suggests that Amar-Suen died before late in his eight or early in his nineth year.[107] Both years were named throughout the empire according to Amar-Suen year-names. Another interpretation of the Umma evidence is to suggest that Amar-Suen and Šū-Suen ruled together for some time.[108]

When a king died, it was customary to settle accounts and measure the arable land of the entire kingdom.[109] Perhaps the circumstances surrounding the transfer of power from one king to the next also prompted the removal of any official whose loyalty lay with a rival branch of the ruling clan. Any royal grants to these subjects were also likely to have been confiscated.[110]

3.5. Šū-Suen

Šū-Suen followed his brother (or father?) on the throne and ruled the empire for nine years. Šū-Suen may have held the position of general (*šagina*) of Uruk and BAD_3.AN[ki] during his father Šulgi's reign.[111] As a prince, Šū-Suen is only known from texts dated to the reign of Amar-Suen, perhaps an indication that he was preparing himself for a place in the line of succession.[112] As we

107 No extant text discloses the time of death of Amar-Suen. See D. Frayne 1997: 242, citing SET 66, with reference to the offerings for the throne of Amar-Suen, which according to W. Sallaberger 1993: 147, occurred only posthumously, suggesting that Amar-Suen was dead before AS 9 xi 26. For SET 66 see now J. L. Dahl nd. (MS 1714).

108 See W. Sallaberger 1999: 166 and fn. 154, for references to the debate.

109 This is above all documented in the land-survey texts (for example, the text MCS 6, 83 [= BM 105334]).

110 The so-called *e_2-du_6-la* texts suggest that the favors which the king bestowed upon his subjects, were reversible at any time. Ur-Lisi, one of the well-known Umma governors, lost all his possessions and possibly his life in the eighth year of Amar-Suen, perhaps, as claimed by K. Maekawa, in connection with the struggle for power at the court (K. Maekawa 1996a: 127). However, see the discussion concerning the nature of this property in W. Heimpel 1997: 63–82.

111 Šū-Suen held the title "general of BAD_3.AN[ki] at some point in his career. This can be inferred from the dedicatory seal on Mesopotamia 12, 93A (AS 9 iii). Following Michalowski (1977a: 83–96), it seems reasonable to argue that the general of Uruk was also the general of BAD_3.AN[ki]. See above for the seal-inscription RIME 3/2 1.2.94 (= BRM 3, 52 = MLC 2357), believed by D. Frayne 1997: 188, following J. Boese and W. Sallaberger 1996: 36, to be an inscription of Šū-Enlil. It is likely, as Michalowski suggested (P. Michalowski 1977a: 84) that BAD_3.AN[ki] of the Ur III period was a locality close to Uruk. See also p. 10 and 19 above.

112 The earliest likely reference to (the prince) Šū-Suen is CTMMA 1, 10 (Š 43 vii 27). Numerous references exist to a person named Šū-Suen with the occupation "runner" or "messenger" (*sukkal / lu_2 kas_4*), he was perhaps son of a captain (see, e.g, MVN 13, 689, obverse line 17). During the late years of Šulgi and the early years of Amar-Suen, numerous references to contributions to (or from) the Drehem livestock made by a person called Šū-Suen may in fact, refer to Šū-Suen the prince. Compare MVN 13, 113 (Š 47), to RA 62, 8 11 (AS 1 i). The title prince is only preserved in the example from AS 1, but could have been present in the first text too. RA 62, 8 11 (AS 1 i), is therefore the earliest certain attestation of the title prince (*dumu lugal*) for Šū-Suen.

have seen, it is possible to argue that Šū-Suen was either a son of Šulgi, or a son of Amar-Suen, but the parallel scenario provided by evidence from the provincial court of Umma, combined with the comparative evidence presented in Excursus 1 and outlined in Chapter 2, above, both weigh in favor of the former solution.

Although the sources were still abundant at the time of Šū-Suen's ascension, they only mention one wife of the king, Kubatum, and one concubine, Ti'amat-bašti. Accordingly, we know of only three children of Šū-Suen, ignoring Ibbi-Suen who I believe could have been another son of Šulgi. The daughters were Tabur-haṭṭum, Šāt-Erra, and Geme-Enlila.

Tabur-haṭṭum and Šāt-Erra are not attested directly as daughters of Šū-Suen, but circumstantial evidence suggests this relationship.[113] Geme-Enlila was perhaps identical with the wife of Ibbi-Suen by the same name;[114] however, her title, daughter of the king (*dumu munus lugal*), need not refer to Amar-Suen, Šū-Suen or Ibbi-Suen. The sole reason for her identification as a daughter of Šū-Suen is her attestation as a daughter of the king in documents dated to the reign of Šū-Suen.

By the time of Šū-Suen, the empire began to experience serious hardship. Judging by the year-date formulae, the south was threatened by a migration from the north, and in the middle of Šū-Suen's reign, the protective wall called Muriq-Tidnim ("Which keeps away the Tidanum") was constructed. Šū-Suen conducted only two campaigns worthy of year names.[115] Still, Šū-Suen was, and is, considered a strong leader and a supporter of the arts. Several self-laudatory hymns concerning Šū-Suen, aimed at glorigying his memory, have survived. These texts have probably been instrumental in creating the image of Šū-Suen as a successful ruler, both in the minds of the ancients as well as the modern reader.

Šū-Suen died no later than the fourth day of the tenth month of his ninth year. From that day on he received funerary offerings.[116]

Šū-Suen, called "great knight" (*lu$_2$ ^{geš}tukul gu-la*) in Amherst 68 (AS 3 xi), might be the prince, but this is not certain at all. An analysis of the hierarchical standing of the military command is necessary to determine whether a prince could serve as a "knight," but that is beyond the scope of this study. Some texts recorded a Šū-Suen delivering bear-cubs to the Drehem pen (see, for example, MVN 11, 140 [AS 5]); the majority of these deliveries were sheep and goats, indicating his special position.

113 See D. Frayne 1997: 337 for their identification.

114 As suggested by D. Frayne 1997: 337. See p. 29 and fn. 120 below for a description of this seemingly incestuous relationship.

115 ŠS 3: Year: "Simanum was destroyed," and ŠS 7: Year: "Zabšali was destroyed."

116 W. Sallaberger 1999: 171

3.6. Ibbi-Suen

Ibbi-Suen, perhaps yet another son of Šulgi, followed Šū-Suen on the throne. Ibbi-Suen ruled twenty-four years.[117] It is very likely that Ibbi-Suen never ruled an empire, but only Sumer during his first five years, and perhaps only the capital Ur from then on.[118]

The year-formula from Ibbi-Suen's sixth year mentions the construction of city-walls surrounding Ur and Nippur. This is believed to indicate fear of an immanent invasion. When paired with the break-away of the provinces, it seems reasonable to interpret this year as the beginning of the end of the Ur III state. The beginning of the end is thus introduced by the following year-name (IS 6):

mu ^{d}i-bi$_2$-^{d}suen lugal uri$_2$^{ki}-ma-ke$_4$ nibru^{ki} uri$_2$^{ki}-ma-ke$_4$ bad$_3$ gal-bi mu-du$_3$
Year: "Ibbi-Suen the king of Ur built great walls of Nippur and Ur."

The destruction of the Ur III Empire was not only caused by outside forces—internal problems also facilitated the decline. A shortage of grain and a resulting collapse of the system of stable equivalencies can be seen as a result of unrest in the northern provinces as well as an inner problem fueled by that conflict.[119] The collapse of the system of stable equivalencies began during Ibbi-Suen's fifth year, and accelerated during the following three years.

By the time of Ibbi-Suen's reign, information about the royal family had begun to decrease dramatically. Only two royal children can be ascribed to Ibbi-Suen: Mammertum and Šulgi-simti, and Ibbi-Suen is mentioned in connection with only one wife, Geme-Enlila, and no concubines. It is not unthinkable that the union of Ibbi-Suen and Geme-Enlila was incestuous. Whether she was a sister-queen or a niece-queen is uncertain. Incestuous relationships, inbreeding, is a well-known phenomenon in history; it is usually restricted to stratified societies and, in particular, is well-known from the uppermost social levels of society, in patrilineal clans, and in royal households where the king had access to a large harem (polygamy naturally reduces the risks associated with inbreeding).[120]

117 The last administrative documents from the Ur III period date to the twelfth month of IS 23 (UET 3, 711 and UET 3, 712). SKL gives Ibbi-Suen 24 years on the throne.

118 Umma texts cease from the fourth year of Ibbi-Suen following a rapid decline in numbers during Ibbi-Suen's first three years. The last Ur III text from Girsu was written in IS 5, from Drehem IS 8, and from Nippur in IS 8.

119 See Th. Jacobsen 1953: 36-47, and T. Gomi 1984: 211-242.

120 Incestuous relationships have a higher sterility rate than non-incestuous relationships. See P. Van Den Berghe and G. Mesher 1980: 300–317. According to Van Den Berghe and Mesher, royal incest is a "high-risk, but also an extremely high-gain, strategy" (p. 304) for the female participant. A royal daughter is left with few alternatives other than to mate with her own brother or father persuing her goal of producing a successful heir. This is, according to the authors, due to the tendency to hypergyny (hypergamy) among most females in stratified societies. For the king the gains are obvious: he may produce an heir with 3/4 of his own genes. The consequences of incest becomes tremendous when analyzed over time, "after just eight generations of full-

Ibbi-Suen was confined to Ur during the approximately twenty years following the break-away of the provinces, and the year-names stemming from these years tell the tale of increasing paranoia, as illustrated in the year-formula from Ibbi-Suen's twenty-third year:

mu ^{d}i-bi$_{2}$-^{d}suen lugal uri$_{2}$^{ki}-ma-ra ugu-dul$_{5}$-bi dugud kur-be$_{2}$ mu-na-e-ra
Year: "the stupid monkey in the foreign land struck against Ibbi-Suen, the king of Ur."

Just a couple of years earlier, Ibbi-Suen's year formula was:

mu ^{d}i-bi$_{2}$-^{d}suen lugal uri$_{2}$^{ki}-ma-ra mar-tu a$_{2}$ im u$_{18}$- ul-ta uru^{ki} nu zu gu$_{2}$ im-ma-an-ga$_{2}$-ar
Year: "the Amorites, the powerful south wind who, from the remote past, have not known cities, submitted to Ibbi-Suen the king of Ur."

The large account from Ur, UET 3, 1498, dating to IS 15 (from the first to the last month), is a good example of the desperate economic situation in Ur after the empire had deteriorated. The text, an account of the workshops of the royal household, is mainly concerned with the recycling of precious materials. As in all Ur III accounts, care is taken to record even very small quantities. In this text, however, it seems as if this principle is followed with a special rigidness, as if resources were in short supply.[121]

Approximately a century after Ur-Nammu's first year as an independent ruler, the capital, Ur, was sacked, and its last king, Ibbi-Suen, taken as prisoner to Elam.[122]

---

sibling matings, father and son have an r [relatedness coefficient] = .95." In other words, the heir is a regular clone of the father (see p. 305). However, incestuous mating is not to be encouraged "under monogamy, [when] the risk of not producing a fit heir with a sister or a daughter would be too high." (p. 304). See also fn. 4 ibid, in cases of absolute hegemony interdynastic marriages are not seen as an atractive strategy for the royal daughter, who will be more inclined to mate within her clan. Note, finally, that brother-sister unions are the most common form of incestuous mating, second is father-daughter unions, whereas mother-son relations are almost unknown (see. p. 305 ibid).

121 M. van de Mieroop 1999/2000: 111-129. See also W. Sallaberger 1999: 276–283

122 That Ibbi-Suen died somewhere in Iran is suggested by several later texts: see D. Edzard 1957: 51.

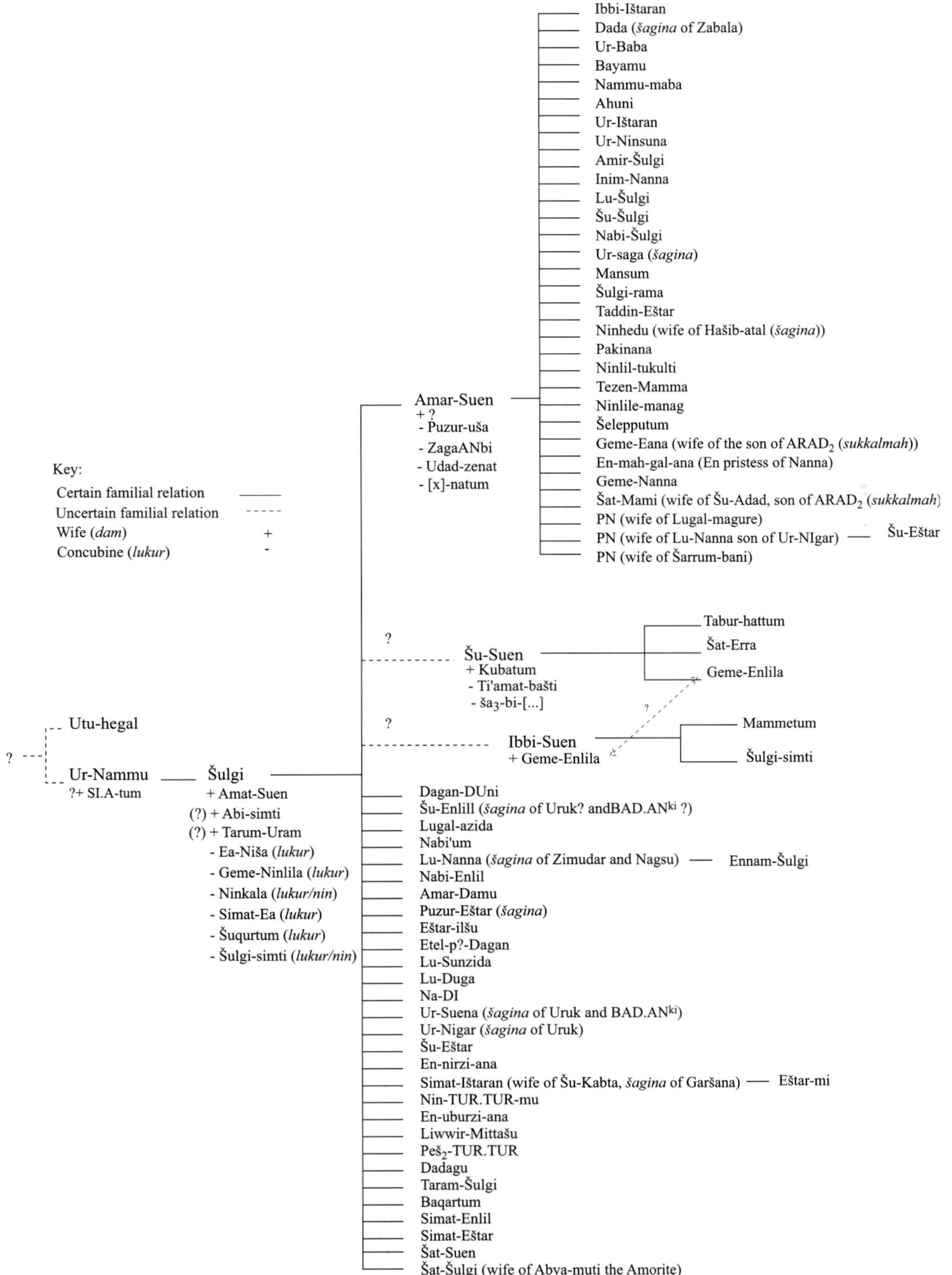

Figure 4: The royal family of Ur

Why did the succession proceed as it did? What determined that Amar-Suen ascended to the throne, although he was apparently not a strong candidate? A prince who did not enjoy the support of a large segment of both the royal family, as well as the provincial governors and other important members of society, is unlikely to be successful, according to the simple rules of succession outlined above. His claim to succession would be contested, and another prince whose career had allowed for the formation of connections and the building of alliances would prevail. It is likely that some sort of principle existed dictating that the next in seniority was supposed to follow Šulgi, and it is possible that it was precisely the circumstances of Šulgi's long rule that had resulted in this system.[123] It is likely that Šulgi outlived any brothers he might have had, thereby eliminating the threat from the senior generation. Babati's supposed distinctive position in the social hierarchy can thus be explained as deriving from his position as a senior member of the royal family exercising his influence through his sister's sons.

The genealogy that has been suggested for the royal family of Ur divides most of the male princes between Šulgi and Amar-Suen.[124] This is done according to the earliest attestation of the title "son of the king" (*dumu lugal*) for each of these persons. It is therefore safe to say that the progeny of Šū-Suen and Ibbi-Suen was restricted, and that Šulgi, and probably Amar-Suen too, had multiple male heirs. This might have been a conclusive factor in determining the succession since Amar-Suen, perhaps himself weak, had the support of many sons who themselves held important offices and hoped for a place in the line of succession, as well as the support of important allies married to his daughters.[125]

It is remarkable that a term equivalent to "heir apparent," or crown prince, is unknown from the Ur III documents.[126] However, if we choose to follow R. Burling 1974, and see the absence of such a title as a conscious choice of the ruler aimed at preventing patricide, this makes sense. The existence of an unwritten system of succession in the ruling family of Ur, resembling that of the House of Saud as formulated by Abd al-Aziz, seems equally likely.[127]

---

123 Compare with R. Burling 1974: 7–8.

124 This division is based largely on the information given in D. Frayne 1997.

125 See also Excursus 1.

126 The Sumerian word *ibila*, which is the closest Sumerian equivalent to English "heir" (German "Erbsohn") is a loanword from Akkadian (see D. Edzard 1960: 256). *ibila* presumably refers to property rights rather than to (royal) succession (see J. Renger 1976: 368).

127 See Excursus 1.

CHAPTER 4. THE RULING FAMILY OF UR III UMMA

4.1 Introduction

Umma[128], located north of Girsu and north-east of Ur on the Umma-canal (*i_7-umma^{ki}*), an outlet from the Tigris[129], was already an ancient city during the Ur III period four thousand years ago. Umma has been identified with Tell Djokha, one of the largest sites in Mesopotamia, although it has never been scientifically excavated.[130] Umma's location in close proximity to the important cult center Zabala, and controlling the junction of the Tigris ("Eastern Euphrates") and the Iturungal, is likely to have been a reason for its importance in both pre-Sargonic as well as Ur III times.

Only very few Umma texts from the pre-Sargonic period have been published, and the abundant historical inscriptions from the neighboring city-state of Lagaš have been almost the only source when attempting to reconstruct the history of that area of Sumer.[131] Umma texts from the period immediately prior to the Ur III period, the Old Akkadian period, have long since been known; albeit poorly understood they are an important source for the history of Umma.[132]

The thousands of Ur III documents from Umma were excavated during the early years of the twentieth century by the local population and quickly found their way to the markets of Europe and North America. Recent illicit excavations at Umma are said to have produced an abundant record

---

128 Written *GEŠ.UH$_3^{ki}$*.

129 Earlier believed to be the "Eastern Euphrates" or the Iturungal canal. The recent study by P. Steinkeller 2001: 22–84, is used here as a reference to the geography of the Umma province.

130 For a concise and contemporary account from the times of the massive plunder of Umma, see G. Contenau 1915. For an eyewitness account of the tell at the time of the lootings, see W. Andrae 1902-03: 20–22. Brief excavations at Umma (Djokha; 31°40'3.63" N 45°53'15.00" E), and its sister site Umm Al Akrab (31°37'16.65" N 45°56'0.09" E), immediately prior to the American-led attack on Iraq in 2003 suggested that the city-state of Umma went through a development not unlike that of Girsu, and that Umm Al Akrab may have been Umma of the pre-Sargonic period. The failure of international forces to protect Iraq's cultural heritage sites following the 2003 invation has, according to rumors, led to the near total destruction of both sites. The large structure excavated prior to the 2003 attack on Iraq has been proven to be the temple of Šara rebuild in Šū-Suen's 9th year (presentation by Nawala Mahmoud of the Iraq National Museum, held at the 53rd RAI (Moscow/Petersburg), 2007).

131 The CDLI project counts seventeen stone objects from Umma (thanks are due to Klaudia Englund for making her Umma files available to me) dating primarily to the pre-Ur III period (two Ur III inscriptions). Based on these few fragmentary historical inscriptions and the Lagaš historical record, D. Edzard published a genealogy of the pre-Sargonic rulers of Umma (D. Edzard 1959: 22).

132 B. Foster published a genealogy of the rulers of Umma during the Sargonic period (B. Foster 1982: 154-156). A web-presentation of the Old Akkadian material is planned within the frame-work of the CDLI project. Note that Umma may have been a stronghold of the Gutian rulers of the post-Akkadian period; see P. Steinkeller 2001: 31.

of texts from all periods, even texts from the earliest periods of Mesopotamian civilization, the Late Uruk period.

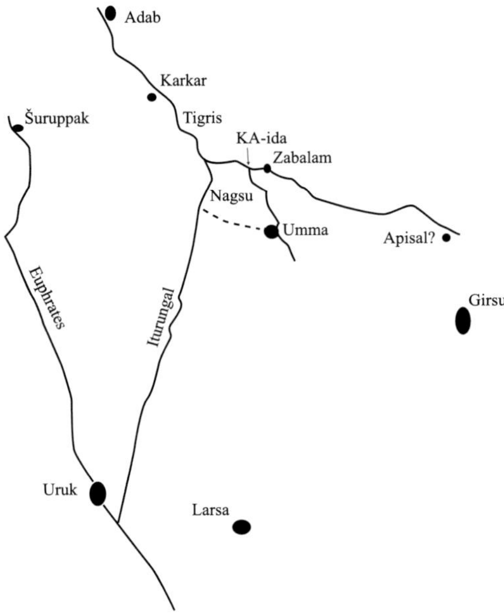

Figure 5: Map of the Umma province, adapted from P. Steinkeller 2001: 50

Since no archaeological description of Umma is available, I will not venture into any discussion of the possible layout of that city; rather I will limit this introduction to a description of the administrative layout of the province as recorded in the cuneiform record, with a particular focus on the ruling elite. A much broader study of the geography and history of Umma is planned within the framework of the CDLI; see in that regard also the projected study by P. Steinkeller on the topography and hydrology of the Umma province.[133]

The city of Umma was the capital of the province bearing the same name, and consequently the only city with a governor. The only other economically important city in the province of Umma was Apisal (*a-pi*$_4$*-sal*$_4$^{ki}). The cities Zabala (see fn. 149 below) and KI.AN^{ki}, although frequently mentioned in the records, were presumably cities of minor economic relevance, but held some religious significance. The districts of Gu(e)dena[134] and Mušbiana, often grouped together, were

133 For an outline of Steinkeller's projected study, "Population Density, Settlement Patterns and Rural Landscape in Southern Babylonia under the Ur III Dynasty: The Case of the Province of Umma," see P. Steinkeller 2001: 23.

134 Gu(e)dena of Ur III Umma is perhaps identical with the famous Gu'edena mentioned numerous times in the historical inscriptions of the pre-Sargonic Lagaš-rulers. In Ur III Umma sources the area Gu(e)dena is written primarily *gu*$_2$*-de*$_3$*-na*, but occasionally *gu*$_2$*-eden-na*; it is possible that the former writing is a phonological

perhaps without any large permanent settlements.[135]

The province of Umma was divided into three agricultural territories: Da-Umma, Apisal, and Gu(e)dena and Mušbiana. Da-Umma, often simply called Umma or aša Umma, was the most important of these three districts, and the one which by far generated the largest yield of economic documentation as well as the largest cereal production.[136] The fact that whenever the districts were listed together Da-Umma was always mentioned first, and Apisal second, followed by Gu(e)dena and Mušbiana, support this observation. The tablet container record Aleppo 433 (M 3779), archiving documents from the two years Š 45 and Š 46, is useful in that it illuminates the structure of the agricultural territories of Umma:[137]

Aleppo 433 (M 3779) (Š 45 to Š 46)

1. pisan dub-ba	Tablet container;
2. x ⸢nam⸣-ša$_{3}$-tam	... of the *šatam*-administrators of
3. ugula nam-1(u)-ke$_{4}$-ne	"foremen of ten"[138]
4. da-umma^{ki}	(concerning the districts of) Da-Umma,
5. a-pi$_{4}$-sal$_{4}^{ki}$	Apisal,
Reverse	
1. gu$_{2}$-eden-na	Gu(e)dena
2. u$_{3}$ muš-bi-an	and Mušbiana,
3. i$_{3}$-gal$_{2}$	are present.
4. mu 2(diš)-kam	From two years.
5. mu ur-bi$_{2}$-lum	Year: "Urbilum (was destroyed),"
6. u$_{3}$ mu ki-maš^{ki}	and Year: "Kimaš (was destroyed)."

MCS 6, 83, BM 105334 (AS 2), which is likely to have been a survey of all the lands of the province of Umma, divided it into three areas of almost equal size. The first third recorded the domain land (*GAN$_{2}$ gu$_{4}$*), divided into 100 units of 6 *bur$_{3}$*, each managed by a "cultivator" (*engar*). With some additional prebend-lands (*šuku*), this was the core of the Umma state lands. An area of the

variant of the later.

135 See also G. van Driel 1999/2000: 80.

136 See for example BM 110116 (cf. K. Maekawa 1987: 25–82), a record of the yield from Da-Umma. The total area of Da-Umma recorded in that text was 339 *bur$_{3}$* and 1 *iku* (2,197 hectares). See also K. Maekawa 1989: 49–50 and table 2.

137 Compare to MCS 1, 26, BM 113020 (IS 2), a tablet container holding the documents concerning inspections of various cattle from the same districts.

138 For the use of interchangeable titles in the agricultural sector (*ugula* >< *nu-banda$_{3}$ gu$_{4}$* >< *šabra gu$_{4}$*) see fn. 319 below.

exact same size was said to be left fallow.[139] The last section computed another third of the total lands, designating it as cultivated prebend-land for allotment holders.[140] The total amount of agricultural land in Umma as recorded in this text comes to more than 2,000 bur_3 (presumably only half of this could be harvested at the same time), making Umma about a quarter of the size of Lagaš insofar as cereal agriculture is concerned.[141]

The expected yield from 600 domain units—using a 20 *gur* per bur_3 ratio[142]—is matched in AAICAB 1, 1912-1143 (Š 28), recording an expected yield of 15,000 *gur* (ca. 4 1/2 million liters) from the domain units of Umma; this product was controlled centrally by the imperial court.[143] Unfortunately these key texts, so important to the reconstruction of the Ur III Umma geographical layout, do not inform us about the fraction of Umma domain units located in any of the main districts, Da-Umma, Apisal, and Gu(e)dena and Mušbiana.

Although the names themselves may help us locate the three main districts of Umma (Da-Umma as bordering the city of Umma, Apisal, as being in the vicinity of the city Apisal, and Gu(e)dena and Mušbiana as bordering the Girsu province), a more precise identification is not possible at the moment.[144]

The traditional Mesopotamian pantheon of the late third millennium was honored in the city of Umma, and we find references to temples dedicated to local deities as well as gods from other provinces, and perhaps even to deities from outside Sumer.[145] The chief deity of the Umma pantheon, Šara, held a pivotal position in Umma, together with his spouse Nin-ura, and Inanna, Šara's mother. The main temple of Šara was the Emah, which appears as an element in some Ur III Umma personal names; names formed with the theophoric element Šara are among the most common in Umma. In the ninth year of Šū-Suen's reign, the central administration constructed (anew?) the main sanctuary

139 AnOr 1, 303 (no date), supports this interpretation; the first entry in that text is an area of 1200 bur_3 called the domain land (GAN_2 gu_4). Unfortunately, the size of the fallow lands is not discernible due to the fragmentary state of this text.

140 See K. Maekawa 1987: 38–39, and table 7.

141 K. Maekawa 1974: 11, estimated that the Girsu area to be harvested (domain units and the allotments for the cultivators (*šuku engar*) was ca. 3,664 bur_3. This area produced ca. 24 $guru_7$, 2,691 *gur* and a few $sila_3$, or more than 22 million liters of barley. The yield of Girsu domain land, therefore, was perhaps also four times the yield harvested from the Umma domain land.

142 In comparison, the yield in Girsu during the latter half of Šulgi's reign and the first half of Amar-Suen's reign averaged 30 *gur* per bur_3. See for instance K. Maekawa 1974: 11. However, K. Maekawa 1989: 49, seems to suggest a 24 to 30 *gur* per bur_3 yield in Umma.

143 AAICAB 1, 1912-1143 (Š 28), rev. 8, reads "copy of sealed tablet exists in the palace," (*gaba-ri* $kišib_3$ e_2-*gal* gal_2-am_3). See also p. 50 for a discussion of this text.

144 See also G. van Driel 1999/2000.

145 See for example the reference to Nanše of Umma in NABU 1989, 95 9 (IS 4). See M. Cohen 1996, for a study of the province of Umma from the point of view of regionalism in the cult.

of Šara in Umma. This event was important enough to give the year its name (see also fn. 130 above).

The city of Apisal,[146] perhaps identical with the site known as Muhallaqiya, located downstream from the outlet of the Umma-canal on the Tigris river ("Eastern Euphrates"), was the second most important city in the Umma province.[147] The substantial tell at Muhallaqiya has never been excavated. A large number of Umma tablets refer to activities that take place in Apisal, suggesting that this city was governed entirely from Umma.[148] The pantheon of Apisal seems to have been a local variant of that of Umma; its main deities were the Apisalite Šara, and the Apisalite Ninura, among others. Apisal is thought to have been an important center for herding activities.

The city of Zabala,[149] which seems to have been of minor economic importance,[150] was an

---

146 For the reading Apisal see (with reference) P. Steinkeller 2001: 54 and fn. 127.

147 See P. Steinkeller 2001: 54–55.

148 See T. Jones & J. Snyder 1961: 337–338, suggesting that Ur-E'e held a position connected with the rule of Apisal.

149 For a possible identification of Zabala with Ibzaykh, see P. Steinkeller 2001: 54, and fn. 124. There seems to be some confusion concerning the writing of Zabala. Following Ellermeier, the following values are accepted:

Ellermeier	Borger AbZ	# of attestations in Ur III sources
zabala | ZA.MUŠ$_2$.UNUG	zabala (586)	0
zabala$_2$ | ZA.MUŠ$_3$.UNUG	zabala$_2$ (586)	0
zabala$_3$ | MUŠ$_3$.UNUG	zabala$_3$ (103)	62
zabala$_4$ | MUŠ$_3$.ZA.UNUG	zabala$_4$ (103)	9
zabala$_5$ | MUŠ$_3$.AB	zabala$_5$ (103)	8 (9?)
zabala$_6$ | AB.MUŠ$_3$	zabala$_6$ (128)	4
zabala$_x$ | MUŠ$_3$.UNUG.ZA		1 (ITT 3, 4954)
zabala$_x$ | MUŠ$_3$.TE.UNUG		0
zabala$_x$ | MUŠ$_3$.ZA.AB		0
zabala$_x$ | ZA.AB		0
zabala$_x$ | ZA.MUŠ$_2$.AB		0
| UNUG.MUŠ.ZA		1 (AUCT 1, 805)

For this survey, 86 attestations from the published record have been checked against published photographs or autographs (when no such record was available to me, the attestation in question was left out). *zabala$_3$* is by far the most frequent writing of the city-name.

150 For a possible reference to a mayor of Zabala see AUCT 1, 225 (Š 25 vi), rev. 8–9: ⸢x⸣ x(=2(diš)?) ha-za-an-num$_2$ / zabala$_4^{ki}$. AUCT 1, 26 (AS 3 viii to xii), mentions a general of Zabala by the name of Dada (presumably a member of the royal family, see above), obv. 2–3: mu da-da ⸢šagina⸣ zabala$_3^{ki}$-ka-[še$_3$] / kišib$_3$ šu-i$_3$-li$_2$ ⸢x-x⸣. MVN 16, 683 (AS 7), mentions a *galamah*-priest of Zabala, rev. 3: gala-mah zabala$_3^{ki}$. See also G. van Driel 1999/2000: 83.

important cultic center, in particular in the period after ŠS 1,[151] during which the "queen-dowager" Abī-simtī visited the city four times in five years.[152] Zabala was the city of Inanna of Zabala, and the oldest Ur III sources from this town (the records were presumably kept in Umma) mention a temple of Inanna at Zabala.[153] Prior to the coronation of Šū-Suen, references to Zabala primarily recorded minor deliveries for the cult of Inanna of Zabala.[154]

The only travelers to Zabala mentioned before Abī-simtī were a number of gods who received rations during their journey there:[155]

TCS 346 (AS 6 i):

Obverse

1. 2(diš) udu 1(diš) maš$_2$	two sheep, and one billy goat,
2. ^{d}nin-nun-gal	Nin-nungal,
3. zabala$_x$^{ki}-še$_3$ gen-na	having gone to Zabala.[156]
4. 1(diš) gukkal	one fat-tail sheep,
5. ^{d}igi-zi-bar-ra	Igizi-bara,
6. zabala$_x$^{ki}-še$_3$ gen-na	having gone to Zabala.

Reverse

1. ki a-lu$_5$-lu$_5$-ta	From Alulu
2. zi-ga iti še-KIN-ku$_5$	booked out. Month "Harvest."
3. mu-us$_2$-sa en unu$_6$-gal ^{d}inanna	Year after: "Enunugal-Inanna

151 One reference from AS 9 suggests that Abī-simtī visited Zabala during that year too; see UTI 3, 2003.

152 See p. 10 above for a discussion of Abī-simtī, the wife of either Šulgi or Amar-Suen. Here she is called "queen-dowager" in opposition to Kubatum who is called "queen," although both were written with the Sumerian sign *nin*. W. Sallaberger briefly described Abī-simtī's visits to Zabala in Sallaberger 1993: 45 and fn. 189. See also M. Such-Guitiérrez 2001: 98 and fn. 87.

153 The household had a small permanent staff; see, for example, AAICAB 1, 1911-229 (Š 28 viii). See also AnOr 1, 88 (AS 5), which mentions conscriptions for *bala* service from among the staff of Inanna of Zabala (the structure of the text is similar to TCL 5, 6038).

154 See for example BIN 5, 19 (Š 33), a text describing the wool meant for the "lofty garnment" of Inanna of Zabala, from Ur-E'e (for ^{tug2}*mah* see H. Waetzoldt 1972: xxi ("Prachtgewand"), and see xxiii fn. 77 for a possible reading *šutur* for ^{tug2}*mah*). Zabalam is also mentioned with some frequency in the texts from Garšana.

155 See also UTI 4, 2563 (AS 8), a list of minor food-stuff offerings designated for "Nin-gipar having ascended to Usag(?)," (obv. 11: ^{d}nin-gi$_6$-par$_4$ u$_2$-sag-še$_3$ e$_3$-a), and "Igizid-bara having gone to Zabala" (rev. 8: ^{d}igi-zi-bar-ra zabala$_3$^{ki}-še$_3$ gen-na). The delivery was made by Ur-Šulpa'e (rev. 21: ki ur-^{d}šul-pa-e$_3$), and sealed by the governor (rev. 22: kišib$_3$ ensi$_2$) of Umma, Ur-Lisi, according to the seal.

156 This reading could not be checked against any graphic representation of the signs; it has not been included in the previous analysis (fn. 149), and Boson's reading (*MUŠ$_3$.TE.UNUG*) has been retained here.

(was installed)."

The first reference to the "queen-dowager" Abī-simtī's yearly visits to Zabala comes from an account concerning Lu-kirizal, the pig-herder:[157]

SNAT 436 (ŠS 1):

Reverse

...

6. 2(diš) šah$_2$ gur$_4$ nita$_2$	Two "fat" male pigs,
7. igi-kar$_2$ nin zabala-še$_3$ gen-na	provisions[158] for the "queen-dowager," having gone to Zabala.
5. 4(diš) šah$_2$ nita$_2$	Four male pigs,
8. kišib$_3$ nu-ra-a ensi$_2$-ka	Unrolled seal of the governor.

...

The vast majority of texts mentioning Zabala from the following five years were concerned with the annual visits of the "queen-dowager."[159] The fragmentary text MVN 18, 508 (ŠS 1?), even alludes to a house of the queen in Zabala.[160] The deliveries for the cult of Inanna of Zabala as well as the provisions for the "queen-dowager's" visits were mostly sealed by the governor of Umma or members of his administration; one of these, Ur-Šulpa'e was perhaps a royal representative at the governor's court.[161]

Twelve or thirteen texts from ŠS 1 mention Zabala; the majority of these texts were not dated by month, but the five that have a month-name were dated to either month three, four, or five.[162] Seven of the texts from ŠS 1 mention the "queen-dowager" by title, or specifically Abī-simtī by name. All other texts from the same year seem in some way to be related to the "queen-dowager's" visit to

157 See also J. L. Dahl 2006, for a brief introduction to third millennium BC pig-herding in southern Mesopotamia.

158 See P. Steinkeller 1982: 149–151.

159 Although no royal visitor was mentioned in Šū-Suen's second year, it is still possible to suggest that Abī-simtī paid a visit to Zabala that year as well.

160 See also MVN 16, 796 (ŠS 4 vii), obv. 9, which mentions a house of the queen, although the location of this house is not specified.

161 See, for example, MVN 18, 463 (ŠS 1). For the role of Ur-Šulpa'e, see also fn. 327 below.

162 SNAT 436; MVN 18, 508 (ŠS 1 ?); YOS 18, 93; UTI 4, 2602; MVN 18, 463; Torino 2, 524; Princeton 1, 243; BPOA 2, 2548 (BM 105353); ITT 5, 6983 (month 3); MCS 3, 43 12 (= BM 105502) (month 4); SET 288 (month 4); UTI 4, 2321 (month 4); and Ontario 2, 5 (ROM 967.287.39) (month 5).

Zabala;[163] it is likely that the governor of Umma went to Zabala at the same time.[164] The texts from ŠS 1 which do mention the "queen-dowager" were all related to basic household functions.[165]

Since the only text with a month-name concerned with the "queen-dowager's" visit to Zabala dates to month four, it seems likely that Abī-simtī visited Zabala during the fourth month of that year. Three texts from ŠS 1 mention Ennum-ili, the equestrian (*ra$_2$-gaba*); he may have been the queen's personal commissary.[166]

Only two texts from ŠS 2 mentioning Zabala have been published; neither of these mention the queen,[167] but both record deliveries for the *siskur*-offerings[168] of the king to the cult in Zabala.[169]

Eight of the eleven texts from ŠS 3 that mention Zabala also mention the "queen-dowager" Abī-simtī.[170] Two texts (MVN 16, 837, and SNAT 481) record the provisions for the "queen-dowager"

---

163 One text (Torino 2, 524) records the oil-rations (*i$_3$ ba*) for two members of the imperial staff (Ennum(mi)-ili, the equestrian, and Šū-Mamitum, the door-keeper, *i$_3$-du$_8$*) and a *ereš-dingir* priestess of Inanna of Zabala from the *sukkalmah*; another text (BPOA 2, 2548 (BM 105353)) records the royal offerings for Inanna of Zabala via Ninmar(ka), the cup-bearer (*sagi*) (For Ninmarka (the cup-bearer) see also fn. 253 in this study.) A Girsu text from month three (ITT 5, 6983) records the man-power for shipping flour to Zabala from Girsu; another text records the delivery of baskets from Ur-Šulpa'e received by a person named Gurzan in Zabala. A text records the dispatch of three *NIG$_2$* garments (perhaps an error for *^{tug2}nig$_2$-lam$_2$*) to Zabala (YOS 18, 93) (sealed by Gurzan son of x-layabi, the cook of the governor), the last text from ŠS 1 not to mention Abī-simtī (Ontario 2, 5 (ROM 967.287.39)) mentions the beer rations for Urra-il(?), the general, sealed by the governor (A(ya)kala) in Zabala.

164 Ontario 2, 5 (ROM 967.287.39) (ŠS 1 v), is a simple receipt for an allotment of ten *sila$_3$* of good beer for the general, from Alli, A(ya)kala's chief brewer, sealed by A(ya)kala the governor in Zabala.

165 Apart from the pigs mentioned in SNAT 436, one text mentions the work-days of a team of workers under Lu-balasag concerned with the "queen-dowager's" journey to Zabala (UTI 4, 2602); another text records a delivery of sesame(?) oil (*i$_3$ geš*) for Abī-simtī going to Zabala, sealed by Ur-Šulpa'e; one text records pottery booked out (from the account of the "queen-dowager") while on the way to Zabala (*zi-ga nin zabala$_3^{ki}$-še$_3$ gen-na-aš*) (Princeton 1, 243, rev. 3). One text mentions seventeen *hal*-baskets for messengers, filled with leather (eight skins) (*1(u) 7(diš) ^{gi}hal kin-gi$_4$-a kuš si-ga / kuš-bi 8(diš)-am$_3$*) for the "queen-dowager," while in Zabala (SET 288 [ŠS 1 iv]); another text records the same bags booked out of Zabala via the "queen-dowager" (UTI 4, 2321 [ŠS 1 iv]).

166 Ennum-ili is known to have been an officer in the imperial administration; see, for example, MVN 13, 549 (AS 9 vi); Ontario 1, 115 (ROM 567 910X209.151) (AS 9 xii*min* 14). He is perhaps identical with the well-known officer responsible for multiple deliveries to the Drehem administration (see, for example, PDT 2, 1135 [Š 43 i]; PDT 2, 1184 [Š 45 xii 24 to 29]).

167 AnOr 7, 377 (ŠS 2 to 4), however, does mention a journey by an unknown person (text is broken) to Zabala.

168 Following W. Sallaberger 1993: 41-42.

169 MVN 16, 877 (no month name), and MVN 4, 174 (from the first month).

170 MVN 16, 960; MVN 16, 916; MVN 16, 837; SNAT 481; BIN 5, 31; Princeton 1, 238; MVN 16, 1092

going to Zabala: the first listed gold, the second baskets and garlic. Both deliveries were made by Lu-kala, the chief household administrator of the governor; the first was sealed by the governor (A(ya)kala), the second by Šarakam.[171] MVN 16, 960, records the garment provisions for Abī-simtī on the way to Zabala, following a smaller provision for the child born to the queen, Kubatum,[172] and in turn followed by several entries recording provisions for gods and imperial officers, from I-kala, sealed by the governor.

While traveling to Zabala, in ŠS 3, the queen received animals from Ušmu (a leading Umma animal fattener, see pp. 116 ff., below)—the animals were termed *mašdaria* (*maš*$_{(2)}$*-da-ri-a*)[173]—the transaction was sealed by the governor (MVN 16, 916). Abī-simtī transferred some animals as *siskur*-offerings (*siskur*$_2$) for Inanna of Zabala (BIN 5, 31).[174] The queen herself received *siskur*-offerings while in Zabala.[175]

The last text from ŠS 3 to be mentioned here recorded the transfer of beer and bread to Zabala while the queen was travelling there:

(month 2); and AnOr 7, 235 (month 2). Three texts dating to ŠS 2 do not mention the "queen dowager" but Zabala: One text (JCS 39, 125 13 [month 2]) records the provisions for (the divine?) Zabala, Enlil, Ninhursag, and the (divine?) *kab*$_2$*-ku*$_5$ of *en-gaba-ra*$_2$, from Šarakam—one of A(ya)kala's provisioners—sealed by the governor (A(ya)kala) (reverse line 6–8, kab$_2$-ku$_5$ en-gaba-ra / ki ^{d}šara$_2$-kam-ta / kišib$_3$ ensi$_2$-ka). It is, of course, not uncommon to find geographical names among the deities receiving offerings in Ur III text. The *kab*$_2$*-ku*$_5$ of *en-gaba-ra*$_2$, is, however, never again attested in this context. For the geographical name The *kab*$_2$*-ku*$_5$ of *en-gaba-ra*$_2$, see, for example, Princeton 1, 477 (Š 36), recording work done there, obv. 4: kab$_2^{ab}$-ku$_5$ en-gaba-ra$_2$ A.DUN gub-ba. The "the field across from the lord" (*a-ša*$_3$ *en-gaba-ra*$_2$) is well attested in Ur III Umma sources (it is also possible to read this field-name *a-ša*$_3$ *en-du*$_8$*-du*, a reading for which an interpretation remains warranted; see also T. Ozaki 2004: 221–222 for a short discussion of this name). Another similar text (Nik 2, 326 [month 9]) records provisions for miscellaneous deities. SNAT 487 (month 9) records the garment rations for the permanent staff of Zabala (rev. 10: tug$_2$-ba giri$_3$-se$_3$-ga zabala$_3^{ki}$).

171 Šarakam, Alli, among others, functioned as supply officers of the governor. Several hundred tablets sealed by A(ya)kala confirm this. The documents all relate to minor deliveries of beer, flour, and other basic commodities.

172 Obv. 3; igi-kar$_2$ ku-ba-tum nin-e dumu tu-da.

173 Following W. Sallaberger 1993: 160–170, *mašdaria* is understood as a sort of regular delivery for the imperial court and not an offering, although it was destined for the religious festivals in the capital and Nippur, and sometimes diverted to cult-offerings.

174 Although both MVN 16, 916, and BIN 5, 31 record different kinds of livestock, there is no direct indication that the animals recorded in the one text were the same as in the other.

175 See Princeton 1, 238, obv: 7(diš) ^{gi}pa$_4$-ti-um 5(diš) sila$_3$ esir$_2$ su-ub-ba / siskur$_2$ nin / ša$_3$ zabala$_3^{ki}$ / ki a-gu-ta, "Seven *patium* baskets holding 5 *sila*$_3$, coated with bitumen, *siskur*-offering of the "queen-dowager" (while) in Zabala, from Agu," and MVN 16, 1092 (ŠS 3 ii) (not specified as *siskur*): 1(u) 5(diš) ku$_6$ ^{gi}kaskal / kun-zi 3(u)-ta / ki nin-še$_3$ / ša$_3$ zabala$_3^{ki}$ // ki ur-^{d}ba-ba$_6$-ta / kišib$_3$ ensi$_2$ ..., "fifteen travel-baskets for fish, thirty *kun-zi* fish each, for the "queen-dowager" (while) in Zabala, from Ur-Baba, sealed by the governor ..."

AnOr 7, 235 (ŠS 3 ii):

1. 2(u) 2(diš) guruš u$_4$ 2(diš)-še$_3$	twenty-two workers for two days,
2. kaš ninda zabala$_3^{ki}$-še$_3$	having brought beer and bread
	to Zabala,
3. de$_6$-a u$_3$ zabala$_3^{ki}$-a gub-ba	and having stayed in Zabala,
4. a-bi$_2$-si$_2$-im-ti nin i$_3$-im-gen-na-a	while Abī-simtī the queen,
	was travelling.
Reverse	
1. [...]-x	x x
2. ⸢kišib$_3$⸣ [lu$_2$]-kal-la	Sealed by Lu-kala.
3. iti sig$_4$-geš i$_3$-šub-ga$_2$-ra	Month "placing the brick in the mold."
(seal)	
4. mu-us$_2$-sa ma$_2$ ^{d}en-ki	Year after: "the boat of Enki."
Seal	
1. lu$_2$-kal-la	Lu-kala,
2. dub-sar	scribe,
3. dumu ur-e$_{11}$-e šuš$_3$	son of Ur-E'e,
	chief livestock administrator.

Abī-simtī perhaps visited Zabala during month 2 of ŠS 3, the only month attested in several texts relating to her visit.

Five of the eight texts from ŠS 4 mentioning Zabala also mention the "queen-dowager." Three of these texts record provisions for the queen.[176] One text records *siskur*-offerings for Inanna of Zabala transferred by the queen.[177] The last text from ŠS 4 to mention Abī-simtī was MVN 16, 796, from month seven, recording household items booked out (for) the "queen-dowager" while traveling to Zabala from A(ya)kala (the chief of the leather workers), once again sealed by Lu-kala.

Two of the three texts from ŠS 4 which mention Zabala, but which do not mention the "queen-dowager," were concerned with textile offerings to Inanna of Zabala.[178] The textiles of these texts were termed *su-si ^{d}inanna zabala^{ki}-še$_3$*.[179] The last text from that year (UTI 4, 2705) documents

176 MVN 16, 1330; MVN 16, 713; and BM 106073 (unpubl.) (month 7).

177 AnOr 7, 241 (month 7).

178 MCS 8, 90 (=BM 105544), and MCS 2, 76 (=BM 113031).

179 The term *su-si* occurs a mere nine times in the published Ur III record, and always in connection with a female divine name. It appears to be a term used to describe different fabrics given to gods, such as regular *^{tug2}uš-bar* or *^{tug2}uš-bar* with various qualifications. The texts are: MCS 2, 76, BM 113031 (ŠS 4): Inanna of Zabala; MCS 8, 90, BM 105544 (ŠS 4): Inanna of Zabala; MVN 14, 244 (AS 7 to 8): Gula; Rochester 145 (no year, month 9): Gula; TJAMC FM 51 (pl. 47) (ŠS 5): Inanna of Zabala; BM 108269 (Š 47) : Nin-Egal; UTI 3,

field work. Since the only month-name on tablets from Zabala during ŠS 4 mentioning the "queen-dowager" was the seventh, there is reason to believe that this was the month she visited Zabala that year.

SAT 3, 1568 (ŠS 5), is the only extant text following ŠS 4 which records the "queen-dowager's" presence in Zabala (reverse line 1; nin zabala^{ki} gub-ba).[180] That text records the labor involved in bringing certain products to Zabala from Umma and back again; the document was sealed by the provisions officer of the Umma governor, Šarakam.[181]

There is no indication that Abī-simtī visited Zabala at a certain time of ŠS 4. In ŠS 1 she presumably went there during month 4, in ŠS 3 during month 2, and in ŠS 4 during month 7.

The last text to mention the city of Zabala is AAICAB 1, 1911-206 (ŠS 9), recording the delivery of a few hides (of sheep?) for Inanna of Zabala. Based on the relatively low number of texts mentioning Zabala altogether, this text cannot be used as a terminal date for Ur control over Zabala.

Numerous records mention the city KI.AN^{ki}, and in particular deliveries for the cult of Šara there.[182] The names of shrines for many other deities as well as many cultic activities are recorded in the extant record. Little evidence exists, however, that links the city of KI.AN^{ki} with either the royal family of Ur, or the gubernatorial court of Umma in any other way than basic administrative activities.

In the following description of the ruling family of Ur III Umma several pages are devoted to the earliest generations of that family, including Ur-nigar, who is considered the actual paterfamilias, and to GIRI$_3$.NI, who is here considered a (semi-)legendary ancestor of the Umma ruling family. The following section will deal with the governors of Umma, mentioning first of all the paucity of data recording any governor prior to Ur-Lisi, followed by a discussion of Ur-Lisi and his two brothers and successors, A(ya)kala and Dadaga. This section also includes discussions of all known female members of the ruling family. We shall then look at the role of the children of the governor and address the vital question of succession within the clan of Ur-nigar. Hereafter a lengthy section is devoted to Ur-E'e and the office of the chief livestock administrator. Following Ur-E'e are two sections: the first deals with Lu-Haya, Ur-E'e's son and presumed successor as chief livestock administrator, while the second is about Lu-kala, Ur-E'e's other son. Lu-kala is, following A(ya)kala, the second best documented person from Umma. The discussion of Lu-kala and his office will also deal with A(ya)kala, Dadaga and Gududu, who seem to have held the same office as Lu-kala at some point in

---

2018 (ŠS 1): Gula of Umma; UTI 3, 2069 (ŠS 1): Ninsun; SACT 2, 280 (ŠS 2): for several gods; and MVN 18, 626 (no date): Nin-x.

180 Abī-simtī must have died prior to ŠS 9 xii 17, when her first *ki-a-nag* offering is recorded (see ASJ 3, 92 3).

181 See also M. Such-Guittérez 2001: 94 and fn. 60 and table 13, p. 17, and add SAT 3, 1595 recording the journey of the princess Me-Ištarān to Zabala in SS 5.

182 See for example the account of deliveries for Šara of KI.AN^{ki}, concerning Dada (perhaps identical with the *sanga*-priest called Dada?) BCT 2, 143 (Š 48), rev. iv 20: [nig$_2$]-⸢ka$_9$⸣-ak mu-DU ⸢d⸣šara$_2$ ⸢KI⸣.AN^{ki}.

time. After our discussion of Ur-E'e, his office and the careers of his sons we will investigate another member of the ruling family whose career in some ways resembled that of Ur-E'e: $ARAD_2$(mu). This section also discusses the office of the Umma chief of the granary, as well as the administration of agricultural production in Umma. The final section discusses, and lists, the other less known sons of Ur-nigar.

Figure 6 below is a graphic representation of the genealogy of the ruling family of Ur III Umma:

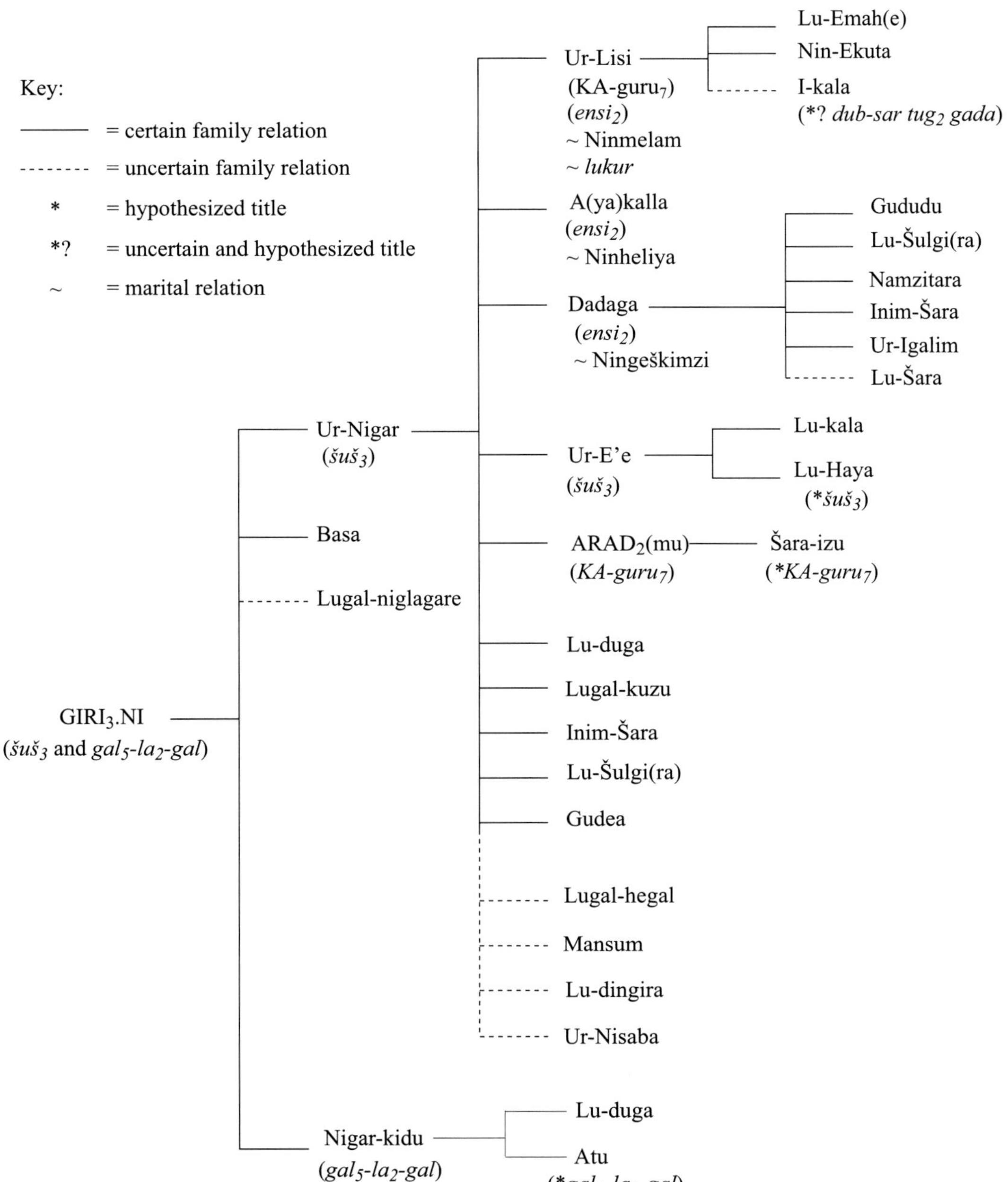

Figure 6: The ruling family of Ur III Umma

4.2. THE EARLIEST GENERATIONS

In their seal-inscriptions both Nigar-kidu (*nigar*^{gar}*-ki-du*$_{10}$)[183] and Ur-nigar (*ur-nigar*^{gar}) claimed to be sons of GIRI$_3$.NI.[184] According to these seal-legends,[185] GIRI$_3$.NI held two titles, chief of the *galla* (*gal*$_5$*-la*$_2$ *gal*),[186] and chief livestock administrator (*šuš*$_3$),[187] titles which were to be divided between his two sons; Nigar-kidu became chief of the *galla* (*gal*$_5$*-la*$_2$ *gal*), and Ur-nigar became chief livestock administrator (*šuš*$_3$). GIRI$_3$.NI had another son named Basag[188] whose title is still unknown.[189] Few documents are available from the time when we expect GIRI$_3$.NI to have been active, making it difficult for us to say anything about him. No impression of his own seal has been recovered, and no text can be ascribed to him with certainty. I therefore find it advisable to describe GIRI$_3$.NI as a semi-legendary ancestor of the Umma clan rather than an administrative figure with his own place in the administration.

Ur-nigar, one of GIRI$_3$.NI's two sons, became father of the most powerful generation of

---

183 *U.UD.KID* = *NIGIN*$_3$ = *KWU 512 (ABZ 447a)*. In Ur III administrative texts, *NIGIN*$_3$ primarily occurs together with the phonetic compliment GAR. The exceptions seem mainly to be the consequence of copying or scribal errors. Following H. Waetzoldt (1975: 383), and M. Krebernik (1984: 197 and fn. 119) a reading nigar is accepted here. The word *nigar* was used almost exclusively in the personal names *geme*$_2$*-nigar*^{gar}, *nigar*^{gar}*-ki-du*$_{10}$, and *ur-nigar*^{gar}, except for a few references to an *e*$_2$ *nigar* (Nik 2, 290 [ŠS 6 viii 6 to 7]; SAT 3, 2145 [month iv 12]; and BE 3-1, 165 [no date]). *nigar* is interpreted here as a short form of a temple-name.

184 Also read *kiri*$_x$*-zal* by some, presumably seen as a phonetic variant of *kiri*$_4$*-zal*. A reading GIRI$_3$.NI is preferred to leave open any interpretation. My suggestion is that the name is an abbreviation of *giri*$_3$*-ni-i*$_3$*-sa*$_6$, a common Ur III name.

185 The seal of Nigar-kidu was rolled on MVN 1, 182 (Š 26), together with the seal of Lu-Nin-x the "grand scribe of the king" (*dub-sar mah lugal-ka*). The document recorded the transfer of a large amount of barley from Ur-nigar to the palace.

186 The title *gal*$_5$*-la*$_2$ *gal* is problematic. Obviously the *gal* makes for an interpretation as "chief of the *gal*$_5$*-la*$_2$," leaving us with the *gal*$_5$*-la*$_2$. An equation with Akkadian *gallû(m)*—a word for an evil demon—must be abandoned for obvious reasons; rather, "police chief, gendarme, deputy, or bailif;" is more reasonable, although the etymology remains obscure.

187 Ur-nigar's seal inscription has not been preserved on any tablet (strike MVN 1, 136, cf. already R. Mayr 1997: catalogue no. 807). However, an actual seal of Ur-nigar, son of GIRI$_3$.NI, the chief of the *galla*, has been preserved; see L. Speleers 1917: 106–107, seal no. 625 (L. Speleers noted that the title of GIRI$_3$.NI was also found in the Obelisk of Maništusu, xii 2, and xiii 11 (both times in the phrase *ši gal*$_5$*-la*$_2$*-gal*, "the one of the chief of the *galla*"). See R. Mayr 1997: 149 and fn. 582 for a brief discussion of the seal of Ur-nigar. The text FAOS 17, 88, independently supports the point that Ur-nigar was the son of GIRI$_3$.NI. For a discussion of the office of the *šuš*$_3$, see section 8 of this chapter.

188 Written *ba-sa*$_6$*-ga* in his seal, and sometimes *ba-SIG*$_5$ in the texts, clearly supporting the reading *sag*$_{10}$*(SIG*$_5$*)* used throughout this study.

189 A possible further son of GIRI$_3$.NI is Lugal-niglagar'e mentioned in SACT 2, 98 (Š 34 vi).

administrators governing Umma, counting among others three well-known governors. Ur-nigar's title, chief livestock administrator (*šuš*$_3$), is almost exclusively known from the seals of his sons.

NYPL 318 (Š 24(?)),[190] an early text dealing with barley, is the only possible attestation of Ur-nigar, chief livestock administrator (*šuš*$_3$), and thereby the only certain attestation of Ur-nigar the father of three governors altogether.[191] It is possible to speculate that a prospering private economic sphere existed, parallel to the centralized economy of the empire, and that even members of the ruling family of Umma were involved not with state-affairs but rather dealings of their own, leaving no traces in the records of the central households. It is also plausible that the administration of the early years of Ur hegemony had yet to experience the excessive bureaucracy of the late years of Šulgi and the reign of his two sons Amar-Suen and Šū-Suen, and that Ur-nigar and his predecessors were state-employees functioning in an administrative machinery based less on written records and more on personal charisma and will. One may also suggest that the office of chief livestock administrator was not controlled by Ur in the early days of the dynasty.

Nigar-kidu is an even more elusive figure, partly because several people in Umma were called Nigar-kidu, and partly because Nigar-kidu's son Lu-duga primarily sealed documents described as sealed by either his brother Dadaga, or his cousin, Dadaga's son, Gududu, and finally, because Nigar-kidu's brother Ur-nigar also had a son named Lu-duga.

Nigar-kidu is only attested in MVN 1, 182 (Š 26), in which he certifies the transfer of a large amount of barley from his brother Ur-nigar to the palace. The document is sealed with his seal along with the seal of a "grand scribe" of the king.

Lu-duga the son of Nigar-kidu never appears in any text sealed with his own seal; he is, nevertheless, attested independently in a few texts.[192] It seems possible to claim that he did not partake in the state-run administration, and that his cousin Dadaga, for whatever reason, used his seal to seal certain transactions. Likewise Nigar-kidu's brother had a son named Lu-duga, who, in a similar fashion either sealed transactions for his cousin or simply deposited a seal with him. Nigar-kidu had another son, Atu, who may have followed him in the office as Chief of Police.[193] This Atu

---

190 The year information reads *mu 3(diš)-kam us*$_2$*-bi*. This is perhaps an abbreviated writing of *nig*$_2$*-ka*$_9$*-ak al-la-ka mu 3(diš)-kam us*$_2$*-sa-bi* = Š 24 (compare with MVN 21, 272 [Š 24 xi]).

191 Collated by the author October 2006. Although it is possible that the text has *ur-nigar*^{gar} ⌜*šuš*⌝, this cannot be verified. The broken parts of the text seems to allow for more signs than one (i.e. *SAHAR*), see also the online documentation at http://cdli.ucla.edu/p122856.

192 SA 76 (AS 4): obv. ii 3; MVN 11, 162 (Š 38 xii): rev. 3; CHEU 30 (Š 46): obv. 7; Nisaba 6, 11 (BM 106050) (IS 1?): mentions the wife of Lu-duga, the son of Nigar-kidu (rev. v 12: dam lu$_2$-du$_{10}$-ga dumu nigar^{gar}-ki-du$_{10}$).

193 This is suggested by the following unpublished Umma text (kept in a French private collection) (ŠS 6 ix – to ŠS 7 xii):

Obverse

1. 1(diš) nig$_2$-u$_2$-rum	One (person) Nigurum,

is also scarcely present in the extant records (see MVN 18, 286 (= AnOr 7:286) from ŠS 6 viii 21).

---

2. en-nu-⸢ga$_2$⸣ ti-la	living in the prison,
3. iti ^{d}li$_9$-si$_4$	from the month "Lisi,"
4. mu na-ru$_2$-a ⸢mah$^{?}$⸣ ba-ru$_2$-ta	of the year: "when the lofty stela was erected,"
Reverse	
1. iti ^{d}dumu-zi	to the month "Dumuzi,"
2. mu ma-da za-ab-ša-li^{ki} ba-hul-še$_3$	of the year: "when Madazabšali was destroyed."
3. ugula lu$_2$-ku$_3$-[..]	Overseer: Lu-ku...
4. kišib$_3$ a-⸢tu⸣	Sealed document of Atu.
Seal	
1. a-tu dub-sar	Atu, the scribe,
2. dumu nigar^{gar}-ki-du$_{10}$	Son of Nigar-kidu,
3. gal$_5$-la$_2$ gal	Chief of the *galla*.

4.3. THE GOVERNOR

When describing the ruling family of Umma it seems reasonable to begin with its most prominent members, the governors. The office of the governor (*ensi*$_2$) of Umma belonged throughout the entire duration of our documentation to the ruling family of Umma. When we research the earliest generations of the Ur III society we are constrained by the paucity of the sources, and it is speculative to comment on either the lineage or the administrative activities of any Umma governor prior to Ur-Lisi. One text has survived documenting the involvement of the ruling family of Umma in the administration of Umma during the early days of Ur hegemony: DC 236, presumably from Š 28.[194]

DC 236 (Š 28?) :

Obverse	
1. 1(geš'u) 2(geš$_2$) 3(u) ⸢3(aš)$^{?}$⸣ ⸢1(barig)$^{?}$⸣ še gur lugal	753 *gur* and 1 *barig* of barley according to the royal measure,
2. ⸢ki ab⸣ -ba-mu ⸢ensi$_2$⸣-ka-ta	From Abbamu the governor,[195]
3. ur-^{d}⸢li$_9$-si$_4$ KA-guru$_7$-ke$_4$⸣	Ur-Lisi, the chief of the granary,
Reverse	
1. šu ba-ti	received.
2. x-gi-na-⸢tum⸣ [...] ⸢^{d}šara$_2$⸣	...
3. giri$_3$ a-kal-⸢la⸣ [...] ab-ba-mu ⸢ensi$_2$⸣	Via A(ya)kala [... of ?] Abbamu the governor.
4. iti e$_2$-iti-6(diš)	Month *e-iti-6*.
5. mu en ^{d}en-ki ⸢x ba⸣ -[hun?]	Year: "the En-priest of Enki x x was installed in office."

The break in the text (reverse line 3) may have given either the official or the familial relationship of A(ya)kala and Abbamu. A reading [*šeš*] would conform with our knowledge of the familial structures of the Umma ruling family, but it is obscured by the lack of any reliable genealogy of Abbamu. The kinship term "brother" was used only in a limited number of relations, see Excursus 2.

---

194 The full formula of this year is: *mu en-nam-šita*$_4$*-*^{d}*šul-gi-ra-ke*$_4$ *ba-gub-ba(-še*$_3$*-šu*$_3$*-sag) en* ^{d}*en-ki eridu*^{ki}*-ga dumu šul-gi nita kalag-ga lugal uri*$_2$^{ki}*-ma lugal an ub-da limmu-ba-ke*$_4$ *ba-a-hun*, "Year: Ennamšita-Šulgirake-bagubaše-šusag, the son of Šulgi, the strong man, the king of Ur, the king of the four quarters, was installed as *en*-priest of Enki in Eridu." The name of this son of Šulgi, who is otherwise never attested in the extant sources, is reminiscent of the 'throne-names' of certain pre-Sargonic rulers.

195 One of the many problems with this text is the possibility to read *ab-ba muhaldim ensi*$_2$ instead of *ab-ba-mu ensi*$_2$ (Abba the cook of the governor, instead of Abbamu governor). Although it is impossible to explain the second genitive post-position on the word *ensi*$_2$ (*/ki abbamu ensi.k-ak-ta/*), it is notably left out in line 3 on the reverse. For this text, see also below.

From the same year (Š 28) another very important document has come down to us, AAICAB 1, 1912-1143 (mentioned above). It is a text computing a large amount of grain (mainly barley, *še*), totaling more than 15,000 *gur*, or more than four and a half million liters. The first entry of that text, 12,066 *gur*, 3 *barig*, 2 *ban$_2$* and 9 *sila$_3$* according to the *Šulgi-measurement*,[196] is the exact yield-estimate corresponding to the 100 domain units recorded in MCS 6, 83, BM 105334 (AS 2) (see above).[197] The total is said to be controlled by Ur-Lisi.[198] Since this document is dated to Š 28, it is my belief that Ur-Lisi, at this point in time operated in the capacity as chief of the granary (*KA-guru$_7$*).[199]

Abbamu has been mentioned above as a candidate for the earliest Ur III governor of Umma, but he remains an almost legendary figure.[200] Abbamu, the governor of Umma, is only mentioned in two texts, these are NYPL 37 (Š 33), and DC 236 (Š 28?) mentioned above. NYPL 37 mentions the *e$_2$ šu-sum-ma ab-ba-mu ensi$_2$-ka*, perhaps a reference to the left-over account of the deceased governor. In CHEU 94 (Š 28 viii), the house of Ur-saga the "slave" (*ARAD$_2$*) of Abbamu is mentioned, also A(ya)kala is present in this short text. No seal-impression of Abbamu the governor has survived to our time. Essentially, all of the texts that have been used as evidence for Abbamu as an early governor of Umma are ambiguous.[201] Other possible early governors of Umma are Ahua, Kuli, and Malakum.

FAOS 17, 88* (dating to before Š 33) is the only extant text which mentions Ahua as governor of Umma (obv. 26: u$_4$-ba a-hu-a ensi$_2$ umma^{ki}, "on the day Ahua (was/became) governor of Umma"). The text is very interesting in that it mentions the purchase of a house by Ur-nigar, the son of GIRI$_3$.NI, the chief of the *galla*. There are no other Umma texts mentioning Ahua dated to the early years of Šulgi. Some undated Umma texts mention Ahua; however, these do not mention any title of Ahua. See, for example, the undated text TSU 92 (= RIAA 188) which has as a concluding line *inim a-hu-a-ta*, "on the command of Ahua," suggesting a high office for this person. On the terminology, *inim PN-ta*, see p. 57 and fn. 216.

196 AAICAB 1, 1912-1143, obv. 1: 3(guru$_7$) 2(geš'u) 1(geš$_2$) 6(aš) 3(barig) 2(ban$_2$) 9(diš) sila$_3$ 1(u) 5(diš) gin$_2$ še gur ^{d}šul-gi.

197 12,066 *gur*, 3 *barig*, 2 *ban$_2$* and 9 *sila$_3$* divided by twenty is approximately 603 1/3. However, these two text still present some problems, and the reconstruction here is only tentative. The texts mentioned here were first discussed by K. Maekawa, however for slightly different purposes (K. Maekawa 1974: 1–60).

198 AAICAB 1, 1912-1143, rev. 11: ur-^{d}li$_9$-si$_4$ i$_3$-dab$_5$.

199 See fn. 204.

200 T. Maeda 1990: 71, table 1.

201 Abbamu, the governor of Umma, is only mentioned in two texts, these are, NYPL 37 (Š 33), and DC 236 (Š 28?), mentioned above. NYPL 37 mentions the *e$_2$ šu-sum-ma ab-ba-mu ensi$_2$-ka*, perhaps a reference to the left-over account of the deceased governor. In CHEU 94 (Š 28 viii), the house of Ur-saga the "slave" (*ARAD$_2$*) of Abbamu is mentioned, also A(ya)kala is present in this short text.

Only two references exist to Kuli the governor of Umma (Nebraska 44 (Š 39 to AS 3), obv. iv 32: $giri_3$ ku-li ⸢$ensi_2$⸣, and Ontario 2, 282 (ROM 925.62.420) (no date)) (see also fn. 257). For Malakum serving as governor of Umma, only one reference exists (Nisaba 9, 100 (BM 108029) (no date)).

4.4. UR-LISI

Ur-Lisi is recorded as governor of Umma for the first time in the thirty-third year of Šulgi, seven years after numerous sources appear for the first time at Umma.[202] Ur-Lisi is attested in a number of texts before Š 33, when he perhaps held the position as chief of the granary (*KA-guru*$_7$) of Umma.[203] This is not only inferred from the text given above (DC 236) but also from the administrative activities of Ur-Lisi before Š 33.[204]

Since Ur-Lisi is mentioned as the son of Ur-nigar, the chief livestock administrator (*šuš*$_3$),[205] and since both ARAD$_2$(mu), and A(ya)kala, well-known members of the ruling family, claimed to be "brothers of the governor" (*šeš ensi*$_2$) at the same time as Ur-Lisi held office,[206] Ur-Lisi must have

---

202 See the seal of Ur-Lisi, the governor (BMC Roma 8, 10 3 [Š 33 viii]); the seal of Šešani (?) dedicated to Ur-Lisi, the governor (Aleppo 147 (M 3936) [Š 33]) (the text was collated September 2006, a reading of Ur-E'e as the owner of the seal can be excluded although the reading of Šešani is not absolutely certain); the seal of Lugalebansa(g), dedicated to Ur-Lisi, the governor (MVN 14, 133 [Š 33 xi]); the seal of Habaluke, dedicated to Ur-Lisi, the governor (Syracuse 485 [Š 33 vii]); the seal of Atu, dedicated to Ur-Lisi, the governor (YOS 4, 151 [Š 32 ix to Š 33 i]).

203 See also T. Maeda 1996: 255.

204 Ur-Lisi is mentioned in several texts from the early days of Ur III, occupying a position similar to that of the *KA-guru*$_7$. He delivered barley for the cult, small quantities of barley for the regular offerings for Šara in Hirose 341 (Š 32 i to vi); for rations, large quantities of barley as rations for the ox-drivers and the engineer-troops (*ša*$_3$*-gu*$_4$ *ša*$_3$*-sahar-ra*: the *ša*$_3$*-sahar-ra* were male workers mainly specializing in excavating, often grouped together with the ox-drivers) in CHEU 2 (Š 31 iv to xi); and he received barley from various persons, for example, a large amount of barley from the governor of Adab, on the order of the governor of Umma as recorded in SANTAG 6, 16 (copy of Umma 92 = ICP 422) (Š 31 ix), (sealed by ARAD$_2$(mu) instead of Ur-Lisi, obv. 3–4: ki ensi$_2$ adab^{ki}-ta / inim ensi$_2$ umma^{ki}-ta, rev. 1–4: ur-^{d}li$_9$-si$_4$ / šu ba-ti / mu ur-^{d}li$_9$-si$_4$-še$_3$ / kišib$_3$ ARAD$_2$ i$_3$-gal$_2$). Compare these examples with the responsibilities of ARAD$_2$(mu) described below Chapter 4: Section 11.

205 See the seal of Ur-Lisi (*ur-*^{d}*li*$_9$*-si*$_4$ */ dub-sar / dumu ur-nigar*^{gar}); AUCT 3, 286 (Š 31 xi); AUCT 3, 427 (Š 31 xii); and MVN 21, 272 (Š 24 xi): 6(geš$_2$) še gur lugal / uri$_2$$^{[ki]}$-še$_3$ / giri$_3$ ur-^{d}li$_9$-si$_4$ // dumu ur-nigar^{gar} šuš$_3$-ka / iti pa$_4$-u$_2$-e / mu nig$_2$-ka$_9$-ak al-la-ka mu 3(diš)-kam us$_2$-bi, "360 *gur* of barley, to Ur, via Ur-Lisi the son of Ur-nigar, chief livestock administrator. Month *Pau'e*, Year: 'third year after the year the accounts of the hoe? (were put in order)'." Only very few seal-impressions of the simple seal of Ur-Lisi are known since he ruled Umma almost from the time when the first numerous archives appear. He came to be known primarily as "the govenor."

206 For ARAD$_2$(mu) see BPOA 2, 2641 (BM 105554) (Š 34 ii), obv. 3: ARAD$_2$ šeš ensi$_2$ umma^{ki}, "ARAD$_2$(mu), the brother of the governor." For A(ya)kala see OrSP 47-49, 500 (no date), obv. ii 15: a-kal-la šeš ensi$_2$, "A(ya)kala, brother of the governor." The text also mentions ARAD$_2$(mu) with the title "chief of the granary" (obv. Iii 17), indicating that Ur-Lisi had already taken office as governor, and Nigar-kidu (the uncle of Ur-Lisi) as "chief of the *galla*" (rev. iv 4: nigar^{gar}-ki-du$_{10}$ ugula gal$_5$-la$_2$ gal, note the unique occurence of the title *ugula* in front of *gal*$_5$*-la*$_2$ *gal*). See also JCS 28, 215 26 (Š 43): 3(u) guruš u$_4$ 1(diš)-še$_3$ / ku$_6$ ga$_6$$^{?}$-ga$_2$$^{?}$

been a member of the ruling family and a son of Ur-nigar, the chief livestock administrator (*šuš*$_3$).

During the early years of Ur-Lisi's tenure it was normal for office-holders in the administration to have seals dedicated to the governor rather than to the king, as was common in later years. More than forty people held seals dedicated to Ur-Lisi.[207] Although most of these dedicatory seals were used from the accession of Ur-Lisi in Š 33 until around the time of Šulgi's fortieth year, it is not possible to say when exactly this custom was abandoned. Some of the problems faced when using the seals of the Ur III administrators to describe the social system of the state can be seen from the following few examples. A(ya)kala had a seal dedicated to Ur-Lisi and at the same time a seal with no dedication (see fn. 206); Kugani had a seal dedicated to Ur-Lisi before the latter became governor, and a different seal dedicated to Ur-Lisi after he had become governor.[208] Some seals dedicated to Ur-Lisi remained in use long after Ur-Lisi's death, when A(ya)kala had become governor (see fn. 206). Nevertheless, it is seen as an attempt by the king to strengthen his influence in the provinces that officials in the local administration had seals carved with a dedicatory inscription mentioning the king rather than the local governor around year Š 41.[209]

As mentioned above, it is likely that Ur-Lisi was chief of the granary before he became governor. At that time this office passed to his brother ARAD$_2$(mu), who held that office at least until the end of Amar-Suen's reign, and presumably several years longer before being succeeded by his son Šara-izu.[210]

It is very difficult to demonstrate any direct administrative contact between the crown and the provincial administration. Only two letters to Ur-Lisi, the governor of Umma, from the king have

/ a-ša$_3$ en-gaba-ra$_2$ / giri$_3$ a-kal-la / šeš ensi$_2$ // kišib$_3$ a-kal-la / dumu lugal-nesag$_2$-e / ugula da-da / (blank line) / mu en ^{d}nanna maš-e i$_3$-pa$_3$, " thirty work-days, carrying? fish to the field Engabara, via A(ya)kala brother of the governor, sealed by A(ya)kala son of Lugal-nesag'e, foreman: Dada. Year: 'the En-priest of Nanna was chosen'." The obvious reason for the sudden need of an otherwise rare kinship term was to clearly exclude any ambiguity in a text mentioning two persons, both named A(ya)kala (see also excursus 2).

207 See for example the seal of Adaga (ur-^{d}li$_9$-si$_4$ / ensi$_2$ / umma^{ki} // a-da-ga / dub-sar / ARAD$_2$-zu) in use from Š 42 iv (MVN 2, 343) to Š 43 xi (MVN 14, 9) (with one possible attestation from ŠS 2); the seal of A(ya)kala (ur-^{d}li$_9$-si4 / ensi$_2$ / umma^{ki} a-kal-la // dub-[sar] / dumu ⸢ur⸣-[nigar]$^{⸢gar⸣}$ [šuš(?)] / ARAD$_2$-[zu]) in use from Š 39 i (MVN 14, 3) to Š 41 (ArOr 62, 238 I 867)), A(ya)kala also had a regular seal without dedication in use from Š 33 until he became governor himself; the seal of Atu, son of Lugal-saga (ur-^{d}li$_9$-si$_4$ / ensi$_2$ umma^{ki} / a-tu dub-sar / dumu lugal-sa$_6$-ga / ARAD$_2$-zu), in use from Š 33 (Nik 2, 189) to Š 43 (MVN 18, 425)), and the seal of Atu, son of Šeš-kala (ur-^{d}li$_9$-si$_4$ / ensi$_2$ umma^{ki} / a-tu dub-[sar] / dumu šeš$^{?}$-kal-la), in use in Š 40 (JCS 28, 220 42)), and so forth. Several other examples can be cited, see also R. Mayr 1997: 117–120 and fn. 492.

208 Kugani son of Ur-Šulgi (ur-^{d}li$_9$-si$_4$ / ensi$_2$ umma^{ki} / ku$_3$-ga-ni / dumu ur-^{d}šul-gi / ARAD$_2$-zu) in use from Š 34 vii (Aleppo 83 (M 4184)) to Š 38 viii (Aleppo 89 (M 4141)). Rochester 206 (ur-^{d}li$_9$-si$_4$ / ku$_3$-ga-ni / dub-sar / dumu ur-^{d}šul-gi / ARAD$_2$-zu) from Š 32 ix.

209 H. Waetzoldt 1995: 659–64.

210 For a discussion of ARAD$_2$(mu)'s tenure see chapter 4.11.

survived; the first (Scheil RA 24, 44)[211] is an order from the king written in Akkadian to give the *Lumah*-priest of Inanna of Girsu *60 gur* (ca. 18,000 liter) of barley.[212] The other letter written in Sumerian (YOS 4, 117)[213] is an order to Ur-Lisi to give the messengers of the king various objects.[214] It is possible that the first letter should be dated prior to Ur-Lisi's tenure as governor when he was chief of the Umma granary, however this question cannot be solved at present. The presence of messengers of the king, and "followers of the crown," commonly interpreted as a sort of police-force, (*aga*$_3$*-us*$_2$) at the local court in Umma strongly suggests a very real royal presence in Umma.[215]

Evidence for the direct involvement of the governor in the daily management of the province permeates the written record, and it is seen most clearly and explicitly in the references to "the command of the governor" (*inim ensi*$_2$*-ta*). Such terminology resembles a practice known from many contemporary middle-eastern societies where "the order of the king," or the like, is analogous to a legally binding and written order. The same phrase could easily be used with the title governor exchanged with the title of another high-ranking official, however, primarily naming the person rather than the office.[216] The phrase, "on the command of the governor" was sometimes used in

---

211 Edition by E. Sollberger: TCS 1, 369, see also P. Michalowski 1993: 55 (text 74).

212 The letter uses the normal Akkadian letter-fomula and introduces the most important person first: um-ma šar-ru-um-ma / a-na ur-^{d}li$_9$-si$_4$-na / qi$_2$-bi$_2$-ma / 1(geš$_2$) še gur / a-na lu$_2$-mah / ša ^{d}inanna / ša gir$_2$-su^{ki} / i-di$_3$-in // (reverse blank), "Thus (speaks) the king: tell Ur-Lisi to give 60 *gur* of barley to the *lumah* (priest) of Inanna of Girsu."

213 Edition by E. Sollberger: TCS 1, 1, see also P. Michalowski 1993: 54 (text 73).

214 The letter uses the normal third person voice throughout, except for the phrase (reverse line 4–5) lu$_2$ kin-gi$_4$-a-ga$_2$ / he$_2$-na-ab-sum-mu > /lu kiñ.gi-a-mu-ak he-na-b-sum-e/ "he shall give it to my messengers ...." The letter reads: lugal-e / na-ab-be$_2$-a / ur-^{d}li$_9$-si$_4$-na-ra / u$_3$-na-a-du$_{11}$ / 1/3(diš)ša har ku$_3$-babbar / 1(u) 5(diš) tug$_2$ hi-a / 3(ban$_2$) i$_3$ du$_{10}$-ga / 2(barig) i$_3$ geš / 1(diš) gu$_4$ / 1(u) udu maš$_2$ hi-a / kin-gi$_4$-a-ga$_2$ / he$_2$-na-ab-sum-mu, "Thus speaks the king: tell Ur-Lisi: to give my messengers silver-rings (weighing) 1/3 (of a shekel), fifteen assorted textiles, 3 *ban*$_2$ of butter-oil, 2 *barig* of vegetable oil, one oxen, and ten heads of sheep and goat.

215 See, for example, Nik 2, 287 (ŠS 4 viii 21 to 25); Nik 2, 290 (ŠS 6 viii 6 to 7); and Nik 2, 340 (IS 3 i), all concerned with the provisions for royal messengers and emissaries at Umma (on their way to the east or on mission to Umma).

216 See, for example, AAS 92 (Š 39), rev. 3: inim a-kal-la-ta, and compare with BIN 5, 117 (Š 48), rev. 3: inim a-kal-la nu-banda$_3$-ta. Other examples include AnOr 1, 75 (AS 1), rev. 3: inim ur-e$_{11}$-e-ta; AR RIM 4, 22 (AS 8 xii), rev. 1: inim ur-^{d}nun-gal; and BIN 3, 549 (AS 9 viii), rev. 2: inim lu$_2$-kal-la. For examples of the same term used with an official other than the governor, but without mentioning the name of the person, see, for example, MVN 1, 173 (no date), obv. 2: inim ⸢šagina⸣-ta; NYPL 258 (AS 6 xii), obv. 3: inim sukkal-mah-ta; SAT 2, 753 (AS 3), obv. 6: inim ša$_{13}$-dub-ba-ta; and TCL 5, 6047 (no date), obv. i 3: inim lu$_2$-kin-gi$_4$-a lugal-ka-ta. See also the letter: MVN 4, 182 (no date): ur-⸢nigar⸣^{gar}-ra / u$_3$-na-du$_{11}$ / udu lugal-^{geš}gigir-re min-a-ba / šu he$_2$-na-a-du$_8$-e // inim ensi$_2$-ka-ta-am$_3$, "To Ur-nigar speak: 'The sheep of Lugal-Gigir, both of them, you shall release them to him! On the command of the governor'."

inter-city relations,[217] and its usage was not restricted to the Umma province.[218] SANTAG 6, 16, is an instructive text, making use of the phrase "on the command of the governor" applied in an inter-city operation. It dates to Š 31 month 9, that is, two years before Ur-Lisi became governor; hence, the governor referred to is likely to have been Abbamu. Ur-Lisi was chief of the granary by this time, and apparently ARAD$_2$(mu) was already his "apprentice." The text relates how Ur-Lisi received a large amount of barley and wheat from the governor of Adab; the transaction was sealed by ARAD$_2$(mu) rather than Ur-Lisi and was part of the formal exchange between the provinces otherwise known as the "*bala.*"

SANTAG 6, 16 (Š 31 ix):

Obverse	
1. 1(u) 8(aš) 3(barig) 4(diš) 2/3(diš) sila$_3$ gig gur lugal	18 *gur* 3 *barig* 4 2/3 *sila$_3$* of wheat, according to the royal measure.
2. 1(u) 9(aš) 1(barig) 5(ban$_2$) 4(diš) 2/3(diš) sila$_3$ ziz$_2$ gur lugal	19 *gur* 1 *barig* 5 *ban$_2$* 4 2/3 *sila$_3$* of emmer, according to the royal measure.
3. ki ensi$_2$ adab^{ki}-ta	From the governor of Adab.
4. inim ensi$_2$ umma^{ki}-ta	On the order of the governor of Umma.
Reverse	
1. ur-^{d}li$_9$-si$_4$	Ur-Lisi
2. šu ba-ti	received.
3. mu ur-dli$_9$-si$_4$-še$_3$	Instead of Ur-Lisi,
4. kišib$_3$ ARAD$_2$ i$_3$-gal$_2$	the seal of ARAD$_2$(mu) is present.
5. iti ezem-^{d}li$_9$-si$_4$	Month "Festival of Lisi."
6. ša$_3$ bala-a	In the period of the *bala*.
7. mu a-ra$_2$ 2(diš)-kam-aš kara$_2$-har^{ki} ba-hul	Year: "the second time Karahar was destroyed."

When Ur-Lisi became governor he also became the head of a large household, and from that time on he is almost exclusively referred to as the governor, or the governor of Umma, and only very rarely with his own name. From the same time we also begin to learn about the family of

217 See, for example, SANTAG 6, 16 (Š 31 ix), obv. 4: inim ensi$_2$ umma^{ki}-ta; TCS 1, 130 (no date), rev. 5: inim e$_2$-gal-kam; and UTI 4, 2972 (ŠS 2), obv. 3: inim ba-ba-ti-še$_3$.

218 See, for example, TUT 168 (Š 44 ix), rev. 1: inim ur-^{d}ba-ba$_6$ dumu ensi$_2$-ka-ta; and TBM 1, 308 (Š 44 x), rev. 3: inim sanga ^{d}nin-gir$_2$-su.

the governor.

Several high-ranking members of the Umma administration were primarily referred to according to their title and not their name. In addition the names of the wives of many of these persons were not given, they were referred to simply as the wife of PN (*dam PN*).

Ur-Lisi had a son, Lu-Emah, with his wife Nin-melam. However, she was not his only consort. He also had a concubine (*lukur*)[219] who bore him another son, I-kala, as well as a daughter, Nin-Ekuta. Nin-melam is not attested prior to Ur-Lisi's tenure.

ASJ 18, 163 nr. 6 (= BM 110263) (ŠS 4), given here in excerpt, might shed some light on the situation of women in Umma:

ASJ 18, 163 nr. 6 (= BM 110263) (ŠS 4)

Obverse

4. 1(bur'u) 4(bur$_3$) 3 (iku) GAN$_2$	14 *bur$_3$* 3 *iku* of land,
5. 2(eše$_3$) 3(iku) GAN$_2$ kiši$_{17}$(UDgunû) u$_2$	2 *eše$_3$* 3 *iku* of land with weed and grass,
6. 1(bur$_3$) GAN$_2$ mur$_7$(LAK 193)	1 *bur$_3$* of land of .....,
7. 1(iku) 1/2(iku) GAN$_2$ e	1 1/2 *iku* of land is dikes,
8. a-ša$_3$ gid$_2$-da	in the long field;
9. nin-me-lam$_2$ dam ensi$_2$-ka	Nin-melam,
	wife of the governor.
10. 6(bur$_3$) GAN$_2$	6 *bur$_3$* of land,
11. 1 1/2(iku) GAN$_2$ du$_6$	1 1/2 *iku* of *du$_6$* land,
12. 1 (iku) GAN$_2$ a-muš-DU	1 *iku* of ..... land,
13. 1 (eše$_3$) 1/4(iku) GAN$_2$ a nu-e$_{11}$	1 *eše$_3$* 1/4 *iku* of land where
	the water does not come down,
14. [a]-ša$_3$ du$_6$-^{d}šara$_2$	in the field Du-Šara;
15. ⸢nin⸣-e$_2$-ku$_3$-ta dumu lukur ensi$_2$-ka	Nin-Ekuta, daughter of the
	concubine of the governor.

The text is a calculation of the size of six plots in the province of Umma distributed to high-ranking members of the local court.[220] The size of Nin-melam's field is around fifty times larger

219 Three ration lists concerning the "concubines" of Šara have been published; AAICAB 1, 1924-0668 (ŠS 2), rev. iv 7: i$_3$-ba lukur ^{d}šara$_2$, "oil-rations for the concubines of Šara," (with its parallel text AAICAB 1, 1911-480 [Š 42]), and AnOr 7, 296 (no date), rev. iv 9: [še-ba] ⸢lukur⸣ ^{d}šara$_2$, "barley rations for the concubines of Šara." Each text lists approximately 55 women; their position in society remains obscure. See also Excursus 2, and fn. 57 above for more on Ur III concubines.

220 The total and the colophon of ASJ 18, 163 6 (= BM 110263) reads:

Reverse

than the average field allotments of the workers in Umma.[221] The field of Nin-Ekuta, the daughter of Ur-Lisi's concubine, is about half the size of Nin-melam's field.[222] Evidence exists that Nin-melam also owned a date-palm plantation,[223] and that she continued to possess this property even after her husband had fallen from power in AS 8. However, such unexpected achievements are likely to have been restricted to women at the absolute top of the hierarchy.

The parentage of Nin-melam is unknown. Ur-Lisi's concubine is not named in the extant records, nor is it certain that Ur-Lisi had only one concubine (*lukur*). The texts mentioning Nin-melam, the wife of Ur-Lisi, suggest that she headed some kind of independent household.[224] Nin-melam was not an uncommon name during the Ur III period. One or more female workers in Umma bore that name, and at least one woman in Nippur.[225]

Ur-Lisi, the head of a large household, was heavily involved in the agricultural production of the province. It is conceivable that all of the arable land within the province of Umma was under the direct jurisdiction of Ur-Lisi. The same can be postulated for Abbamu on the basis of AAICAB 1, 1912-1143 (quoted above). For understanding Ur-Lisi's control of Umma agricultural production we rely

---

...

7. ŠU+NIGIN$_2$ 1(bur'u) 6(bur$_3$) 1(eše$_3$) GAN$_2$	Total: 16 bur$_3$ 1 eše$_3$ of land.
8. ŠU+NIGIN$_2$ 2(bur$_3$) 1(eše$_3$) 2(iku)	Total: 2 bur$_3$ 1 eše$_3$
1/4(iku) GAN$_2$ mur$_7$(LAK 193)	2 1/4 iku of murgu land.
9. ŠU+NIGIN$_2$ 1(iku) 1/2(iku) GAN$_2$ e	Total: 1 1/2 iku of land is dikes.
10. nig$_2$-gal$_2$-la	"things present."
11. lu$_2$-sa$_6$-ga in-gid$_2$	Lu-saga measured.
(blank space)	
12. mu-us$_2$-sa si-ma-num$_2^{ki}$ ba-hul	Year after: "Simanum was destroyed."

221 See also J. L. Dahl 2002: 334.

222 Compare that to the field of the governor, which in one text (AnOr 1, 303) is recorded as more than 60 *bur$_3$*. Compare with MCS 6, 83, BM 105334.

223 See MVN 16, 742. That text is among the documents reviewed in K. Maekawa 1996a, see page 129.

224 SAT 2, 19 (YBC 3681) (Š 38), suggests that Nin-melam had access to means of her own, and was able to contribute to the economy. YOS 18, 123 (AS 9), testifies that she was able to continue these activities even after the dethronement of her husband.

225 See, for example, NATN 530 (AS 9 x 17), with the seal *nin-me-lam$_2$ / geme$_2$ ^{d}nin-e$_2$-gal*. It is, of course, intriguing to see the texts as evidence that Nin-melam, the widow of Ur-Lisi, went to Nippur shortly after the death of her husband. This cannot, of course, be confirmed although another governor's wife (Ninheliya) is believed to have traveled (see p. 66–67 below). Six out of the seven Nippur texts mentioning Nin-melam date to between AS 9 vii and xii. Only one text is without year (TMH NF 1-2, 212), it is, nevertheless, dated to month 11, day 7. All seven texts were concerned with the delivery or receipt of wool and garments, and all transactions included a certain Lugal-magure. The texts are (in chronological order): NATN 542 (AS 9 vii 7); TMH NF 1-2, 195 (AS 9 ix); NATN 530 (AS 9 x 17); TMH NF 1-2, 197 (AS 9 xi 22); and TMH NF 1-2, 229 (AS 9 xii 7).

on MCS 6, 83, BM 105334, mentioned above. The text is a survey of Umma land conducted in AS 2; the colophon reads, "account of the measured field, concerning Ur-Lisi, governor of Umma."[226] It also mentions the prebend field of the governor, which measured 60 *bur*$_3$, an area capable of yielding up to 1,800 *gur* of barley.[227] From other documents we know that the prebend field of the governor was made up of smaller lots in many different fields.[228]

Ur-Lisi ruled Umma from Šulgi 33 until the death of Amar-Suen sometime during AS 8, in total 23 years. The exact date of Ur-Lisi's fall from power cannot be established, but it seems to coincide with the downfall of Amar-Suen.[229] We have already mentioned the time of the death of Amar-Suen, the evidence of which is closely linked to the political situation in Umma: from the sixth year of Amar-Suen, texts appear that label A(ya)kala as the governor of Umma, and A(ya)kala used a seal which mentions Šū-Suen as the king of Ur in a dedicatory inscription.[230] A(ya)kala also had a seal dedicated to Amar-Suen, but he used it only occasionally from AS 8 ix to ŠS 5 vii, that is, after Amar-Suen had already died.[231] The seal-inscriptions of A(ya)kala from these years show no simple

---

226 Rev. ii 12–13: nig$_2$-ka$_9$-ak a-ša$_3$ gid$_2$-da / ur-^{d}li$_9$-si$_4$-na ensi$_2$ umma^{ki}. An account (*nig$_2$-ka-ak(a)*) was divided into three sections. The first section, the "debits," was terminated by the administrative term *sag-nig$_2$-gur$_{11}$-ra-kam* ("the goods which are in the top (of the account)"), the second section, the "credits," was framed by the term *ša$_3$-bi-ta .... zi-ga* ("is torn out"). An operating balance would be recorded in the third section if the values of the first and the second section were not equal. The third section would also record the name of those responsible for the accounted goods, and sometimes the nature of these as well as calendrical information.

227 See also MVN 16, 934 (ŠS 3 iii); UTI 3, 1687 (ŠS 3); and MVN 21, 334 (ŠS 8), three texts that record the subsistence (*šuku*) grain of the governor (see J. L. Dahl 2002: 337–338).

228 The evidence for Ur-Lisi's prebend fields is fairly limited, whereas abundant evidence exists for the plots making up A(ya)kala's and Dadaga's allotment. See, for example, BIN 5, 276 (ŠS 9) (published with no regard to placement of the text on the different surfaces of the tablet):

1. 1(bur$_3$) 1(eše$_3$) 2(iku) 1/2(iku) GAN$_2$	1 *bur$_3$*, 1 *eše$_3$*, and 2 1/2 *iku* of field,
1(u) la$_2$ 1/2(diš)-ta	with 9 1/2 furrows per *ninda*.
2. še-bi 3(u) 1(aš) gur	its barley is 31 *gur*
	(= yield ratio of ca. 21 *gur* per *bur$_3$*).
3. šuku ensi$_2$	(It is the) subsistence of the governor,
4. a-ša$_3$ igi-e$_2$-mah-še$_3$	(in the) field Igi-Emahše.
5. ⸢a-ša$_3$⸣ gid$_2$-da buru$_{14}$	Measured field, to be harvested.
6. mu e$_2$ ^{d}šara$_2$ ba-du$_3$	Year: "the house of Šara was built."

229 The seal of Ur-Lisi dedicated to Amar-Suen was used until the tenth month of AS 8 (MVN 4, 74). See also K. Maekawa 1996a: 126ff.

230 A survey of the seal-impressions of A(ya)kala during the final years of Amar-Suen's reign suggest that A(ya)kala used two seals during this period both dedicated to Šū-Suen, but with a different writing of his own name (either */a/* or */a-a/*). Note also Hirose 365 (AS 7), with the unique attestation of a seal of Ur-Lisi dedicated to Šū-Suen.

231 A survey of the seal-impressions of A(ya)kala's seal dedicated to Amar-Suen shows that these date

development; rather, the inscription freely alternates between mentioning Amar-Suen and Šū-Suen and using the writing *a-a-kal-la* instead of the reduced form *a-kal-la*, both presumably nominalized a(ya)kala, or similar.[232]

During the six years following Ur-Lisi's fall from power, and possible death, a group of texts were written dealing with his possessions.[233] These texts all have the critical subscript "the covered house of Ur-Lisi, the governor of Umma" (*e_2-du_6-la ur-$^d li_9$-si_4 $ensi_2$ $umma^{ki}$-ka*).[234] Several texts from AS 9 together with the document AAS 81—an account of the confiscated properties following Ur-Lisi's fall from power, that spans several years from the twelfth month of AS 8 to the second year of Šū-Suen's reign—suggest that Ur-Lisi had died some time during Amar-Suen 8. Based on MVN 16, 627 (see below), we may suggest that Ur-Lisi's tenure ended in AS 8 month 10 or 11.

---

between AS 8 month 9 and ŠS 5 month 7, and that A(ya)kala, almost without exception is written *a-a-kal-la*.

232 K. Maekawa 1996a: 128.

233 The sequence of *e_2-du_6-la* texts concerning Ur-Lisi runs from AS 8 to ŠS 5 (AAS 81 is an account of the *e_2-du_6-la* of Ur-Lisi the governor running from the twelfth month of AS 8 till ŠS 2; MCS 6, 10, BM 106041, and MCS 1, 54, BM 106045 both date to ŠS 5), and perhaps even until ŠS 7 (YOS 4, 237). See p. 93 ff. and fn 327.

234 See K. Maekawa 1996a: 103-168. According to Maekawa the *e_2-du_6-la* was the former private property of an official later confiscated due to political misunderstandings. Whereas I agree that the *e_2-du_6-la* was indeed confiscated property, I disagree on the nature of this property which I see as an allotment to an office rather than the private possessions of the officeholder.

4.5. A(YA)KALA

A(ya)kala followed his brother as governor of Umma late in the year AS 8. He ruled until ŠS 7 ii. The earliest credible mention of A(ya)kala as acting governor of Umma is from the eleventh month of AS 8. The first certain attestation of the transfer of the office of governor from Ur-Lisi to A(ya)kala is MVN 16, 627.

MVN 16, 627 (AS 8 xi):[235]

Obverse	
1. 5(geš$_2$) 3(barig) še gur	300 *gur* 3 *barig* of barley,
2. 2(u) 7(aš) 4(barig) ziz$_2$ gur	27 *gur* 4 *barig* of emmer.
3. še geš e$_3$-a	Levied(?) barley,
4. e$_2$ šu-sum-ma	of the remainder,[236]
5. ša$_3$ e$_2$-gal gu$_2$-eden-na	in the palace of Gu(e)dena.
Reverse	
1. a-a-kal-la	A(ya)kala,
2. ensi$_2$ umma^{ki}	governor of Umma.
(blank line)	
3. iti pa$_4$-u$_2$-e	Month: *Pau'e*.
4. mu en eridu^{ki} ba-hun	Year: "the En-priest of Eridu was installed."

A(ya)kala's career prior to his tenure as governor is well known.[237] Although A(ya)kala is only attested with the titles scribe (*dub-sar*), captain (*nu-banda$_3$*), and finally governor (*ensi$_2$*), there is evidence to suggest that A(ya)kala held the office of chief household administrator of the governor (*šabra e$_2$*) during some part of the tenure of his brother, Ur-Lisi (see below, chapter 4, section 10).

The personal name A(ya)kala is rather frequently attested in the Umma records; A(ya)kala, the chief of the leather workers was, apart from A(ya)kala, the son of Ur-nigar, the best known A(ya)kala in Umma.[238] Since the chief of the leather workers and the son of Ur-nigar operated on entirely

235 See also the parallel text MVN 16, 621 (AS 8 xi).

236 The use of the technical term *e$_2$ šu-sum-ma* is in Umma sources restricted to three chronological periods, early, middle and late. The majority of the texts from the middle group date to AS 8, some running from AS 8 to ŠS 2. Most texts from AS 8 are dated to month 11. The texts from the early period form no coherent block, while the late texts seem to concentrate around ŠS 7 month 2. Since the texts mentioning an *e$_2$ šu-sum-ma*, with few exceptions, were restricted to these times of leadership change, I find it likely that the term referred exclusively to property transferred from one person to another.

237 See also W. Yuhong 1995: 130–134.

238 The seal of Inim-Šara, A(ya)kala's son, rolled on CHEU 24 gives explicitly the title "chief of the leather

different levels of the economy, the two are therefore rather easily distinguished.

A(ya)kala, the son of Ur-nigar, is attested from Š 33[239] until ŠS 7—in total thirty-two years. Texts from Š 33 suggest that A(ya)kala may already have been the chief household administrator from the year his brother, Ur-Lisi, took office as governor. Several texts testify to the fact that A(ya)kala received the "field interest" (*maš a-ša$_3$-ga*) from agricultural overseers as early as Š 33.[240] This function is understood as an important part of the office of the chief household administrator.[241] It was only after Š 36 month 10, however, that A(ya)kala came to seal multiple tablets, each recording the delivery of a few dead sheep and goats, texts that have been used in this study to build the sequence of holders of the office of chief household administrator of the governor. A(ya)kala held that office until Š 39 month 2, when he was succeeded by his brother Dadaga. The sequence of people holding the title chief administrator of the governor's household will be described below (p. 103 ff. and figure 9). A(ya)kala used the title "captain" (*nu-banda$_3$*) from Š 40[242] until AS 8, when he became governor of Umma. He used that title primarily in documents concerning work[243] and the administration of fields.[244] While operating as chief household administrator of the governor, A(ya)kala used the title captain only once.[245] I suggest, therefore, that while holding the title captain, A(ya)kala effectively held the position as a provincial administrator.[246]

workers" (*ašgab gal*) to A(ya)kala.

239 See, for example, MVN 14, 34 (Š 33 viii); and MVN 14, 100 (Š 33 viii).

240 MVN 14, 188 (Š 33 xi), obv. 2–4: maš a-ša$_3$-ga / a-ša$_3$ ka-ma-ri$_2$ / giri$_3$ ur-^{d}nin-su; MVN 14, 190 (Š 33), obv. 2–4: maš a-ša$_3$-ga / ki lugal-e$_2$-mah-e šeš a-ab-ba-ta; OrSP 47-49, 163 (Š 33): 2(diš) 2/3(diš) ma-na 1(diš) gin$_2$ la$_2$ 2(u) še ku$_3$-babbar / maš a-ša$_3$-ga a-ša$_3$ ^{d}šara$_2$ / ki lugal-e$_2$-mah-e-ta / a-kal-la / šu ba-ti // mu us$_2$-sa a-ra$_2$ 3(diš)-kam si-mu-ru-um^{ki} ba-hul; SAKF 58 (Š 33 v), obv. 2–3: maš a-ša$_3$ lugal-ka / ki ur-^{d}nin-su-ta; BM 108004 (Š 33), obv. 2–3: maš a-ša$_3$-ga a-pi$_4$-sal$_4^{ki}$ / ki ur-e$_{11}$-e-ta; and Aleppo 448 (M 3807) (Š 33), obv. 2–3: ku$_3$ maš <a-ša$_3$>-ga a-ša$_3$ muš-bi-an-na / ki lugal-^{geš}kiri$_6$-ta.

241 Compare with P. Steinkeller 1981: 113-145, in particular 116–119.

242 Two texts date to Š 34 (MVN 18, 395 [Š 34 x]; and Syracuse 17 [Š 34 v]), and one text dates to Š 38 (JCS 40, 112 3 [Š 38 vii]).

243 See, for example, Aleppo 187 (M 3715) (Š 48 v); MVN 4, 11 (AS 5); and MVN 16, 818 (AS 8 iii).

244 See, for example, OrSP 47-49, 467 (AS 1 i to ii); TCS 333 (AS 5 v); and Syracuse 384 (AS 7 iii).

245 JCS 40, 112 3 (Š 38 vii).

246 This is in part supported by the unpublished document PTS 1457 (= Princeton 2, 497) (Š 47), rev. 3: kišib$_3$ nam-ša$_3$-tam a-kal-la nu-banda$_3$ (sealed with the seal of A(ya)kala son of Ur-nigar, the chief livestock administrator). A(ya)kala is attested frequently as the supervisor of agricultural lands. In BIN 5, 117 (Š 48), A(ya)kala gave the order (rev. 3: inim a-kal-la nu-banda$_3$-ta) that Lu-gina as a provincial administrator should seal a document regarding field-work (*šatam*) (rev. 2: [kišib$_3$] ⌜nam⌝-ša$_3$-tam lu$_2$-gi-na). Lu-gina was a member of the family of Dada discussed below, suggesting that A(ya)kala was directly involved in the administration of a specific area of the agriculture. A(ya)kala was the conveyer of the produce of a number of different tracts of land (CHEU 10 [AS 1 xii]; OrSP 47-49, 467 [AS 1 i to ii]; and BRM 3, 80 [AS 7 x]), and he interacted

One of the main theses of this study is that members of the ruling family and other high-ranking administrators in Umma acted as supervisors of larger units of agricultural lands; that is, units larger than those administrated by either the captain of (plow-)oxen (*nu-banda$_3$ gu$_4$*) or the scribe of ten oxen (*dub-sar gu$_4$ 1(u)* perhaps synonymous to *šabra gu$_4$*[247]). That office is tentatively referred to here as the office of a provincial administrator, since all of the people postulated to have held this office were said to occasionally have sealed transactions relating to the agricultural administration with a particular seal of *šatam-ship*, a *nam-šatam* seal (*kišib$_3$ nam-ša$_3$-tam*).[248]

As governor A(ya)kala sealed transactions regarding the Umma *bala* contribution,[249] including Umma contributions to the feasts and festivals of the empire, in both the Umma province and abroad.[250] As a natural consequence, the governor would appear in numerous records receiving goods, and contributing to the exchange and the production of the province. There is also evidence to suggest

---

with the chief household administrator (first Dadaga, then Lu-kala) as the administrator of one or more large agricultural units (BIN 5, 146 [Š 44]; and TCS 333 [AS 5 v]).

247 K. Maekawa 1987: 39–40.

248 Based on an analysis of the documents sealed with a *nam-šatam* seal, it is my belief that that term referred to the seal rolled on documents relating to a larger agricultural unit. Groups of five to ten agricultural foremen, variably called *nu-banda$_3$ gu$_4$* or *ugula*, often worked closely together. See, for example, the texts: UTI 4, 2399 (ŠS 2), a record of work-days weeding plots in Gu(e)dena and Mušbiana; MVN 11, 164 (ŠS 4), a record of levied? barley from Gu(e)dena; AnOr 7, 313 (no date), an account of the total output of grain from Gu(e)dena and Mušbiana; UTI 4, 2864 (ŠS 2), a record of disbursements of wool and hides for the cultivators of Gu(e)dena and Mušbiana; UTI 3, 2126 (ŠS 4 iv), a record of "fallen" (*ri-ri-ga*) oxen and their fodder. All these texts mention some (or all) of the members of the following group of agricultural foremen: Ur-Abzu, Ur-Enun(a), Lu-dingira, GuTAR, Ur-Ninsu, Dada, Ur-Enlila, Ipa'e. These foremen are all attested with the titles foreman (*ugula*) (in relation to the cultivators under their command), captain of (plow-)oxen (*nu-banda$_3$ gu$_4$*) (when relating to the plow-oxen), and administrator (of domain units) (*šabra (gu$_4$)*) (when relating to the yield). Often the same person from within the group, or a member of the ruling family sealed the transactions with his *nam-šatam* seal, forming the basis of my suggestion. Certain texts clearly relate the ruling family to these groups (for instance MVN 16, 751 (no date), treated below), others only suggest such a relationship. In the following, the title provincial administrator is used to describe the title of an administrator of a larger unit of land covering twenty-five to fifty domain units. There is no consensus as to a translation of the term *šatam* (or *kišib$_3$ nam-šatam*), but it may relate to the physical seal or the act of using another person's seal.

249 See, for example, BIN 5, 82 (ŠS 2), recording deliveries of butter-oil (*i$_3$ nun*) and "*gazi*-cheese" (*ga gazi*) from the chief livestock administrator, Atu, destined for the palace, as part of the *bala*, sealed by A(ya)kala, the governor. See also, for example, Aleppo 421 (M 4080) (ŠS 2); AnOr 1, 199 (ŠS 4 vi); and Babyl. 8 Pupil 13 (ŠS 5).

250 See, for example, BPOA 2, 2620 (BM 105508) (ŠS 2 iii), recording provisions for the *sukkalmah*, and JCS 40, 113 5 (ŠS 4), recording deliveries for Babati. See also, for example, AnOr 7, 221 (ŠS 1); BRM 3, 44 (AS 8 iv).

that the governor was the official responsible for the major temples of the Umma province,[251] and less evidence in support of a vivid independent temple-household economy as seems to have been the case in Ur III Girsu.[252] In a great number of texts recording deliveries from the governor's household to members of the imperial court or to deities, a certain Ur-Šulpa'e was involved.[253] These documents were often sealed by the governor.[254] The governor seems to have sealed tablets relating to the Umma contributions to both the empire and the official cult, whereas the chief household administrator of the governor sealed documents relating to the daily business of the province.

A(ya)kala's wife was named Ninheliya.[255] It is likely that Ninheliya headed her own office, just as Nin-melam, her predecessor as primary consort of the governor had done. Ninheliya is never attested before her husband became governor, and when she is mentioned in the official records it is often together with him.[256]

One text suggests that Ninheliya went to Nippur, and since we have witnessed the "queen-dowager" making multiple cultic voyages, it is equally possible that the wife of the governor traveled to Nippur for a similar purpose.

---

251 See, for example, BIN 5, 2 (ŠS 4 iv), a lengthy list of *mu-DU* deliveries for Šara sealed by A(ya)kala the governor (rev. 16-19: mu-DU ^{d}šara$_2$ / <e$_2$> ku$_3$-an ku$_4$-ra / ki lugal-nir-ta / kišib$_3$ ensi$_2$). See also G. van Driel 1999/2000.

252 As noted elsewhere in this study, the archives of the central administration of Umma seem to suggest that the major temple-households of Umma were all run from the household of the governor. For example, the flocks of the temple-households were all managed by a restricted number of chief livestock administrators directly subordinate to the governor, and not to the chief administrators of any of the temple households to which these flocks presumably belonged. It is therefore my working hypothesis that the household of Šara (*e$_2$ ^{d}šara$_2$*) was identical to the household of the governor (*e$_2$ ensi$_2$*).

253 In transactions involving food-stuffs, the cup-bearer Ninmarka is often mentioned (CST 784 [ŠS 3]). Ur-Šulpa'e was active prior to A(ya)kala's tenure (DC 257 [AS 6 i]).

254 See, for example, CST 715 (ŠS 2 vii).

255 According to P. A. Parr 1974: 90, Ninheliya used two different seals with two different othographies. The first (used on the majority of the tablets) reads: *nin$_9$-hi-li$_2$-a / dam a-a-kal-la / ensi$_2$ umma^{ki}-ka*, the second (according to P. A. Parr rolled only on JCS 26, 99 1 [ŠS 1 viii], see now also MVN 18, 467 [ŠS 1 viii]) reads: *nin$_9$-hi$_2$-li$_2$-a / dam a-a-kal-la / dumu ur-^{d}da-mu*. The ambiguity of this seal-inscription is not easily resolved. The most obvious way to analyze the inscription is to understand both "wife of" and "child of" as appositions to the seal-owner, Ninheliya. However, it may still refer to the wife of a person other than the governor named A(ya)kala (see also R. Mayr 1997: 106 and fn. 446).

256 Ninheliya received wool from Ur-Dumuzida (JCS 26, 99 1 [ŠS 1 viii]; and JCS 26, 101 3 [ŠS 2 viii]), as well as resins and spices from Ur-Dumuzida (JCS 26, 102 4 [ŠS 2]; and JCS 26, 106 8 [ŠS 4]). She received leather products from A(ya)kala, the chief of the leather workers (*ašgab gal*) (JCS 26, 103 5 [ŠS 3 iv]; JCS 26, 104 6 [ŠS 3]; JCS 26, 105 7 [ŠS 4 xi]; JCS 26, 107 9 [ŠS 4]; and JCS 26, 110 12 [ŠS 5]). She received livestock for the cult from Alulu, the fattener (JCS 26, 108 10 [ŠS 5 xii]; and JCS 26, 109 11 [ŠS 5 xii]).

AnOr 1, 304 (ŠS 4(?) ix):

Obverse

1. [...] ⌜x⌝	x
2. ša-ad-da	Šadda.
3. 5(diš) gin_2 gur_4-za-an muhaldim	Five shekel, Gurzan, the cook,
4. zi-ga nin_9-hi-li_2-a nibru^{ki}-$še_3$ gen-na	booked out for Ninheliya, having gone to Nippur.

Reverse

(blank space)

1. iti $^{d}li_9$-si_4	Month "Lisi."
2. [mu bad_3 mar]-tu [ba-du_3]	Year: "the Amorite wall was built."

4.6. DADAGA

The next governor of Umma, Dadaga, was also a brother of the previous two. Dadaga ruled Umma from ŠS 7, month 2, to at least IS 3, when sources become so scarce that we are unable to determine who was governor.

The end of A(ya)kala's tenure as governor of Umma in ŠS 7 seems not to have been related to any dramatic events outside of Umma, and it is therefore likely that A(ya)kala died of old age, judging also from his long career in public service. Accepting that the *e*$_2$-*du*$_6$-*la* of Ur-Lisi was related to his unfortunate fall from power it is likely that exactly the fact that A(ya)kala's end was not related to any crisis explains why no *e*$_2$-*du*$_6$-*la* concerning him was recorded. It is possible that a series of texts under the heading *e*$_2$ *šu-sum-ma* were written instead, however, we lack the sources to prove this at present.[257]

Among the documents registering the transfer of office between A(ya)kala and Dadaga we find one that records the transfer of prestige household objects from the former governor to the new.

Nik 2, 528 (ŠS 7 ii):

Obverse

1. 3(diš) gal zabar	Three bronze bowls,
2. 3(diš) za-hum zabar	three *zahum*-containers of bronze,
3. 1(diš) šen a$_2$-la$_2$ zabar	one bronze *ala* drum,
4. 1(diš) gi-gid$_2$ zabar	one bronze measuring stick,
5. ki-la$_2$-bi 5(diš) ma-na	its (combined) weight: 5 *minas*.

257 We have already mentioned above (fn. 236) that the *e*$_2$ *šu-sum-ma* texts seems to have been written at the times of leadership change. The brief text RA 25,45 1, dated to the first month of Š 33 may lend further credibility to this theory, while generally strengthening the argument of this book, that the family of Ur-nigar took power of Umma in Š 33. The text reads:

RA 25, 45 1 (Š 33 i):

Obverse

1. 1(u) udu niga	Ten fattened sheep,
2. 2(diš) gukkal niga	two fattened fat-tail sheep,
3. e$_2$ ku-li-ta	from the household of Kuli,
4. ba-sa$_6$ i$_3$-dab$_5$	Basa seized.
5. e$_2$ šu-sum-ma	It is (of?) the? *e*$_2$ *šu-sum-ma*.
Reverse	
1. iti AN-še-sag-ku$_5$	Month "Divine? Harvest."
2. mu us$_2$-sa a-ra$_2$ 3(diš)-kam si-mu-ru-um^{ki} ba-hul	Year after "the third time Simurum was destroyed."
(blank line)	

For Kuli, a possible early governor of Umma, see p. 53, above and note that one member of the early generation of the ruling family of Umma was named Basag (i.e., the son of GIRI$_3$.NI, see fn. 188).

Reverse

1. 1(diš) urudu šen	one copper drum,
2. ki-la$_2$-bi 2(u) ma-na	its weight: 20 *minas*.
3. 1(diš) urudu šen-šu$_2$	one *šu*-drum of copper,
4. ki-la$_2$-bi 5(diš) 2/3(diš)	its weight: 5 2/3
5. e$_2$ ⸢šu!(KI)⸣ sum-ma	Of the *e$_2$ šu-sum-ma*.
6. ki a-a-kal-la ensi$_2$-ta	From A(ya)kala, the governor,
7. da-da-ga ensi$_2$	Dadaga, the governor,
8. šu ba-ti	received.
9. iti maš-da$_3$ gu$_7$	Month "Eating the gazelle."
10. mu ma-da za-ab-ša-li ba-hul	Year: "the district of Zabšali was destroyed."

Another set of records related to the transfer of office from A(ya)kala to his brother Dadaga were subscribed as *sila* (mostly written *si-il$_8$-la*). These texts are exclusively concerned with livestock and its products, but were written at all times, not only coinciding with rulership changes although they could be part thereof.[258]

One of these texts concerned the transfer of livestock from the old governor, A(ya)kala, to the new governor, Dadaga. It is given here in excerpts.

YOS 4, 237 (ŠS 7 ii):

Reverse, column 8.

(blank space)

1. ŠU+NIGIN 1(šar$_2$) 1(geš'u) 2(geš$_2$) 5(u) 8(diš) udu hi-a	Grand total: 4,378 assorted sheep.
2. ŠU+NIGIN 2(geš'u) 4(geš$_2$) 4(u) 8(diš) ud$_5$ maš$_2$ hi-a	Grand total: 1,488 assorted goats.
3. 1(šar$_2$) 3(geš'u) 7(geš$_2$) 4(u) 6(diš) udu maš$_2$ hi-a	5,866 assorted sheep and goats.
(blank line)	
4. udu si-il$_8$(ILxKAR$_2$)-la	"*sila*" sheep.
5. ki a-a-kal-la ensi$_2$-ta	From A(ya)kala the governor,
6. da-da-ga ensi$_2$-ke$_4$ i$_3$-dab$_5$	Dadaga the governor seized.
7. ša$_3$ ⸢umma⸣[^{ki} giri$_3$$^?$ ur$^?$-]-^{d}ba-ba$_6$ u$_3$ šu-ur$_2$-zi	In Umma via? Ur?-Baba and Šurzi.

258 *si-il$_8$-la* is perhaps related to *sila.a* = "on the road." See R. K. Englund 1990: 41 and fn. 142 quoting K. Butz. The Umma texts mentioning the term sila are few and do not form any meaningful sequence.

8. iti maš-da$_3$ gu$_7$	Month “Eating the gazelle.”
9. mu ^{d}šu-^{d}suen lugal uri$_5$^{ki}-ma-ke$_4$	Year: “Šū-Suen, the king of Ur
ma-da za-ab-ša-li^{ki} mu-hul	destroyed the district of Zabšali.”

When a new governor took office, perhaps in the middle of a year, it is likely that the entire household of the governor was inventoried. At the time of a peaceful change of office, it is likely that the estate was simply transferred to the debits of the new governor. At the time of a hostile takeover, when the old governor was ousted, it is possible that the estate was taken apart and the “operating balance” of the province settled through the administrative means of an *e$_2$-du$_6$-la*, the confiscated property of the old governor.

The two documents quoted above help us to establish the time of the transfer of governorship from A(ya)kala to Dadaga at around the first or the second month of ŠS 7.

Dadaga’s career mirrored that of his brothers, he too held the office of chief household administrator. Although he is only attested once with the title captain, it is still likely that he too acted as a provincial administrator.[259] Since Dadaga was the only high-ranking person, and indeed one of the very few people, in the Umma province with that name, it is unlikely that we will ever find any substantial documentation of Dadaga using any title other than scribe, and eventually governor, after ŠS 7.

Dadaga is often attested from Š 30 until Š 39, month 9,[260] when he became chief household administrator of the governor, following A(ya)kala; however, no seal-inscription mentioning Dadaga is known prior to AS 9 (perhaps AS 8).[261] All of the texts said to be sealed by Dadaga prior to Š 43 were sealed with the seal of Lu-duga, the son of Nigar-kidu.[262] Texts said to be sealed by Dadaga between Š 43 and AS 9 were all sealed with the seal of Lu-duga, the son of Ur-nigar.[263] Although it may seem likely that the two people called Lu-duga were identical, it still remains pure speculation.[264]

Dadaga sealed documents relating to the agricultural administration prior to becoming chief household administrator, and we should probably include him among the members of the ruling

259 RA 10, 210, BM 103413 (AS 4 i to xii).

260 See MVN 14, 66 (Š 39 ix).

261 Dadaga’s simple patronymic seal reads *da-da-ga / dub-sar / dumu ur-nigar^{gar} šuš$_3$*. See, for example, UTI 4, 2424 (AS 9); OrSP 47-49, 395 (ŠS 1); and UTI 4, 2909 (AS 8).

262 For the seal of Lu-duga, the son of Nigar-kidu, see, for example, MVN 14, 10 (Š 42 i): ur-^{d}li$_9$-si$_4$ / ensi$_2$ / umma^{ki} / lu$_2$-du$_{10}$-ga // dub-sar / dumu nigar^{gar}-⌜ki⌝-[du$_{10}$] / gal$_5$-la$_2$ gal / ARAD$_2$-zu.

263 For the seal of Lu-duga, the son of Ur-nigar, see, for example, MVN 10, 201 (Š 48 vii): lu$_2$-du$_{10}$-ga / dub-sar / dumu ur-nigar^{gar}.

264 Note in this regard that the seal of Lu-duga, the son of Nigar-kidu was dedicated to Ur-Lisi, and that it seems to have been rolled for the last time in Š 42 month 1 (see MVN 14, 10), corresponding well with the change in seal-inscriptions noted above (p. 16 and fn 56, and p. 54 and fn. 207).

family holding office as a provincial administrator. It is possible that Dadaga became provincial administrator once again after leaving office as chief household administrator of the governor at the end of the reign of Šulgi.[265]

The wife of Dadaga, Nin-geškimzi, is attested in very few texts, and never prior to her marriage to Dadaga. Nin-geškimzi was a common Umma female name; two concubines of Šara were also named Nin-geškimzi.[266]

The seal of Nin-geškimzi is preserved on only one tablet, UTI 4, 2898 (ŠS 7 to 8), a receipt of a number of containers (*gipisan*) received from Zugali, and entered into the house of the governor.[267] The seal reads:

UTI 4, 2898 (ŠS 7 to 8)

Seal.

1. nin-geškim-zi	Nin-geškimzi,
2. dumu ur-gi_6-par_4	child of Ur-gipar,
3. dam da-da-ga	wife of Dadaga.[268]

The last two texts that mention Dadaga as governor were both from IS 3. One, AUCT 1, 304 (IS 3), is a text dealing with large amounts of barley, presumably the produce of some or all of the prebend fields of the governor. Another, NABU 1996, 131 (IS 3 ii 27), is a record of the *bala* of Dadaga, the governor of Umma, consisting mainly of livestock. During that same year Dadaga was still identified as governor of Umma in the seal-inscription of his son Gududu.[269] The final certain reference to a governor of Umma, MVN 16, 792 (IS 3 v), does not give his name.[270]

Ibbi-Suen's third year is the last year with substantial numbers of Umma texts. None of the

265 Last text concerning the delivery of dead animals said to be sealed by Dadaga is Aleppo 395 (M 3534) (Š 48 xii).

266 AAICAB 1, 1924-668 (ŠS 2): obv. i 12 and 24; and AnOr 7, 296 (no date): obv.i 15' and rev.iii 1. Since we do not know anything about the social status of either the "concubines of Šara" (*lukur* *dšara*$_2$), or the wives of the governors prior to the tenure of these men, it is improper to exclude the possibility that Nin-geškimzi, the "concubine of Šara," was identical with the wife of Dadaga.

267 Rev. 4: e_2 ⸢$ensi_2$⸣ ku_4(KWU 636)-ra.

268 Since it is unlikely that Ur-Gipar (a man) was the wife of Dadaga (another man), we need to reconsider our rigid interpretation of the structure of the seal-inscriptions and also reconsider our rejection of the seal of Ninheliya (cited above), dismissed by R. Mayr, as the seal of the wife of A(ya)kala the governor. However, note that this is the singular attestation of this seal, and the information obtained from it should therefore be treated with caution.

269 Seal of Gududu; see, for example, MVN 16, 855 (IS 3); and MVN 16, 1043 (IS 3).

270 It is a receipt of wood from the governor of Umma received by Ur-Enlila, the general. The text is sealed with the seal of Ur-Emah, the son of Lugal-kugani.

twenty published Umma texts dating to IS 4 mention the governor. His son, Gududu, is mentioned in a few of these texts, but never with his seal or other form of identification.[271]

271 UCP 9-2-1, 43 (IS 4 i), obv. 4: ki gu-du-du-ta; SAT 3, 2006 (IS 4), obv. 5: ki gu-du-du-ta; CST 677 (IS 4 i), obv. 4: ki gu-du-du-ta; and MVN 13, 883 (IS 4 xii), obv. 2: ki gu-du-du-ta.

4.7. THE CHILDREN OF THE GOVERNORS

Lu-Emah(e), I-kala, Nin-Ekuta, Namzitara, Gududu, and Lu-Šulgi(ra)

The persons discussed in this section are of great importance for understanding neo-Sumerian rules of succession. Having reviewed the succession of the office of the governor of Umma we may ask "why the brother of the governor and not his own son succeeded him?" To answer this question it seems reasonable first to limit our question in particular to the cases where the governor had not yielded to political misunderstandings, i.e., supposedly the cases of Ur-Lamma in Girsu and Ur-Lisi in Umma. In other words, taking into consideration Maekawa's interpretation that the fall of Ur-Lamma affected the social standing of the governor of Girsu's entire family,[272] it makes sense to suggest that the office of the dismissed governor would not be handed over to his sons, but rather to his brother or even out of the hands of the ruling family of that city altogether. In Nippur, it seems that the ruling family lost its influence early in the reign of Amar-Suen and regained its former positions only with the accession of Šū-Suen. The majority of succesions to high-office in Nippur did not happen at the times of leadership changes in Ur. In Umma, as we have seen, the office of the governor remained at all times within one family. Succession passed from brother to brother regardless of whether each individual case can be viewed as independent or in relation to succession conflicts at the royal court. The question posed in the beginning of this section is therefore justified by the conditions. To answer that question we will now describe the careers of the sons of the governors of Umma.

It is the thesis of this study that the sons of the governor faced two challenges, first of all that the system of succession during the neo-Sumerian period did not particularly favor primogeniture, and secondly that the private sphere of the economy as well as the state administration could offer valuable opportunities for a high-ranking member of society. Should the prospective heir decide to withdraw from the line of succession, he might also very well have disappeared from the official records of the state. It is equally likely that each member of the ruling family (and other privileged families), even after venturing into the private sphere of the economy, could (or were obliged to) re-surface in the state administration on special occasions to take part in official transactions for whatever purpose.

The extant documents have only revealed the names of three of Ur-Lisi's children—whether he had more remains unclear. He fathered these three children with two women. His wife Nin-melam was the mother of Lu-Emah(e); his concubine (*lukur*) was the mother of I-kala and Nin-Ekuta.

Lu-Emah(e), the son of Ur-Lisi and Nin-melam, had his own seal with an inscription calling him the son of Ur-Lisi, governor of Umma. The seal lacks a dedication.[273] This seal was, however,

---

272 K. Maekawa 1996a: 121–122.

273 See, for example, AAICAB 1, 1911-190 (ŠS 1 vi), or MVN 4, 92 (AS 7 vii). In this seal-inscription, Ur-Lisi is sometimes spelled *ur-^{d}li$_{9}$-si$_{4}$-na* and sometimes only *ur-^{d}li$_{9}$-si$_{4}$*. Likewise Lu-Emah(e) is sometimes spelled Lu-Emah-e. It is impossible to say whether he had more seals, if the inscription had been recarved, or whether this is the result of inaccurate transliteration until adequate photo documentation of Ur-III texts is

never used in any transactions where Lu-Emah(e) was mentioned as the sealing party in the texts; in fact, Lu-E(e)mah is never attested in any text outside of his seal-inscription. Lu-Emah(e)'s seal was used exclusively on tablets said to be sealed by Lu-Šulgi(ra) or Lu-duga. The majority of these seal-impressions are found on tablets mentioning Lu-Šulgi(ra); only three texts from the eigth month of AS 7 were said to be sealed by Lu-duga, but rolled with the seal of Lu-Emah(e).[274] Texts sealed with Lu-Emah(e)'s seal were dated to the years AS 7, AS 8 and ŠS 1. No texts from AS 9 have been recovered. All these documents recorded minor transactions.[275]

Both Lu-duga and Lu-Šulgi(ra) can be identified as members of the ruling family of Umma. Both were probably Lu-Emah(e)'s uncles, although Lu-Šulgi(ra) might have been his cousin (for a discussion of Lu-duga and Lu-Šulgi(ra) see below).[276] For these reasons Lu-Emah(e) remains a difficult character to understand.

The whereabouts of I-kala,[277] Ur-Lisi's son by a concubine, is even more obscure. I-kala the foreman of the Umma textile factory was the highest ranking person by that name in Umma.[278] His familial relations are not well understood. This I-kala should not be confused with the agricultural overseer by the same name. I-kala, the chief of the weaving-mill, seems to have been a high-ranking member of society, fulfilling some of the duties also carried out by other members of the ruling family such as weighing out wool and garments (*PN in-la*$_2$),[279] but the sources are silent about his familial

---

available.

274 MVN 1, 128; NYPL 301; and SACT 2, 229.

275 For example, the delivery of one ewe with fleece, and one ram with fleece from Urru (SACT 2, 229 [AS 7 viii]: 1(diš) u$_8$ bar gal$_2$ / 1(diš) udu nita$_2$ bar gal$_2$ / ki ur-ru-ta / kišib$_3$ lu$_2$-du$_{10}$-ga // iti iti-6(diš) / (blank space) / mu hu-hu-nu-ri^{ki} ba-hul // lu$_2$-e$_2$-mah / dub-sar / dumu ur-^{d}li$_9$-si$_4$-na /ensi$_2$ umma^{ki}-ka); or ten work-days to punt a boat (that is, pushing the boat up-stream with a punting-pole, Sumerian: *ma*$_2$ *gid*$_2$*-da*) from KA-ida (*KA-i*$_7$*-da*, literally "the mouth of the river") to Umma, and to unload the barley (*še ba-al-la*, literary "excavate the barley"), credited to the overseer Nigdupa'e (MVN 16, 1526 [AS 7] see p. 79 below).

276 The seal on AAICAB 1, 1924-698, a document certainly dated to AS 8 viii (and not Š 28 as suggested by J.-P. Grégoire in his notes to the text), has the sole attestation of a seal of Lu-Šulgi(ra), son of Ur-Lisi, the governor of Umma. This reference is excluded from this investigation since the reading of the seal inscription is doubtful. A person named Lu-Šulgi(ra) is attested as son of both Dadaga and Ur-nigar.

277 In both UTI 3, 2139 (no date) (concerning the transfer of a garden plot belonging to I-kala to the god Šara), and SANTAG 6, 192 (AS 8 vii) (the corresponding account listing all the "gifts" to Šara from that month), we read: *i*$_3$*-kal-la dumu lukur ensi*$_2$. Note SAT 3, 1765 (ŠS 6), obv. 3: i$_3$-kal-la <dumu> lukur$^!$.

278 According to H. Waetzoldt 1972: 101, I-kala held the title *dub-sar tug*$_2$ *gada*, a title translated by Waetzoldt as "Schreiber für Stoffe und Leinen."

279 The term *PN in-la*$_2$ was used exclusively for garments and metal-wares. It is likely that the official who weighed these objects was responsible for the accuracy of the weights. A limited number of administrators weighed garments and metals. For garments these were: the governor (fourteen texts from Š 46 iii to AS 9 vi); Dadaga (two texts from Š 47 x to Š 48 vi) (both texts together with I-kala); I-kala (eight texts from Š 47 x to

relations. The ruling family of Umma did not entirely control weights and measures in Umma; rather, members of the archivist family of Ur-Šara took part in this important administrative activity.

It remains speculative at this point to assert whether I-kala, the son of Ur-Lisi and a concubine, is identical to I-kala the high ranking Umma textile official, or whether he remained entirely outside the sphere of the state administration.

Nin-Ekuta, the daughter of Ur-Lisi by a concubine, is known only from the text quoted above (ASJ 18, 163 nr. 6, see p. 59) and remains otherwise completely unknown.

The extant documents from Umma mention no important children of A(ya)kala, the following governor of Umma.[280] Three people in Umma had seals claiming to be sons of A(ya)kala, but these three can be neither excluded, nor can it be positively asserted that they were the sons of the governor A(ya)kala.[281]

The last governor of Umma, Dadaga, had one son who is particularly well known. This son, named Gududu, figures among the most active Umma administrators at any time. He held an important office in the administration of Umma, an office also held by his father, Dadaga, his uncle A(ya)kala, as well as by his cousin, Lu-kala. It is possible that he was designated as his father's successor to the governorship of Umma. Gududu will be discussed at the end of this section.

Dadaga had more sons than any other Ur III Umma governors. However, only Gududu was to hold an important office in the city administration. Namzitara is known only from two fragmentary seal impressions naming Dadaga, the governor of Umma, as his father.[282] He is scarcely present in the administrative records. Inim-Šara seals a few receipts concerning work instead of his brother Gududu.[283] Ur-Igalim is only attested in MVN 8, 143 sealing for a couple of dead sheep and goats, instead of his father Dadaga.[284] Among the other sons of Dadaga, we find Lu-Šulgi(ra), who like

---

ŠS 2 iii); Ur-E'e (fifteen texts from AS 2 viii to ŠS 5 iv); Lu-kala (seven texts from AS 7 vi to ŠS 3 vi); Dingira (one text in AS 7viii); Gududu (two texts from ŠS 9 to IS 1 i). For metal wares these were: Ur-Šara (seventy-two texts from Š 36 ix to AS 7 vii); the governor (ten texts from Š 45 xii to AS 1 v); ARAD$_2$(mu) (three texts from Š 46 vi to AS 1 vii); Lu-kala (with Ur-Šara) (two texts from AS 4 xii to AS 5 i); Lu-kala (alone) (nine texts from AS 7 xii to ŠS 7 i); Ur-Nungal (the son of Ur-Šara) (three texts from AS 5 vi to IS 2 vi); Dingira (two texts from AS 7 v to ŠS 1 vii); and Ea-šar (one text in ŠS 7 viii).

280 Lu-dingira mentioned by W. Yuhong 1995: 134, cannot for certain be included as a son of A(ya)kala.

281 Ur-gipar (see, for example, MVN 1, 85 [Š 48]; and MVN 9, 202 [ŠS 4 i]). Lu-sa'izu (see, for example, BIN 5, 138 [ŠS 1]; and MVN 16, 1287 [ŠS 3]). Abba (see, for example, MVN 21, 158 [Š 47 vi]). Abba is only attested in five texts from Š 46 and Š 47.

282 See SACT 1, 122 (ŠS 8 x), and SACT 1, 124 (ŠS 9 i). Another similar seal inscription which does not include Dadaga's title is known from SACT 2, 241 (ŠS 9 iv), a text dealing with the same commodities as the two previous ones: sheep hides as regular offerings for Šara of Apisal.

283 BCT 2, 39; MVN 16, 1532; NYPL 364; OrSP 47-49, 429; SNAT 501; UTI 4, 2927; SAT 3, 1525; SAT 3, 1718; UTI 6, 3532+3552; SANTAG 7, 85. See also pp. 128 ff.

284 Add perhaps Lu-dingira attested in MVN 16, 1018; and Lu-Šara attested in UTI 6, 3583.

Gududu had a seal dedicated to the king. Since the inscription of Lu-Šulgi(ra) is from the time before Dadaga became governor, calling Dadaga scribe, it lacks the second piece of evidence necessary to rule out entirely any confusion regarding the identity of the seal-holder.

In this study we have already encountered a person called Lu-Šulgi(ra) more than once, and we can now distinguish three different persons with that name: a son of Dadaga was called Lu-Šulgi(ra), someone who used the seal of Lu-Emah, the son of Ur-Lisi, was named Lu-Šulgi(ra), and finally Ur-nigar the chief livestock administrator had a son called Lu-Šulgi(ra). Therefore, Lu-Šulgi(ra) might hold the key to understanding the practice—well known from Ur III sources, and a continuous source of confusion—of people supposedly altering their lineage/parentage.

The texts in which a member of the ruling family named Lu-Šulgi(ra) sealed with his own seal (i.e., Lu-Šulgi(ra) the son of Dadaga, or the son of Ur-nigar) or used the seal of Lu-Emah, produce a very intriguing sequence when arranged according to date (see table 1). Namely, Lu-Šulgi(ra) is shown to have used the seal of Lu-Emah, his cousin, from AS 7 to ŠS 1. In the following two years, ŠS 2 and ŠS 3, he used a seal in which Ur-nigar is named as his father, and finally from ŠS 5 to ŠS 8 Lu-Šulgi(ra) sealed with a simple patronymic seal claiming to be the son of Dadaga. From IS 1 to IS 3 he used a dedicatory seal mentioning the king at Ur,[285] still claiming Dadaga to be his father.

years	name in text	seal legend
AS 7 to ŠS 1	Lu-Šulgi(ra)	lu$_2$-e$_2$-mah dub-sar dumu ur-^{d}li$_9$-si$_4$ ensi$_2$ umma^{ki}
ŠS 1to ŠS 3	Lu-Šulgi(ra)	lu$_2$-^{d}šul-gi-(ra) dub-sar dumu ur-nigar^{gar} šuš$_3$
ŠS 5 to ŠS 8	Lu-Šulgi(ra)	lu$_2$-^{d}šul-gi-(ra) dub-sar dumu da-da-ga
IS 1 to IS 3	Lu-Šulgi(ra)	^{d}šu-^{d}suen lugal kala-ga lugal uri$_2$^{ki}-ma lugal an-ub-da limmu-ba - lu$_2$-^{d}šul-gi-(ra) dub-sar dumu da-da-ga

Table 1: The activities of Lu-Šulgi(ra)

285 For some bizarre reason this seal, which is only attested from Ibbi-Suen's first three years, has a dedication to the previous king Šū-Suen!

The transactions sealed by Lu-Šulgi(ra) do not form a perfect continuum; for example, it was only when he sealed receipts of dead sheep and goats that he used the seal of Lu-Emah. However, if we compare MVN 16, 1526 (AS 7), UTI 3, 2217 (ŠS 3), and SNAT 522 (ŠS 8), three primary receipts concerning work, such a continuum may become apparent.

MVN 16, 1526 (AS 7)[2862]	UTI 3, 2217 (ŠS 3 iv)[287]	SNAT 522 (ŠS 8)[288]
Obverse	Obverse	Obverse
1. 1(u) guruš u$_4$ 1(diš)-še$_3$	1. +3(u) 2(diš) guruš u$_4$ [*n*-še$_3$]	1. 3(u) 2(diš) guruš u$_4$ 1(diš)-še$_3$
2. KA-i$_7$-da-ta ⸢gub⸣-[ba]	2. ki-su$_7$ i$_7$ lugal gub-ba	2. kab$_2$-ku$_5$ i$_7$ sal$_4$-la^{ki}-ka
3. umma^{ki}-še$_3$		
4. ma$_2$ gid$_2$-da		
5. še ba-al-la		
Reverse		
1. ugula nig$_2$-du$_7$-pa-e$_3$	3. ugula lugal-ku$_3$-zu	3. ugula a-gu
2. kišib$_3$ lu$_2$-^{d}šul-gi	4. kišib$_3$ lu$_2$-^{d}šul-gi-ra	4. kišib$_3$ lu$_2$-^{d}šul-gi-ra
(seal)	Reverse	
	5. iti nesag$_2$	
	(Seal)	Reverse
3. mu hu-hu-nu-ri$^{[ki]}$ ba-hul	6. mu si-ma-num$_2$^{ki} ba-hul	1. mu ^{d}šu-^{d}suen lugal
		uri$_5$^{ki}-ma ma$_2$-gur$_8$ mah
		^{d}en-lil$_2$-la$_2$-ra mu-na-dim$_2$
Seal.	Seal.	Seal.
1. lu$_2$-e$_2$-mah	1. lu$_2$-^{d}šul-gi	1. lu$_2$-^{d}šul-gi-[ra]
2. dub-sar	2. dub-sar	2. dub-sar
3. dumu ur-^{d}li$_9$-si$_4$	3. dumu ur-nigar^{gar} šuš$_3$	3. dumu [da-da]-⸢ga⸣
4. ensi$_2$ umma^{ki}		

It is of course possible to hypothesize that only one Lu-Šulgi(ra) was behind the four seals, as

286 Translation: Ten work-days, punting a boat from KA-ida to Umma, emptying the barley (from the boat). Foreman: Nigdupa'e. Sealed by Lu-Šulgi(ra). Year: "Huhnuri was destroyed." Seal: Lu-Emah, scribe, son of Ur-Lisi, governor of Umma.

287 Translation: Thirty-two (+?) work-days(?), spent on the threshing-floor of the "royal-canal." Foreman: Lugal-kuzu. Sealed by Lu-Šulgi(ra). Month "First fruits." Year: "Simanum was destroyed." Seal: Lu-Šulgi, scribe, son of Ur-nigar, chief livestock administrator.

288 Translation: Thirty-two work-days, spent at the pond of the Salla-canal. Foreman: Agu. Sealed by Lu-Šulgira. Year: "Šū-Suen, the king of Ur, fashioned the lofty barge of Enlil." Seal: Lu-Šulgi(ra?), scribe, son of Dadaga.

is suggested by the three texts just quoted. Indeed, some of the tablets witnessing Lu-Šulgi(ra)'s involvement in the administration of labor do increase in complexity, suggesting the prosperous career of a single person.[289]

The evidence is not conclusive but does advocate a more complex scenario than previously considered and does not need to include the use of nick-names or altered lineages. It is possible to speculate that Lu-Šulgi(ra), a son of Dadaga, worked with his younger cousin, the son of the governor, and used his seal. When Ur-Lisi lost power, Lu-Šulgi(ra) might have had a seal claiming to be the son of Ur-nigar, the chief livestock administrator, a seal which would have granted him some immunity and detached him from the fallen governor. After the clarification of succession, he would at last have been able to acknowledge his relations and allegiance to Dadaga, the later governor. But it is equally possible to suggest that two different persons were called Lu-Šulgi(ra): one the son of Ur-nigar and the other a son of Dadaga.[290]

Lu-Emah(e)'s seal was rolled exclusively on tablets commonly sealed by other members of the ruling family, that is, receipts of a few dead animals (see under chapter 4, section 10), or rather simple primary receipts from the administration of the agricultural work.[291] In sum, it appears that Lu-Emah(e) was obliged to roll his seal on a number of documents, but otherwise did not take part in the affairs of the state-run administration. The reason behind this practice is unknown, but we might propose two solutions. First, that Lu-Emah(e) was a minor whose responsibilities were taken care of by his uncles, and that he died before he came of age and was unable to conduct his own affairs, or secondly, that Lu-Emah(e) was primarily occupied in the private sphere of the economy, but maintained certain privilegies or obligations for which he made available his seal to his uncles, or cousins. Under either scenario, Lu-Emah(e) had to seal certain administrative activities, mainly the regular receipt of (a few) dead animals from shepherds, and the records of the same type as the documents sealed by the provincial administrator, that is, documents relating to a particular group of agricultural overseers.

R. Mayr has argued for a different solution and has streamlined the genealogies of a number

---

289 See, for example, SNAT 516 (ŠS 7); and BM 105340 (unpubl.) (IS 1).

290 A final investigation concerning the identity of Lu-Šulgi(ra) concerns the spelling of his name. Is the spelling of the name Lu-Šulgi(ra)—with or without final *-ra*—dependent on the person sealing? Is it a result of the language reform which is supposed to have been implemented with the coronation of Šū-Suen, or is it perhaps completely random and an expression of the character of neo-Sumerian archival orthographic practice? It does seem that the spelling with a final *-ra* is more prevalent in the later texts when Lu-Šulgi(ra) used a seal naming Dadaga as his father. In the earliest texts, however, as well as in the texts giving the patronym Ur-nigar, the chief livestock administrator, in the seal-inscriptions the writings with affixed *-ra* prevail. This spelling is the most correct, according to our understanding of Sumerian grammar, and conforms with our suggestion that reforms took place around the coronation of Šū-Suen, which would enforce a more correct orthography such as "*a-a*" over "*a*," supposedly for *aya*.

291 These documents were of the same sort often sealed with a *nam-šatam* seal.

of families by introducing the possibility of the use of pseudonyms in the Ur III onomasticon.[292] Mayr's prime example was the very large and complex family of agricultural overseers, in this study referred to as the family of Dada. However, the interpretation offered here eliminates the need for streamlining any genealogies. Attention should be paid to the system of familial involvement in the state-economy, and especially the system of apprenticeships amply attested in the administrative sources, and explicitely described in the key text SAT 2, 77 (Š 33 vi), concerning the family of Dada.[293] Also, the possibility that people would readily vacate their official positions, letting family members take over their responsibilities, must be further studied in order to understand the complex lineages of neo-Sumerian families.

The most famous, and certainly the most important of all the sons of the three governors of Umma was Gududu, the son of Dadaga. Gududu, who is first attested in AS 5,[294] operated as a high-ranking state administrator until the end of Ur domination over Umma. He is mentioned several times in the last twenty texts of Umma documentation dating to IS 4. In his early years, Gududu used the seal of a certain Inim-Šara, who was either his brother or his uncle, but most likely the latter. Gududu's own seal was dedicated first to Šū-Suen, then to Ibbi-Suen, in both cases naming him a son of Dadaga—in the latter seal Dadaga is mentioned as the governor of Umma.

292 R. Mayr 1997, for example, pp. 140, 147, 149, and 150–152.

293 Dada might have had as many as ten sons, who, except for Šešani, all functioned as mid-level administrative overseers. The fact that one or perhaps two of Šešani's nephews were also named Šešani, coupled with the intricate chronological distribution of the use of the seals and the complex relationship between the information in the body of the texts themselves and the inscriptions of the seals, forced R. Mayr to suggest that not only did Šešani's father—according to Mayr Lugal-niglagar'e—use the pseudonym Šeš-kala, but moreover Šešani would, towards the end of his tenure, use a seal naming his grandfather as his patronymic, following a period where he had referred to either Lugal-niglagar'e or Šeš-kala as his father. This interpretation is based on the assumption that the term *dumu* can refer to almost any familial relationship, and on the possibility of the existence of pseodonyms in the Sumerian onomasticon, as well as the assumption that the same Lugal-niglagar'e, who was the son of Dada, was the father of Šešani. The seal of Lugal-ezem and that of (his brother) Ur-Emahe appears on about fifty tablets from AS 7 to ŠS 6, all dealing with agricultural work. In the same tablets, a certain Agugu is named as the sealing party. This Agugu can be shown to have belonged to the same social group of persons as Lugal-ezem, Ur-Emahe, and the twelve other agricultural overseers mentioned in the same fifty texts. This situation is not unique to these people; actually, it can be observed frequently with regard to the same group of tablets. SAT 2, 77 (Š 33 vi), describes the structure of one of these units, mostly organized according to family lines. It is entirely possible that some of the sons of Dada were occupied with other (private?) business and had their group of cultivators administered by another family member. See also D. McGuiness 1982: 324–342, who suggested that neo-Sumerian naming practice involved naming after a paternal uncle. This can in fact be observed in several families; e.g, the family of Ur-Meme (W. Hallo 1972: 87-95).

294 See, for example, SACT 2, 120 (AS 5), sealed by Inim-Šara, scribe, son of Ur-nigar, chief livestock administrator.

Since it is credible that Gududu, following his cousin Lu-kala in ŠS 9 month 3,[295] was the last person to hold the office of chief household administrator of the governor, it is the working hypothesis of this study that Gududu was aspiring to become the next governor of Umma, following his father Dadaga. Gududu is likely to have been successful since it is reasonable to believe that most of the senior members of the ruling family were dead by the end of the tenure of Dadaga. Ur-Lisi and A(ya)kala would certainly no longer have presented a challenge to Gududu's candidacy. ARAD$_2$(mu) and Ur-E'e, two other senior members of the Umma clan, were probably also dead by the end of Šū-Suen's reign; both would have been serious contestants to the governorship, since the chief of the granry and the chief livestock administrator were both offices intimately connected with the line of succession. Most of the other sons of Ur-nigar were presumably also dead before Ibbi-Suen's coronation, or judging from their careers had presumably already been bypassed in succession (see Section 12 below). Lu-kala and Gududu were the most prominent members of the younger generation and the only ones whose career resembled that of the three previous governors. Since Lu-kala may have died late in the reign of Šū-Suen, it seems reasonable to assume that Gududu had successfully positioned himself as the next in line for succession to the governorship of Umma. Unfortunately the sources for this interesting period of time are nowhere to be found.

Two other people in Umma held seals with the patronym Dadaga, but neither of them can be shown to have been sons of Dadaga the governor.[296]

Several texts mention people who claimed to be sons of Gududu.[297] Only one high-ranking person called Gududu has been recognized in the extant Umma material—this person is never attested with any title save for the honorary title of his seal inscription, scribe, used by all persons from all levels of society (save for the dependent workers).[298] Gududu was never given the title "captain" used by his uncle A(ya)kala, and perhaps by his father Dadaga. It is therefore likely, but impossible to prove,

---

295 MCS 2, 55, BM 112948 (ŠS 9 iii).

296 Inim-Šara (see, for example, BCT 2, 39 [ŠS 5]; MVN 16, 1532 [ŠS 5]; and NYPL 364 [ŠS 6 i to xii]), and Lu-dingira, only attested in one text (MVN 16, 1018 [AS 8xii]). Wu Yuhong argued that Inim-Šara was a brother of Gududu who sealed with his seal in ŠS 5 and 6. See W. Yuhong 1995: 140–142.

297 Ur-Baba is attested with patronym in only two Umma texts and is a likely candidate as a son of Gududu (see, for example, BM 105339 (unpubl.) [AS 6], and perhaps the account SAT 2, 423 [Š 45]). The father of a Lu-Šara mentioned in MAOG 4, 191 3 (ŠS 9) is presumably not identical with our Gududu. He is in that text called messenger of the king (*sukkal lugal*), a title otherwise never attested for Gududu. Three persons are mentioned only once as the son of Gududu, neither can be positively certified to have been related to the ruling family of Umma. They are: Ur-Ninsu (MVN 16, 908 [AS 8 iii]), Inim-Inanna, and Ur-Suen (Nik 2, 447 [AS 3 xi]).

298 Other persons named Gududu include: Gududu, the leather worker (*ašgab*), see SANTAG 6, 26 (Š 35 vi); Gududu, the cultivator (*engar*), see Syracuse 371 (Š 44 ix); Gududu, the messenger (*sukkal*), see ASJ 19, 228 74 (no date); Gududu, the *gudu*-priest of Ninšubur, see Nebraska 63 (IS 2 xii); and Gududu, the shepherd (*na-gada*), see SAKF 36 (Š 46).

that the people in Umma claiming to be the descendants of Gududu were right.

The fact that none of the children of the three well-documented Umma governors, except for Gududu, followed in the footsteps of their fathers and the fact that none of these sons were to occupy high ranking positions in the administration of Umma is puzzling. This situation clearly warrants a reconsideration of the current prevailing understanding of neo-Sumerian rules of succession and the formulation of a new paradigm allowing the fraternal system to be tested against the extant material. When approching the material from a purely theoretical angle, it seems there were three possible career options available to a son of an Ur III Umma governor other than succession to the office of his father. It is possible, but highly unlikely, that a majority of the sons of the governor's died before reaching maturity, leaving only a handful of administrative records. It is also unlikely that the sons of the Umma governor were "caged"—this habit is entirely unknown from ancient Mesopotamia, excluding perhaps the neo-Assyrian period. The most likely senario is that seniority excluded most of the sons of the governors from the line of succession by favoring fratrilineal succession with the prospective heirs chosen from within the generation of the sons of Ur-nigar. This is likely to have forced these sons to enter the private sphere of the economy; these people would, however, still be responsible for certain duties. The backing that membership in the powerful ruler's family would have given the son of a governor might easily have made his business venture very prosperous. Although the private sector of the Umma economy remains esilusive, it is likely that the sons of the governor could exit the state sphere and enter the private sector when no career opportunities existed for them in the state administration. It is unknown at present whether this private sphere corresponded to more than an annuity.

4.8. UR-E'E, THE CHIEF LIVESTOCK ADMINISTRATOR[299]

This section will concentrate on Ur-E'e and one of his sons, Lu-Haya, but it will also include a discussion of the office of the chief livestock administrator (*šuš*$_3$).[300]

Ur-E'e[301] is attested in the Umma records from Š 33(?) to ŠS 8. His thirty-three-year tenure is paralleled by few other administrators. Throughout this period, Ur-E'e functioned as a state administrator and there appears to have been no break in his activities; the last text to mention Ur-E'e included his title, chief livestock administrator (*šuš*$_3$).[302] Although the first certain identification of Ur-E'e comes with a seal-inscription on a document dated to Š 36, month 2,[303] several documents prior to this date suggest that he had already held the office of chief livestock administrator since Š 33. A document from Š 33 recorded wool disbursements which is likely to have constituted part of the regular activities of the chief livestock administrator.[304] That year was also the year that Ur-Lisi took office as governor and perhaps elected his brother A(ya)kala as chief household administrator (and heir?).

In juxtaposition to the great frequency with which the title of Ur-E'e is given in the seal inscriptions of his two sons (Lu-kala and Lu-Haya), it is striking to observe that he himself makes use of it a mere seven times.[305] These examples, running from Š 37 iii to ŠS 4, include the key-texts SET 273, a wool-account concerning Ur-E'e from AS 3. That text and SET 130, a sheep, oil and wool account concerning Ur-E'e from the following year (AS 4) will be dealt with below. The first attestation of a seal-impression of either of Ur-E'e's two sons recording the title of their father is from Š 42 ix.[306]

---

299 The Sumerian title *šuš*$_3$ was during the Ur III period used by people controlling both sheep and goat, a well as cattle (German Kleinvieh and Großvieh), as well as the products obtained from these herds (wool, butter-oil, dry cheese, hides, etc.). Older translations of the title, such as equerry, are therefore misleading, notwithstanding the possible support found in later lexical texts, etc.

300 For the reading *šuš*$_3$ for *SAHAR* see, above all, R. H. Beal 1992: 48.

301 The name Ur-E'e is rare in the Ur III record, Ur-E'e, the chief livestock administrator, son of Ur-nigar, is the only high-ranking Umma official to bear this name. The following persons in Umma were also named Ur-E'e: a cowherd (*unu*$_3$) (see, for example, MVN 3, 208 [Š 45 vii], with the broken seal of Ur-E'e the cowherd); a cultivator (*engar*) (see NATN 376 [Š 33 v]); a fisherman (*šu-ku*$_6$) (see SNAT 294 [Š 45]); a cult-singer(?) (*gala*) (see TCL 5, 6039 [AS 5 ii]); and a *gudu*-priest (*gudu*$_4$) (see Princeton 1, 296 [Š 30 vi]).

302 See AnOr 1, 234 (ŠS 8 x).

303 See MCS 2, 57 (= BM113072). For Aleppo 147 (M 3936) (Š 33), see fn. 202 above.

304 BIN 5, 19 (Š 33).

305 These are Rochester 187 (no date); MVN 15, 390 (Š 37 iii to vii); OrSP 47-49, 201 (Š 37 to 39); SET 273 (AS 3); Aegyptus 26, 158 6 (AS 5); MVN 16, 668 (AS 8 iv); and MVN 8, 202 (ŠS 4).

306 MVN 14, 450 (Š 42 ix), see also Aleppo 399 (M 3818) (Š 42). Both texts have the seal of Lu-kala.

According to the published record, the vast majority of the seal-inscriptions of Ur-E'e do not mention the title of his father Ur-nigar, also chief livestock administrator. Since the distribution of the few seal-inscriptions copied (or transliterated) with patronymic title is completely random, it seems likely that the inclusion of this patronymic title can be deemed a modern copying error. This is likely to be a result of the fact that the most frequently attested seal-inscriptions—mentioning other members of the ruling Umma family—did indeed include the title of chief livestock administrator following the name of Ur-nigar, the ancestor of the Umma clan. Had the occurrence of the title of chief livestock administrator, following Ur-nigar's name, appeared in any meaningful sequence, for example after Ur-nigar is presumed to have been dead, it would be difficult to exclude the inclusion of this title as a copying error. According to Rudi Mayr's unpublished dissertation on the seal inscriptions from Umma, the seal of Ur-E'e never included his father's title.[307] Since we have been unable to find any two high-level officials named Ur-nigar operating at the same time in Umma, I find it likely that some other solution is behind the exclusion of the patronymic title than to conclude that Ur-E'e belonged to an important Umma family other than the ruling family. Ur-E'e's special position as the one who came to inherit his father's title and office might have prompted the exclusion of his father's title from his seal-inscription. A parallel scenario can be observed for at least two other members of the ruling family; neither Lu-Haya, Ur-E'e's own son, nor Šara-izu, the son of $ARAD_2$(mu), the chief of the granary, ever used the same title as their fathers although they most certainly inherited their offices. Again, the position held by Ur-E'e's son Lu-kala, chief household administrator of the governor intimately connected him, and his kin, with the ruling family.

Due to the paucity of sources we must at present conclude that it is likely that Ur-nigar died sometime during the reign of Šulgi, and that Ur-E'e operated as chief livestock administrator from at least Š 37. It is my suggestion, however, that he had already assumed that title in Š 33. In any case this would to some extent mirror the course of events at the time of Ur-E'e's own death. For more on this chapter of the history see below.

The title of chief livestock administrator was not only held by members of the ruling family, as was the case with other high offices; still, there is evidence to suggest that Ur-E'e ranked above the other chief livestock administrators. This will be discussed in greater detail below.

Ur-E'e is mentioned in more than 350 texts, primarily pertaining to the livestock sector of the economy: most of these texts were not sealed. The majority of his sealed texts, on the other hand, recorded activities related to basic agricultural work. Ur-E'e did not use a *nam-šatam* seal in witnessing these transactions, although they resembled very closely the texts that other high-ranking provincial administrators sealed with their *nam-šatam* seal.[308]

In this connection it might also be beneficial to look at two texts demonstrating that EnKAS,

---

307 R. Mayr 1997: 150.

308 Compare, for example, the two almost identical texts MVN 14, 215 (Š 46), a receipt for the work of ox-drivers on the GANmah field sealed by Ur-E'e, and AnOr 7, 199 (AS 2), a similar receipt concerning work on the Kamari field, sealed by the *šabra*-administrator Ur-gigir with his *nam-šatam* seal.

another Umma chief livestock administrator, operated at the same level as a provincial administrator.[309] EnKAS sealed the record UTI 4, 2895[310] (AS 9), with his *nam-šatam* seal. That text is almost identical to MVN 1, 90 (AS 8), sealed by Šeš-kala, a well-known member of the group of agricultural overseers. Šeš-kala did not use a *nam-šatam* seal to seal this transaction although he would occasionally do so on other texts. Both texts were concerned with the *erin*$_2$-work of plowing and harrowing the field Abagal-Enlila; they each included a section devoted to work performed by hirelings, and both were sealed with the regular seals of the two administrators. This strongly suggests that EnKAS as well as Ur-E'e operated as provincial administrators alongside their regular activities as chief livestock administrators.

A handful of texts are said to have been sealed with the *nam-šatam* seal of Ur-E'e. However, most of these texts were not related to agricultural work. Rather, some of them were records concerning metal and metal objects; three of them dealt with silver for emblems and were thereby indirectly related to the administration of the agricultural lands.[311] This is in good accord with the fact that Ur-E'e functioned as an Umma metal supervisor,[312] and with his prominent position within the

309 The name EnKAS is always written *KAS*$_4$ in the texts themselves but *en-KAS*$_4$ in his seal-inscriptions. The reason behind this practice remains obscure to me. *KAS*$_4$ has no known reading implying that EN could be a phonetic complement. For the seal of EnKAS see, for example, MVN 16, 966 (Š 42), a transfer of the deficits of the shepherds of the temple-household of Šara to the account of EnKAS. EnKAS was active from Š 42 (41?) to IS 2 (see, for example, L'uomo 65 [IS 2 xii 13]). It is possible that EnKAS took office following Lugal-azida (see, for example, Princeton 1, 24 [Š 42]; and AAS 59 [Š 42]). According to his seal he was a son of Ur-Ištaran, perhaps indentical with the fattener of the same name who was also the father of Ur-Šulpa'e. Ur-Šulpa'e claimed to be the brother of EnKAS in an independent context—approximately nine texts attest to this relationship—Ur-Šulpa'e was an agricultural overseer at the level of a captain of (plow-)oxen; see, for example, the peculiar tablet container SAT 3, 1368 (ŠS 3). EnKAS himself seems to have operated at the level of a provincial administrator (see, for example, HUCA 29, 87 13 [ŠS 3]), sealing documents concerning the activities of the agricultural overseers at his brother's level (only very few texts give information such as *kišib*$_3$ *nam-ša*$_3$*-tam KAS*$_4$; see, for example, SACT 2, 19 [ŠS 4]; and UTI 4, 2895 [AS 9], with the title chief livestock administrator (*šuš*$_3$)). EnKAS also transferred silver as payments for outstanding deficits from individual shepherds and overseers to the chief household administrator of the governor (see, for example, BIN 5, 329 [Š 47]). Nasa, the well-known Drehem administrator also had a son named EnKAS, but we believe this EnKAS to have been mainly active in Drehem, posing little difficulty for a proper identification (see, for example, Princeton 2, 340 (unpubl.) [AS 3 ii]; and AUCT 3, 298 [AS X i 27]).

310 See also SNAT 418 (AS 9).

311 The texts sealed with the *nam-šatam* seal of Ur-E'e are: OrSP 18 pl.14 40 (ŠS 2), a copper ring; SAT 2, 321 (Š 43), an emblem of Gu(e)dena; SAT 2, 963 (AS 6), an emblem of Gu(e)dena; MVN 5, 12 (Š 42), provisions for female workers employed in the agricultural sector; MVN 16, 1554 (Š 37 to 45), various metals; Princeton 1, 185 (AS 8), dogs; SAT 2, 208 (Š 39), sesame(?) seeds (*še geš-i*$_3$); SAT 2, 288 (Š 41), an emblem of Gu(e)dena in Apisal. The emblems (*šu-nir*) in question were always related to agricultural districts and mostly mentioned in relation to agricultural administrators.

312 See fn. 279 above.

administration of the eastern district of the province, Apisal.[313] Through much of his tenure, Ur-E'e was known as the conveyor of the "field interest" of the entire district of Apisal.[314]

The collected field interest and outstanding debits of the shepherds presumably account for the existence of silver accounts concerning Ur-E'e, and the fact that Ur-E'e appears in numerous accounts concerning the Umma colony of trade agents. The "debits" of TCL 5, 6045 (AS 8 xii), a silver account of Ur-E'e, suggest that the "field interest" as well as the collected debts of the shepherds administrated by Ur-E'e were the personal "debits" of Ur-E'e. The "credits" of Ur-E'e's silver account were made up of some amounts of raw materials received by Lu-Haya, and a substantial delivery (*mu-DU*) of silver as well as minor transfers for specific purposes sealed by Lu-kala. Later, Lu-Haya, the son of Ur-E'e, had a silver account drawn up concerning his silver "debits," testifying to the transfer of Ur-E'e's office to his son. In this text Lu-kala acted as the chief household administrator; the fact that the partners of the transaction were father and son seems to have been of no importance. We can, however, only speculate about the opportunities the members of this favored family may have had when controlling all of the important offices in the local administration.

The economic importance of the office of the chief livestock administrator is elucidated from a broken, but still powerful, series of accounts of sheep and goats and their products from the Umma province. These records include SET 130, SET 273, and the top-level account AAICAB 1, 1924-666, a wool account concerning the governor. The third year of Amar-Suen is particularly well documented since both SET 273 and AAICAB 1, 1924-666 covered that year. Therefore, it is also possible to investigate the interaction between the two texts. Both accounts dealt with wool and both belong to the standard type having a "debits" section and a "credits" section. Further, in both accounts the value of the "debits" surpassed that of the "credits" resulting in a "deficit" recorded just prior to the colophon. One text (SET 273) was a wool account concerning Ur-E'e, the other (AAICAB 1, 1924-666) was a wool account concerning the governor. The three first entries of each account (following the "remainder" (*si-i*$_3$*-tum*)) are identical. The amount of wool recorded in the account of Ur-E'e is approximately one third of the amount recorded in the account of the governor. The account of the governor is likely to have recorded the entire production of the province, making Ur-E'e and his colleague (presumably EnKAS) responsible for the majority of Umma wool production.

313 Ur-E'e often received silver, perhaps in his capacity as a provincial administrator; the silver seems to have come mainly from shepherds and agricultural overseers, and was destined for the state. This suggests that Ur-E'e conveyed field interests from the tracts of land in the district he managed. For the connection between Ur-E'e and the city and countryside of Apisal, see T. Jones and J. Snyder 1961: 334–339.

314 See BM 108004 (Š 33); AAS 75 (Š 37); Princeton 1, 548 (Š 38); BIN 5, 108 (Š 44); and Princeton 1, 409 (AS 2). These texts were first discussed by P. Steinkeller 1981: 116ff. See also fn. 433.

Wool account concerning the governor
Ashm. 1 1924-666 from AS 3

	"debits" section	
A	Remainder:	379 talents 59 mana 1/2 shekel mixed wool
B	From Ur-E'e:	
	1st entry:	48 talents 38 1/2 mana kura wool 102 talents minus 1 mana yellow(?) wool 4 talents 7 2/3 mana dark(?) wool
	2nd entry:	19 talents 22 mana mixed wool
	3rd entry:	40 talents minus 6 mana yellow(?) wool
C	From PN:	
	1st entry:	11 talents 6 mana kura wool 77 talents [x] mana ? wool
	2nd entry:	13 talents 35 mana 10 shekels mixed wool
	3rd entry:	1 talent yellow(?) wool
D	Emblems:	
	1st entry:	[...] +3 1/2 mana [...]-ga
	2nd entry:	[...]
	3rd entry:	3 talents 55 1/2 mana (wool)
	4th entry:	53 mana wool
	5th entry:	2 mana wool 43 2/3 mana wool
	6th entry:	45 mana wool
	Total (A+D):	422 talents 51 mana 10 1/2 shekels
	Total (B+C):	301 talents 17 mana mixed wool
	(its *halmutum*:)	10 talents [2] mana 14 shekel
	Grand total:	734 talents 10! 1/3 mana 4 1/2 shekels mixed wool

	"credits" section	
A	1st entry:	regular deliveries for the gods (sa$_2$-du$_{11}$ dingir-re-ne)
B	2nd entry:	rations for the permanent staff
C	Received by Ur-Nintu	
	3rd entry:	various quantities and qualities of wool for textiles
D	Received by Šeššag (tranfered to the "debits" of his account) (= AAS 135, column 1, line 21 to column 2 line 9)	
	4th entry:	various quantities and qualities of wool for textiles Reverse column 5, lines 4-17
	etc.	

Wool account concerning Ur-E'e, chief cattle administrator
SET 273 from AS 3

"debits" section		
Remainder:	1) 13 talents 11 2/3 mana wool 2) 22 talents 26 2/3 mana wool	A
From Ur-E'e:		B
1st entry:	48 talents 38 1/2 mana kura wool 102 talents minus 1 mana yellow(?) wool 4 talents 7 2/3 mana dark(?) wool	
2nd entry:	19 talents 22 mana mixed wool	
3rd entry:	40 talents minus 6 mana mixed wool	
From EnKAS:		C
1st entry:	21 talents 17 1/3 mana wool 3 talents 50 mana minus 1 mana wool	
From Šakuge		D
2nd entry:	1 talent 5 2/3 mana wool	
From the governor		E
3rd entry:	16 talents 17 5/6 mana wool	
From Ur-Šara		F
4th entry:	10 mana wool	
5th entry:	1 talent 22 mana wool	G
Total (A+B+C+D+E+F+G):	293 talents 41 1/3 mana mixed wool	

"credits" section		
Received by the governor		A
1st entry:	48 talents 23 1/2 mana kura wool 142 talents 14 1/2 mana yellow(?) wool	
Received by Šeššag (see perhaps AAS 135)		B
2nd entry:		
etc.		

Figure 7: Accounts concerning the office of the chief livestock administrator

The "credits" section of Ur-E'e's account again records the same amounts of wool as is recorded in the governor's account, now summarized as (received under) the seal of the governor. This clearly indicates Ur-E'e's position as a civil servant answering directly to the governor. Figure (7) is an attempt to reconstruct parts of these two accounts in a meaningful way, showing the relationship between the two texts.

Although a crucial part of AAICAB 1, 1924-666, is broken, and we are left with only Ur-E'e's wool account from that year to support our interpretation, it remains reasonable to reconstruct the overall structure of the "debits" of this text as seen in figure 7. By doing so, it is clear that Ur-E'e and EnKAS shared the responsibility for the largest part of the Umma sheep and goat production. The "credits" section of the governor's account recorded first of all a long list of regular deliveries to the major temple households of the Umma province, followed by lists of the wool for the rations for the permanent staff of all the important households and groups in Umma. The next section listed the garments to be produced by the textile factories, followed finally by a list of administrative transfers. The "credits" section of the wool-account of Ur-E'e begins, as already noted, with the wool transferred to the account of the governor. This is followed by a few minor deliveries.

Our knowledge of the activities of Ur-E'e are above all derived from the account SET 130 (AS 4).[315] The following figure (8) shows the levels of accounting and the different offices controlled by Ur-E'e according to that text.

---

315 This multiple level account starts out with a rather substantial "remainder" (*si-i$_3$-tum*) from the previous year (AS 3), followed by a "debits" section consisting of, first, the expected production of the shepherds (these were divided into shepherds of native(?) sheep, and shepherds of foreign(?) sheep (*sipa udu eme-gi-ra* [obv. col. 2, line 22] and *sipa udu kur-ra* [obv. ii 33])), followed by the expected production of the goat herders (*sipa ud$_5$-da* [obv. iii 20]), the anticipated production from a number of cow herders (*unu$_3$-de$_3$-ne* [obv. iv 1]), and finally several minor contributions to the "debits" consisting of animals delivered for the cult in either Apisal (obv. v 2) or Zabala (obv. v 7). The rather substantial total of the "debits" section was recorded at the beginning of column six (1–9). The "credits" section, consisting of the actual production of the herders under the supervision of Ur-E'e, begins by listing the animals expended for the regular offerings to the gods (*sa$_2$-du$_{11}$ dingir-re-ne*), more specifically, the deliveries for Šara of Apisal (obv. vii 9), Ninura of Apisal (obv. vii 15), Lamma-Šulgira of Apisal (obv. vii 18), Nin-Zabala of Apisal (obv. vii 24), and Inanna of Zabala (obv. vii 36), as well as the dowry of Dumuzi(d) (obv. vii 41). The next brief section recorded animals which had fallen (*ri-ri-ga*), followed by a longer section (rev. i 13 to rev. ii 4) listing the *siskur*-offerings for various threshing floors in the province. The sealing officials in these cases were all known agricultural overseers (GuTAR, Agugu, etc.), several of whom are mentioned elsewhere in this study. The header (i.e. last line) of this section reads "shall not be transfered to the debits" (rev. ii 4: ugu$_2$-a nu-ga$_2$-ga$_2$), presumably suggesting that these deliveries were meant for consumption and not for further disbursement. Following several minor transfers (some animals were transfered to the "debits" of known shepherds), we find a long list of animals transferred to various persons, both herders and administrators. A minor "surplus" from the previous year was recorded right before the complex totals. The complex "operating balance" recorded both "deficits" and "surplus." The colophon named the text as a sheep, oil, and wool-account concerning Ur-E'e.

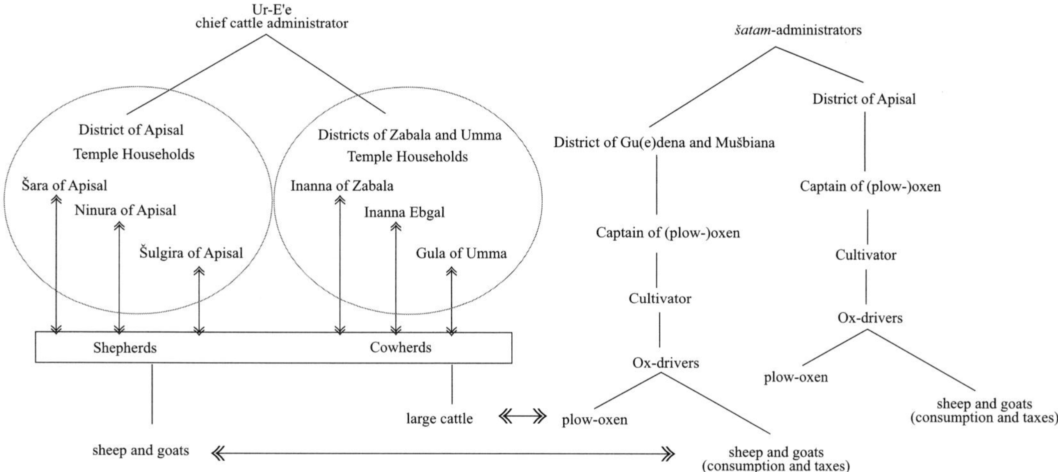

Figure 8: Partial reconstruction of the responsibilities of Ur-E'e based on YOS 4 237; MCS 1, 54; MCS 6, 10; SET 130 and other texts

Ur-E'e administered the shepherds who made deliveries to the temples in the two districts Apisal, Zabala and some parts of Umma.[316] These shepherds were apparently not bound to one particular household, but rather either permanently bound to several households or assigned ad hoc to a variety of households. Exchange between the shepherds and the cultivators was managed by Ur-E'e and a high-ranking agricultural overseer at or above the level of a captain of (plow-)oxen.[317] Likewise, exchange between the shepherds and the fatteners was managed by the chief livestock administrator and the fattener.[318] However, the records of the deliveries of dead animals sealed by members of the ruling family, in this study referred to as sealed by the chief household administrator of the governor, were mostly mediated directly between the shepherd and the chief administrator.

The relations between the administrators of cows and oxen, who also held the title šuš, and the

316 People who were called *sipa(d)* in one text could be referred to as *na-gada* in another. Whether this is due to so-called horizontal terminology, that *sipa(d)* was the general word for any herder, and *na-gada* the only specific (Ur III) word for a shepherd, is still uncertain. See MCS 1, 54, BM 106045 (ŠS 5), for evidence that persons with the title *na-gada* could be summarized as either *sipa* ud_5 (goat herder) or *sipa eme* [gi_7-*ra*] (shepherder of native sheep).

317 As was pointed out by K. Maekawa 1987: 39–40, an agricultural overseer was called by different titles according to the function he held in each particular situation. It seems as if high-ranking members of the ruling family and prominent members from the level of the captains of (plow-)oxen were sometimes mediators between groups of captains of (plow-)oxen and the other Umma offices. It is possible that the family structure of the agricultural overseers, as supported by SAT 2, 77 (Š 33 vi), is indicative of the command-structure of the agricultural administration, i.e., that a "clan-leader," given the formal title *dub-sar* gu_4 *1(u)* or equivalent, was the overseer of the lands managed by his sons or younger brothers who held titles at the ranks of the captain of (plow-)oxen (see fn. 293, 383, and 455 elsewhere in this study).

318 See, for example, SACT 2, 242 (Š 43).

agricultural units are documented in numerous texts. SAKF 54 (Š 45), may be useful in illuminating this relationship since it rather clearly describes the transfer of animals:

SAKF 54 (Š 45)	
Obverse	
1. 3(u) 6(diš) gu$_4$ ab$_2$ hi-a	Thirty-six assorted oxen and cows,
2. ^{geš}apin-ta gur-ra	having returned from the plow,
3. ki šabra gu$_4$-ke$_4$-ne-ta	from the administrators of oxen,[319]
Reverse	
1. KAS$_4$ i$_3$-dab$_5$	EnKAS seized.
2. mu us$_2$-sa si-mu-ru-um^{ki} lu-lu-bu^{ki}	Year after: "Simurum and
a-ra$_2$ 1(u) la$_2$ 1(diš)-kam ba-hul	Lulubum were destroyed for the ninth time."
(blank line)	

Cattle management in the Umma province seems to have been managed above all by EnKAS and Atu, another chief livestock administrator.[320] Ur-E'e seems to have been involved exclusively with the management of sheep and goats.

YOS 4, 237 (ŠS 7 ii) is an account of the livestock transferred between the governors A(ya)kala and Dadaga, when Dadaga took office following the retirement or more likely the death of his brother A(ya)kala.[321] The account has no division between a "credits" section and a "debits" section; rather, it is subscribed udu *si-il$_8$-la*,[322] perhaps suggesting that the document recorded the sheep and goats "found" with the shepherds while surveying the livestock of the province.[323] The counted animals were divided into three groups according to the overseer. In this text, as in other texts concerning livestock, the title foreman (*ugula*) was used where we would expect the title chief livestock administrator

---

319 *šabra gu$_4$* is believed to be the correct title of the *šabra* administrators mentioned in the Umma agricultural record (see K. Maekawa 1987: 40). These people were otherwise called captains of (plow-)oxen (*nu-banda$_3$ gu$_4$*) or foremen (*ugula*).

320 For a discussion of the office of Atu see, above all, R. K. Englund 1995: 377–429.

321 See M. Stepien 1996: 50–53, and in particular the figure on pp. 51–52 for an analysis of this text.

322 See fn. 258 above.

323 See also Buffalo SNS.11-2, 134 4 (ŠS 8 iv); SNAT 526 (ŠS 9 ix); and TIM 6, 46 (IS 3 viii), three texts counting the large cattle of the temple households of Šara, Ninurra, and Šulgi (the last household mentioned only in Buffalo SNS 11-2, 134 4) (see also fn. 324 below for this sequence of Umma temple-households). In the last two texts, Atu is mentioned as the overseer (no doubt instead of his regular title "chief livestock administrator" following the pattern described for EnKAS and Ur-E'e) of the temple household of Šara, and Lu-Haya (the son of Ur-E'e) as the overseer of the cattle of the temple households of Ninurra, suggesting that by ŠS 9 he had taken over the activities of his father.

(*šuš*$_3$), however, since this happens exclusively, in connection with the calculation of the animal belonging to different temple-households, I expect it to be a context-specific terminology meaning "foreman (of the shepherds) of such-and-such temple-household." The first overseer mentioned in YOS 4, 237, is EnKAS. In YOS 4, 237, he was in charge of the shepherds and their animals from the temple-household of Šara (*e*$_2$ *^{d}šara*$_2$).[324] The second overseer, Ur-E'e, was in charge of the shepherds and their animals from several temple-households: the household of Ninura, Šulgi, Inanna of Zabala, Gula of Umma, E'e, and of Ninhilisu.[325] The last overseer, Ur-Nungal,[326] was not mentioned in connection with any household. The animals controlled by Ur-Nungal may be related to the animals belonging to the *e*$_2$*-du*$_6$*-la* of Ur-Lisi. Although this "remainder" of the accounts of the household of the governor Ur-Lisi is not recorded after ŠS 5, there is strong circumstantial evidence which suggests that the animals recorded in this text belonged to a similar administrative category, and perhaps even the same group.[327]

---

324 EnKAS's affiliation with the household of Šara of Umma is above all documented by the large but fragmentary account MVN 13, 618 (AS 7) in which EnKAS is mentioned explicitly as the administrator responsible for the animals of the household of Šara (rev. viii 4–5: e$_2$ ^{d}šara$_2$ / ugula KAS$_4$). The colophon of that text reads:

Reverse, column 10.

10. nig$_2$-ka$_9$-ak sipa udu eme-gi-ra-ke$_4$-ne	Account of shepherds of native sheep, concerning
11. e$_2$ ^{d}šara$_2$	the household of Šara,
12. e$_2$ ^{d}nin-ur$_4$-ra	the household of Ninura,
13. e$_2$ ^{d}šul-gi-ra	the household of Šulgi,
14. e$_2$ ^{d}inanna	the household of Inanna,
15. u$_3$ e$_2$ ^{d}gu-la	and the household of Gula
16. mu hu-uh$_2$-nu-ri^{ki} ba-hul	Year: "Huhnuri was destroyed."

For the sequence of temple households, see also the label (*pisan-dub-ba*) recording accounts of orchards AAICAB 1, 1911-176 (AS 8); compare to YOS 4, 214 (Š 47), an actual record of the orchards of the temple-households of Šara of Ninura; and the unpublished account concerning cattle BM 105329 (AS 7). Now, see also WAM 2000.47 (AS 5) (edition: R. K. Englund 2003).

325 e$_2$ [^{d}nin-ur$_4$]-ra (rev. i 1), e$_2$ ^{d}šul-gi-ra (rev. col. i, 10), e$_2$ ^{d}inanna zabala$_4^{ki}$ (rev. i 29), e$_2$ ^{d}gu-la umma^{ki} (rev. ii 5), e$_2$ ^{d}inanna eb-gal (rev. ii 14), e$_2$ e$_{11}$-e (rev. col. ii 20), e$_2$ ^{d}nin-hi-li-su$_3$ (rev. ii 28).

326 Ur-Nungal, son of Ur-Šara, the accountant (*ša*$_{13}$*-dub-ba*), was himself an accountant; see OrSP 47-49, 412 (AS 1) obv. 4: ša$_{13}$-dub-ba e$_2$ ^{d}šara$_2$, "the accountant of the household of Šara"; and UTI 3, 1692 [ŠS 2 xii]). For the seal of Ur-Nungal; see, for example, MVN 1, 185 (AS 7 viii); MVN 5, 77 (ŠS 6 iv); MVN 14, 372 (ŠS 1). For the dedicatory seal of Ur-Nungal (dedicated to Šū-Suen); see, for example, BCT 2, 81 [ŠS 8]; MVN 15, 355 [ŠS 9]; MVN 16, 834 [ŠS 7]). It is likely that Ur-Nungal was the accountant of the governor's household, and in that regard perhaps directly answerable to the king rather than the governor.

327 Ur-Nungal is never attested as an overseer of shepherds, nor as a chief livestock administrator, but only as an accountant. Ur-Nungal's role in YOS 4, 237 should be compared to MCS 1, 54, BM 106045 (with parallel text MCS 6, 10, BM 106041), where the last entry before the total of the shepherds was the *e*$_2$*-du*$_6$*-la* of Ur-Lisi. The same shepherd (*šeš-kal-la na-gada*) mentioned in YOS 4, 237 (rev. col. ii, 32), is also mentioned in MCS

Whereas EnKAS was the overseer of the shepherds of the temple-household of Šara of Umma, numerous texts mention Ur-E'e in connection with the temple-household of Šara of Apisal.[3283]However, as we have seen (figure 7), both were directly answerable to the governor and not to the temple households. The individual shepherds cannot be used to determine the relationship with the temple households, since, as already pointed out by M. Stepien,[329] the shepherds could be related to several different households at the same time.[330]

In the large account concerning the hides of "fallen" animals (*kuš gu$_4$ udu ri-ri-ga*), MCS 1, 54, BM 106045 (and the fragmentary parallel text MCS 6, 10, BM 106041) from ŠS 5, EnKAS and Ur-E'e were again listed side by side.[331] The first section of this text (until column 2, line 27) recorded the ox hides from the cow-herders, described as "the hides of oxen (?) of the pen, from the cow-herders."[332] The next section listed the fallen animals of the cultivators, grouped according to captains

---

1, 54, BM 106045 (rev. col. ii, 14). Ur-Nungal is attested in three other documents relating to the *e$_2$-du$_6$-la* of Ur-Lisi. (1) Controlling garment rations for the female dependent workers still associated with the *e$_2$-du$_6$-la* of Ur-Lisi, in MVN 14, 564 (AS 9), rev. 1–3: tug$_2$-ba geme$_2$ e$_2$-du$_6$-la ur-^{d}li$_9$-si$_4$ ensi$_2$-ka / ki i$_3$-kal-la-ta / kišib$_3$ ur-^{d}nun-gal, "garment rations for the dependent female workers, of the *e$_2$-du$_6$-la* of Ur-Lisi, the governor, from I-kala, Sealed by Ur-Nungal." (2) Transferring oil from the *e$_2$-du$_6$-la* of Ur-Lisi to Ur-Šulpa'e, perhaps identical with the representative of the palace in Umma, already mentioned on p. 39 and fn. 161, in Syracuse 448 (AS 9), obv. 2 to rev. 5: i$_3$ e$_2$-du$_6$-la ur-^{d}li$_9$-si$_4$ ensi$_2$-ka / ki ur-^{d}nun-gal-ta // ur-^{d}šul-pa-e$_3$ / šu ba-ti, "Oil of the *e$_2$-du$_6$-la* of Ur-Lisi the governor, from Ur-Nungal, Ur-Šulpa'e received." (3) Transferring animals from the *e$_2$-du$_6$-la* of Ur-Lisi to Ušmu, the Umma fattener, in UTI 3, 2275 (ŠS 2), rev. 2–5: gu$_4$ udu e$_2$-du$_6$-la ⌜ur⌝-^{d}li$_9$-si$_4$ ensi$_2$ / u$_3$ udu bar ku$_3$-ga / ki ur-^{d}nun-gal-[ta] / uš-mu i$_3$-dab$_5$, "Oxen and sheep of the *e$_2$-du$_6$-la* of Ur-Lisi, the governor, and *barkuga* sheep from Ur-Nungal, Ušmu seized." The term *bar ku$_3$-ga*, "silvery fleece," is attested in one other text (TJAMC JOS 21 (pl.54) [Š 29 iv], obv. 7–9: 3 udu bar ku$_3$-ga / mu-DU / ^{d}šara$_2$ umma^{ki}), and in one, perhaps two, personal names (CT 10, 28, BM 014316 [AS 2 iii to xii], obv. ii 11: 1(ban$_2$) 5(diš) <sila$_3$> (še) lu$_2$-bar-ku$_3$-ga dumu lu$_2$-bala-sa$_6$-ga, and AUCT 2, 333 [no date], obv. 4: 1(diš) bar-ku$_3$-ga-ni. This personal name is mentioned in a context that seems to exclude a reading *1(diš) bar ku$_3$-ga-ni*, as is possible, and likely, in SNAT 487 [ŠS 3 ix], obv. 4: 1(diš) tug$_2$ bar ku$_3$-ga-ni ma$_2$-lah$_5$, based on an analogy with the preceding and following lines, for example, line 5: 1(diš) tug$_2$ bar nin-za-me AH.AH).

328 See, for example, SAT 2, 1006 (AS 7 xii), recording wool from Šakuge, as a delivery for Šara of Apisal, transfered to the "debits" of Ur-E'e; obv. 2–4: mu-DU ^{d}šara$_2$ a-pi$_4$-sal$_4^{ki}$ / ki ša$_3$-ku$_3$-ge-ta / ugu$_2$ ur-e$_{11}$-e ba-a-gar); SANTAG 6, 106 (AS 1), recording products from Šakuge, as deliveries for Šara of Apisal, received by Ur-E'e, rev. 1–4: mu-DU ^{d}šara$_2$ a-pi$_4$-sal$_4^{ki}$ / ki ša$_3$-ku$_3$-ge-ta / ur-e$_{11}$-e-ke$_4$ / šu ba-ti, compare to the identical text Syracuse 450 (AS 4); MVN 14, 584 (ŠS 2), recording bran as fodder for the birds of the house of Šara of Apisal, from Ur-E'e, obv. 1–5: duh sag$_{10}$ / ša$_3$-gal mušen / e$_2$ ^{d}šara$_2$ a-pi$_4$-sal$_4^{ki}$).

329 M. Stepien 1996: 52.

330 See, for example, the shepherds mentioned in TCL 5, 6038 (AS 7), and compare with the shepherds mentioned in the texts discussed here.

331 See also M. Stepien 1996: 94–96.

332 Obv. ii 26–27: kuš ab e$_2$ tur$_3$-ra / ki unu$_3$-de$_3$-ne-ta. The corresponding line-numbers from MCS 6, 10,

of (plow-)oxen. The first group of captains of (plow-)oxen was directed by two overseers, Abbagina and EnKAS. Abbagina who is not known as a chief livestock administrator may have been a scribe of 10 oxen, controlling a couple of captains of (plow-)oxen.[333] This section (ending in obv. iv 12-13 (22-23)) is identified as part of the household of Gula(?),[334] and it was controlled by EnKAS.[335] The second section (until obv. v 9 (24)) recorded the overseers from (the district of) Gu(e)dena and Mušbiana,[336] the third (until obv. v 18 (33)) recorded the overseers from (the field) Menkara,[337] and the last (until obv. vi 8 (24)) recorded the overseers from (the district of) Apisal.[338] This entire section is designated as "the plow-oxen, from their cultivators."[339] The second main section, approximately corresponding to columns 7 and 8, record the deliveries of the shepherds.[340] The first long list (column 7) records the shepherds under Ur-E'e,[341] the second records the shepherds under EnKAS,[342] and the last records the animals that continue to come from the *e*$_2$-*du*$_6$-*la* of Ur-Lisi.[343] The last section (columns 9 and 10) records transfers of hides from Ur-E'e (until column 9, line 34 (38)), and from EnKAS (until column 10, line 4 (15)). The deliveries from Ur-E'e span the period from ŠS 3 through ŠS 5.

Assuming we understand these texts correctly, Ur-E'e was the main overseer of sheep and goats in the eastern regions of the Umma province, in particular the animals of the temple-households of Ninura, Šulgi, Inanna of Zabala, and Šara of Apisal, together with the temple-households of

---

BM 106041, are given in parentheses after the line numbers from MCS 1, 54, BM 106045, whenever these are different.

333 Abbagina, son of Lugal-magure, was also known as a provincial administrator; see, for example, AAICAB 1, 1911-228. This Abbagina should not be confused with the cow-herder by the same name.

334 The prominent position of the household of Gula in this text is not clear to me. Since this section is otherwise normally occupied by the household of Šara or the Da-Umma district it is possible to speculate that the household of Gula was in some way or another here a pseudonym for the household of Šara.

335 Obv. iv 12–13: gu$_4$ $^{[d]}$gu-la / ugula KAS$_4$.

336 Obv. v 9: gu$_4$ gu$_2$-eden-[na] u$_3$ muš-[bi-an]-⸢na⸣. The agricultural overseers mentioned were Ur-Enun(a), GuTAR, Ur-Ninazu, Ipa'e, and Lu-dingira, all of whom we are by now familiar with (see above all p. 125 ff. and table 4 on p. 126, in this study).

337 Obv. v 18 (33): gu$_4$ me-en-[kara$_2$]. The field Menkara was hardly a district, but perhaps an important field.

338 Obv. vi 8 (24): gu$_4$ a-pi$_4$-sal$_4$^{ki}.

339 Column 6 is broken; it has been reconstructed from MCS 1, 54, BM 106045, obv vi 33–34: gu$_4$ apin / [ki] engar-e-ne-<<ne>>-ta.

340 Obv. viii (ix) 28 (3): ki sipa nam-en-na-ke$_4$-ne-ta.

341 Obv. vii (viii) 26 (1): ugula ur-e$_{11}$-e.

342 Obv. viii 17 (28): ugula KAS$_4$.

343 Obv. viii 36: udu ⸢e$_2$⸣-du$_6$-la ⸢ur⸣-$^{[d]}$li$_9$-si$_4$ ⸢ensi$_2$⸣.

several other less important deities. EnKAS was the person responsible for the sheep and goats of the household of Šara of Umma, an altogether less powerful position than that of Ur-E'e. We may speculate that the proximity to the foothills of the Zagros Mountains made the eastern districts of the province of Umma better suited for sheep and goat herding than the central districts. Atu, another chief livestock administrator, seems to have been in charge of the large cattle of several households, but seems to be unrelated to the administration of sheep and goats, and their products. During the reign of Šū-Suen, Lu-Haya gradually took over more and more of the responsibilities of his father. According to M. Stepien, Lu-Haya also held the title chief livestock administrator, and was connected with the management of the large cattle of the household of Ninura.[344] However, he was never called 'chief livestock administrator' (*šuš*$_3$) in the extant records.

344 M. Stepien 1996: 61, concludes, after comparing Lu-Haya's activities with those of his father Ur-E'e, and the other Umma chief livestock administrators Atu (cattle), Lugal-azida (cattle), and EnKAS (called Girim by Stepien), that Lu-Haya, "must have had per analogiam the same title" (p. 61). Stepien divided the responsibilities of the Umma chief livestock administrators in the following way; Ur-E'e and EnKAS were in charge of sheep and goats while Atu, Lugal-azida, and Lu-Haya were in charge of large cattle. As will be apparent from the preliminary investigation in this study it is likely that the organization was more complex than suggested by Stepien, and that Lu-Haya was in fact about to take over the entire responsibilities of his father, i.e., both sheep and goat as well as cattle.

4.9 LU-HAYA

Lu-Haya, a son of Ur-E'e, is mentioned for the first time in AS 6. He was probably younger than Lu-kala, the best-known son of Ur-E'e who operated much earlier. Lu-Haya was active until at least the end of Ur domination over Umma in IS 4. Lu-Haya's own seal, which mentions the title of his father, chief livestock administrator, was rolled on all the tablets said to be sealed by him.[345] Lu-Haya is never himself mentioned with any title except for the regular expression in his seal, "scribe." No sons or daughters of Lu-Haya are known, nor do we find any reference to his wife in the published records.

Lu-Haya fulfilled three obligations in his service to the state: he assisted his father and perhaps in the end acted as his successor as the chief livestock administrator of the household of Ninura in Apisal. He was a provincial administrator controlling several captains of (plow-)oxen, and functioned as a mediator between the state (or perhaps the household of Ninura in Apisal) and the trade agents (*dam-gar*$_3$).

Lu-Haya's involvement in the activities of the trade-agents is above all ascertained from two accounts SNAT 504 (ŠS 6), and SNAT 518 (ŠS 7). SNAT 504 is a short text which is not a complete account but does record a number of commodities "booked out from the silver-account for the

---

345 See however the following text suggesting that administrators could deposit seals with an institution (or presenting old, outdated seals as presents to the gods?), perhaps accounting for the many different seals attested for some Umma administrators (see, for example, R. Mayr 1997: 155–163).

MVN 16, 628 (ŠS 4 v):

Obverse	
1. 1(diš) kišib$_3$ ^{na4}za-gin$_3$ ka-ba ku$_3$-sig$_{17}$ gar gu-bi ku$_3$-babbar	One lapis seal, its setting mounted in gold, its thread of silver,
3. lu$_2$-^{d}ha-ia$_3$ dumu ur-e$_{11}$-e šuš$_3$	(inscription(?):) "Lu-Haya, son of Ur-E'e, chief livestock administrator."
4. 3(diš) u$_8$ 1(diš) udu nita$_2$	Three ewes, one ram,
5. AG ašgab	? of the leather worker.
6. 1(diš) maš$_2$ ^{geš}tukul ur-^{d}ur$_3$-bar-tab	One goat, the weapon, Ur-Urbartab,
7. 1(diš) maš$_2$ ^{d}nin-hur-sag ur-^{d}a-šar$_2$	one goat, Ninhursag, Ur-Ašar,
Reverse	
1. ŠU+NIGIN$_2$ 1(diš) kišib$_3$ ^{na4}za-gin$_3$ ka-ba ku$_3$-sig$_{17}$ gar gu-bi ku$_3$-babbar	Total: One lapis seal, its setting mounted in gold, its thread of silver.
3. ŠU+NIGIN$_2$ 3(diš) u$_8$	Total: three ewes.
4. ŠU+NIGIN$_2$ 1(diš) udu nita$_2$	Total: one ram.
5. ŠU+NIGIN$_2$ 2(diš) maš$_2$	Total: two goats.
6. mu-DU ^{d}šara$_2$	Deliveries for Šara.
7. iti RI mu ^{d}šu-^{d}suen lugal-e bad$_3$ mar-tu mu-ri-iq ti-id-ni-im mu-du$_3$	Month *RI*, Year: "Šū-Suen, the king, built the Amorite wall (called) Muriq-tidnim."

bala."[346] This text suggests that Lu-Haya was in some way obliged to transfer funds to the central administration; the second text (translated here in full) is essentially an account of the "field interest" (*maš*$_2$ *a-ša*$_3$*-ga*), perhaps of the district of Apisal.

SNAT 518 (ŠS 7), has the format of a regular *dam-gar*$_3$ account:

"Debits" (first section of an account, and the personal debits of the accounted, terminated by the technical term *sag-nig*$_2$*-gur*$_{11}$*-ra-kam*. If the accounted accumulated a deficit (*la*$_2$*-ia*$_3$) in the previous period of accounting it is entered at the start of the debits as a *si-i*$_3$*-tum*):

Obverse

1. [1(diš)] ma-na 3(diš) 1/3(diš) ⸢gin$_2$⸣ [1(u) 1(diš) 1/2(diš) še] ku$_3$-babbar	1 *mina* 3 1/3 shekel 11 1/2 *še* of silver,
2. [ku$_3$ maš$_2$] a-ša$_3$-ga	(is) silver (for the) field interest,[347]
3. 3(diš) 2/3(diš) gin$_2$ ku$_3$ pa mušen	3 2/3 shekel, (is) "silver (for the) bird-feather."[348]
(blank line)	
4. ŠU+NIGIN$_2$ 1(diš) ma-na 7(diš) gin$_2$ 1(u) 1(diš) 1/2(diš) še ku$_3$-babbar	Total: 1 *mina* 7 shekel 11 1/2 *še* of silver.
5. ša$_3$-bi-ta	From that:

"Credits" (second section of an account and the personal credits of the accounted, framed by the technical term *ša*$_3$*-bi-ta ... zi-ga*. The credits recaptures the individual receipts of the accounted accumulated during the period of accounting):

6. 1(diš) ma-na ku$_3$-babbar	1 *mina* of silver,
7. kišib$_3$ gu-du-du	Sealed by Gududu.
8. 2(diš) 5/6(diš) gin$_2$ 2(u) 2(diš) 1/2(diš) še ku$_3$ maš$_2$ a-ša$_3$-ga	2 5/6 shekel 22 1/2 *še* of silver (for the) field interest,
9. gu-du-du	Gududu
10. 1(diš) 1/2(diš) gin$_2$ šu-nir gu$_2$-eden-⸢na⸣	1 1/2 shekel; emblem of Gu'edena

346 *n ku*$_3$*-babbar / nig*$_2$*-ka*$_9$ *ku*$_3$*-ta / .... / bala-še*$_3$ */ ŠU+NIGIN*$_2$ *n ku*$_3$*-babbar / zi-ga-am*$_3$ */ nig*$_2$*-ka*$_9$*-ak dam-gar*$_3$ *lu*$_2$*-*^{d}*ha-ia*$_3$ */ date.*

347 P. Steinkeller 1981: 113-145.

348 "Silver for the bird-feather" appears mostly in a context similar to "silver for the goat-of-the-field," but escapes all other meaningful interpretation. The texts are MVN 21, 344 (AS 8 to ŠS 3); MVN 16, 910 (AS 9); Nik 2, 401 (ŠS 2); SANTAG 6, 315 (ŠS 7 ix); SNAT 518 (ŠS 7); TCL 5, 6045 (AS 8 xii); and VO 8/1, 67 (ŠS 8 xi).

Reverse

(blank line)	
1. ŠU+NIGIN$_2$ 1(diš) ⸢ma⸣-na 4(diš) 1/3(diš) gin$_2$ 2(u) 2(diš) 1/2(diš) še ku$_3$-barbar$_2$	Total: 1 *mina* 4 1/3 shekel 22 1/2 *še* of silver
2. zi-ga-am$_3$	is booked out.

"Operating balance" (third section of an account). If the value of the first section outweighed the value of the second a negative balance would be recorded (*la$_2$-ia$_3$*), if the value of the second section outweighed the first a surplus would be recorded (*diri*)):

3. la$_2$-ia$_3$ 2(diš) 2/3(diš) gin$_2$ la$_2$ 1(u) še ku$_3$-babbar$_2$	Deficit: 2 2/3 shekel minus 10 *še* of silver,
(blank line)	
"Colophon":	
4. nig$_2$-ka$_9$-ak lu$_2$-^{d}ha-ia$_3$	Account concerning Lu-Haya.
5. mu ^{d}šu-^{d}suen lugal-e ma-da za-ab-ša-li^{ki} mu-hul	Year: "Šū-Suen, the king, destroyed the district of Zabšali."

The "debits" of SNAT 518 correspond approximately to half the "field interest" of the district of Apisal when Ur-E'e controlled it.[349] The "credits," consisting of "field interest," as well as silver for the emblem of Gu(e)dena, were in fact received by Gududu, acting as a chief administrator of the governor.

Although Lu-Haya is mentioned in the wool-accounts of both Lu-duga from ŠS 3,[350] and Ur-E'e from ŠS 4,[351] and although we have a short account concerning Lu-Haya himself written in ŠS 4,[352] it was not before ŠS 9 that Lu-Haya became intricately involved in the administration of livestock (see SNAT 526). This coincides fairly closely with the termination of his father's tenure as chief livestock administrator, and it is possible that Lu-Haya inherited his father's office. Two texts dated to the ninth month of ŠS 9, and the eighth month of IS 3, respectively, are among the clearest evidence that Lu-Haya held the office of chief livestock administrator. SNAT 526 (ŠS 9 ix),[353] perhaps related to the

349 However the amount in SNAT 518 is almost identical to the amount found in TCL 5, 6045, the silver account of Ur-E'e mentioned on p. 88 and fn. 314 above.

350 Receiving the entire "credits" in MVN 14, 234 (ŠS 2 to 3).

351 SANTAG 6, 288 (ŠS 4).

352 AnOr 7, 260 (ŠS 4), an account recording less than 100 animals and their wool(-production).

353 See also the parallel text TIM 6, 46 (IS 3 viii).

accounting processes connected with the death of the king, is an account of cattle, subscripted *sila*.[354] The animals belonged to the households of Šara in Apisal and Ninura in Apisal—Atu was foreman of the first group and Lu-Haya of the second. The list of herders recorded in Lu-Haya's section can be compared with a known list of herders associated with that institution.[355] Other texts can also be cited to the effect that Lu-Haya took over the office of his father around the time of ŠS 8 or 9, above all texts such as MVN 14, 525 (IS 2), a text which lists large numbers of sheep and lambs termed *ki-ba ba-a-gar*, booked out from Lu-Haya for the *bala*, and received by Ušmu, the well-known Umma fattener.

Several texts record that a transaction was sealed with the *nam-šatam* seal of Lu-Haya (*kišib$_3$ nam-ša$_3$-tam lu$_2$-^{d}ha-ia$_3$*),[356] adding Lu-Haya to the group of high-level administrators who functioned—Lu-Haya perhaps together with his cousin Lu-Šulgi(ra),[357] the son of Dadaga—as administrators of specific agricultural groupings. The following undated text example (MVN 16, 751) is a list of two administrative groups, one controlled by Lu-Haya, the other controlled by Lu-Šulgi(ra), both were called foremen (*ugula*) in this text. Each of them also figured as the first entry of their group and received the largest rations (assuming this text is a record of rations!). The people mentioned in this text are the same as those mentioned together in several texts as captains of (plow-)oxen.

MVN 16, 751 (no date):[358]

Obverse

1. 3(geš$_2$) gur lu$_2$-^{d}ha-⸢ia$_3$⸣	180 *gur*: Lu-Haya,
2. 1(u) ur-^{d}⸢igi⸣-zi-bar-ra	10 (*gur*): Ur-Igizibara,
3. 4(u) ⸢inim⸣-$^{[d]}$šara$_2$	40 (*gur*): Inim-Šara,
4. 4(u) [...]-a-ga	40 (*gur*): x-aga,
5. 4(u) [?]-mu-U$_2$.U$_2$[359]	40 (*gur*): Mu'u'u (?),
6. 1(u) a-a-⸢kal⸣-[la]	10 (*gur*): A(ya)kala,

354 See p. 70 and fn. 258, above.

355 See R. K. Englund 2003: § 9, and M. Stepien 1996: 54–62.

356 See, for example, MVN 13, 573 (ŠS 9 xi 25 to xii), a text concerned with fodder for dogs (*ša$_3$-gal ur-gi$_7$-ra*) which has the *nam-šatam* seal of Lu-Haya. See also Princeton 1, 185 (AS 8), a similar text sealed by Lu-Haya's father Ur-E'e.

357 See, for example, BIN 5, 258 (ŠS 6), for a reference to the *nam-šatam* seal of Lu-Šulgi(ra), rev. 4: kišib$_3$ nam-ša$_3$-tam lu$_2$-^{d}šul-gi-ra.

358 The text transliterated here might very well be an exercise tablet or a note since it lacks a date and does not mention any institutional information.

359 See SNAT 531 (IS 3 i), for a reference to a person Mu'u'u active in the agricultural sector of the economy, obv., line 7': 4(barig) še šuku ša$_3$-gu$_4$ kišib$_3$ mu-u$_2$-u$_2$, "4 *barig* of barley, is the subsistence of the ox driver, sealed by Mu'u'u."

7. 4(u) lugal-⌜ku$_3$⌝-[ga-ni]	40 (*gur*): Lugal-kugani,
8. 6(aš) lu$_2$-dingir-⌜ra⌝ ⌜dumu⌝ u$_3$-dag-⌜ga⌝	6 (*gur*): Lu-dingira, the son of Udaga,
9. 4(u) lu$_2$-dingir-ra nu-banda$_3$ gu$_4$	40 (*gur*): Lu-dingira, the captain of (plow-)oxen,
10. lu$_2$-^{d}šara$_2$ nu-banda$_3$ gu$_4$	Lu-Šara, the captain of (plow-)oxen,
(blank line)	
11) ⌜6(geš$_2$)⌝ 4(u) 6(aš) ⌜gur⌝	Total: 406 *gur*,
12) [ugula lu$_2$-^{d}]⌜ha⌝-ia$_3$	Foreman: Lu-Haya.
Reverse	
1. 3(geš$_2$) [lu$_2$]-^{d}šul-gi-ra	180 (*gur*): Lu-Šulgi(ra),
2. 3(u) ⌜al⌝-la-palil$_2$(IGI.ŠE.DU)[360]	30 (*gur*): Alla-palil,
3. 4(u) lu$_2$-dingir-ra	40 (*gur*): Lu-dingira,
4. 4(u) ^{d}šara$_2$-kam	40 (*gur*): Šarakam,
5. 4(u) gu$_2$-TAR	40 (*gur*): GuTAR,
6. 4(u) e$_2$-⌜gal⌝-e-si	40 (*gur*): Egalesi,
7. 2(u) ur-[...]-na	20 (*gur*): Ur-[enun?]na,[361]
8. 4(u) ur-^{geš}gigir	40 (*gur*): Ur-gigir,
9. 2(u) inim-^{d}šara$_2$	20 (*gur*): Inim-Šara,
10. 2(u)+[n] lu$_2$-[...]-la	20 + (*gur*): Lu-[...]la,
[(blank line)]	
11. [...]	Total: [...]
12. ugula lu$_2$-^{d}⌜šul⌝-[gi-ra]	Foreman: Lu-Šulgi(ra).

All of the persons mentioned in this text are known agricultural overseers, sometimes mentioned with the title captain of (plow-)oxen (*nu-banda$_3$ gu$_4$*), sometimes as foremen (*ugula*). They each directed a number of cultivators (*engar*) who in turn directed a number of ox drivers (*ša$_3$-gu$_4$*).

Based on a comparison with MCS 1, 54, BM 106045, where some of the same people were mentioned, it seems likely that the second section of MVN 16, 751 recorded the agricultural overseers of Gu(e)dena and Mušbiana. Perhaps the first section recorded the overseers from the Apisal district? Lu-Haya may have been in control of this group of agricultural overseers for several reasons: he could have been the administrator of state or temple lands, or he could have been administrating his

360 See MVN 21, 114 (ŠS 6), for a reference to the seal of Alla-palil. Note that he himself could seal as a šatam, rev., 7 and seal: kišib$_3$ nam-ša$_3$-tam al-la-palil$_2$ // al-la-⌜palil$_2$⌝ / dub-sar / dumu ur-a-a-mu, "sealed with the *nam-šatam* seal of Alla-palil; Alla-palil, the scribe, son of Ur-Ayamu."

361 The reconstruction is based on the fact that Ur-Enun(a) is often mentioned within the same administrative group.

own (prebend) lands (*šuku*).

One group of texts, exclusively written on three-sided bullae, were sealed by either Ur-E'e or one of his sons, Lu-Haya or Lu-kala, sometimes together with Ur-Nungal, the archivist.[362] These bullae all record the regular provisions (*sa$_2$-du$_{11}$*)[363] for the couriers stationed in Umma or at the "tower" (*an-za-gar$_3$*)[364] on the Girsu-canal (*i$_7$ gir$_2$-su^{ki}*).[365]

BRM 3, 12 (ŠS 4 x 30) has been chosen as a typical example of a text from this group:[366]

Side 1.

1. 4(barig) 5(ban$_2$) 5(diš) sila3 kaš sag$_{10}$	4 *barig*, 5 *ban$_2$* and 5 *sila$_3$* of good beer,
2. 1(aš) 4(barig) 5(ban$_2$) kaš DU gur	1 *gur*, 4 *barig*, and 5 *ban$_2$* of regular quality beer,
3. 1(aš) 4(barig) 1(ban$_2$) ninda DU gur	1 *gur* 4 *barig*, and 1 *ban$_2$* of regular quality bread,
4. 1(ban$_2$) 7(diš) 1/2(diš) sila$_3$ igi-sag sum gaz	1 *ban$_2$* and seven and a half *sila$_3$* of best quality crushed garlic,
6. 1(ban$_2$) 1/2(diš) sila$_3$ i$_3$-geš	1 *ban$_2$* and a half *sila$_3$* of sesame (?) oil,
7. 7(diš) sila$_3$ 4(diš) gin$_2$ naga ⌜gaz$_x$⌝(KUM)	7 *sila$_3$* 4 shekel of crushed alkali,
8. sa$_2$-du$_{11}$ kas$_4$ ša$_3$ umma^{ki}	regular provisions for the couriers while in Umma,
9. ⌜giri$_3$⌝ ^{d}šara$_2$-za-me	via Šara-zame.

Side 2.

1. ⌜kišib$_3$⌝ lu$_2$-kal-la u$_3$	Sealed by Lu-kala and
2. ur-^{d}nun-gal-ka	Ur-Nungal,

---

362 Two texts were sealed by the governor: Hermitage 3, 514 (= Erm 15302) (AS 7 iv), and OrSP 47-49, 373 (AS 7 ix 29).

363 Although *sa$_2$-du$_{11}$* is usually translated as "regular offerings" it is certain that a translation "regular delivery" is more correct since it applies to humans as well as gods.

364 For a location of the tower of the Girsu-canal, see W. Heimpel 1994: 9 and 18.

365 The first example from this group of texts is Nebraska 43 (AS 5 ix), which was sealed with the seal of Ur-E'e. The two last texts date to IS 2 month 6, one (CST 872) sealed by Lu-kala, the other (CST 873) by Ur-Nungal. The last text with the seal of Ur-E'e is AR RIM 4, 28 (ŠS 4 vi). However, Ur-E'e is mentioned as late as ŠS 5 viii in the body of MVN 15, 96. Unfortunately the seal on that text is illegible. The first text to be sealed by Lu-kala was Hermitage 3, 512 (= Erm 15010) (AS 7 i), the first to have the seal of Ur-Nungal was Hermitage 3, 515 (= Erm 15280) (AS 8 iii). Ur-Nungal sealed some documents alone, and several together with Lu-kala, but never with anyone else. Lu-Haya sealed only one text: OrSP 47-49, 457 (ŠS 9 viii).

366 See F. Pomponio 1992: 172–179, for a discussion of these texts.

3. iti ezem ^{d}šul-gi u4 3(u)-kam	Month “Festival of Šulgi,” on the thirtieth day,
4. mu ^{d}šu-^{d}suen lugal uri$_{5}$^{ki}-ma-ke$_{4}$ bad$_{3}$ mar-tu mu-ri-ig-ti-id-ni-im mu-du$_{3}$	Year: “Šū-Suen, the king of Ur, built the Amorite wall (called) Muriq-tidnim.”
5. ur-gi$_{6}$-par$_{4}$ [u$_{3}$] lu$_{2}$-sukkal$^{?}$ Ib$_{2}$-gi-[ne$_{2}$]	Ur-gipar and Lu-sukkal made it firm.
Side 3.	
Seal 1	
1. ur-^{d}nun-gal	Ur-Nungal,
2. dub-sar	scribe,
3. dumu ur-^{d}šara$_{2}$	son of Ur-Šara,
4. ša$_{13}$-dub-ba-ka	the archivist.
Seal 2.	
1. lu$_{2}$-kal-la	Lu-kala,
2. dub-sar	scribe,
3. dumu ur-e$_{11}$-e šuš$_{3}$	son of Ur-E’e, the chief livestock administrator.

These deliveries could also include animals. So far, no connection between these texts and any other group of texts has been observed—the fact that Ur-Nungal seals together with Lu-kala on several bullae reinforces our understanding of his position in society as an archivist of the governor, or perhaps better, the state (i.e., the king).

4.10. LU-KALA, CHIEF HOUSEHOLD ADMINISTRTOR

The chief household administrator (*šabra* e_2) of the governor is an office well attested in third millennium sources.[367] However, Umma sources from the time of the Third Dynasty of Ur do not frequently report this title, nor the simpler title chief administrator (*šabra*).[368] Nevertheless, it appears certain that Lu-kala, along with his predecessors Dadaga and A(ya)kala and his successor Gududu, all at some point in their careers held an office comparable to that of chief household administrator of the governor (*šabra* e_2 *ensi*$_2$). This claim will be substantiated in the following section.

From the entire corpus of Umma texts I have found only one in which Lu-kala is not merely called scribe (*dub-sar*). In this text, MVN 16, 1294, Lu-kala is called chief administrator (*šabra*). The title chief household administrator is attested frequently in Ur III Girsu texts, where the office seems to relate to the ruling family and the household of the governor.[369] Since a few Girsu texts also mention a Lukal(kal)a with the title chief administrator (*šabra*) (for example, TCTI 2, 4177 (no date) obv. i 6; udu lu_2-kal-kal-la šabra) great caution must be taken when evaluating the single text that mentions Lu-kala, the *šabra*, in an Umma context.[370]

MVN 16, 1294 (ŠS 3 x):

Obverse

1. 1(diš) u_8 ba-$uš_2$	One ewe, slaughtered.
2. še-ta sa_{10}-a	Bartered for barley,
3. ki lu_2-kal-la sipa-ta	From Lu-kala, the shepherd,

Reverse

1. $kišib_3$ lu_2-kal-la šabra	Sealed by Lu-kala, the chief administrator.
(seal)	
2. iti ezem ^{d}šul-gi	Month "Festival of Šulgi."

---

367 J.-P. Grégoire 1970: xv.

368 For the use of the title *šabra* in the agricultural record, see K. Maekawa 1987: 40.

369 In Girsu the well-known system of a temple administration headed by a sanga-priest and a šabra-administrator is elucidated by texts such as HSS 4, 4 (see also R. K. Englund 1990: 58–63). The existence of an office of chief household administrator of the governor is also amply attested in the sources. See, for example, TUT 259 (Š 48 xi), mentioning Ur-Lamma, chief household administrator. He is otherwise known primarily through his sons. See also TCTI 2, 4226 (ŠS 1) mentioning Lu-Ningirsu the chief household administrator. The activities of the Girsu chief household administrator seem to have been primarily concerned with the daily management of the household. YOS 18, 115 (no date), rev. vii, may allude to the staff of the chief household administrator.

370 Two Umma texts mention a person Lu-kala with the title *šabra*, without any positive means of connecting this person to Lu-kala the son of Ur-E'e: Georgica 8.3.2 (AS 7), obv. ii 23; and MVN 21, 343 (ŠS 3), obv. i 18 and rev. i 1.

2. mu si-ma-num$_2$^{ki} ba-hul	Year: "Simanum was destroyed."
Seal	
1. lu$_2$-kal-[la]	Lu-kala
2. dub-sar	the scribe
3. dumu ur-e$_{11}$-e [šuš$_3$]	son of Ur-E'e [chief livestock administrator].

The seal rolled on this text is the standard seal of Lu-kala which was rolled on more than 500 texts. Had this text been a random receipt from an unknown person, its relevance would have been more restricted. This receipt from the rather well-known shepherd Lu-kala[371] is part of a long sequence of receipts of dead animals, sealed by Lu-kala, son of Ur-E'e, during his tenure as chief household administrator of the governor. The phrase "bartered for barley" appears in four texts sealed by Lu-kala, the son of Ur-E'e; twice the shepherd was Imani (title inferred),[372] and twice the shepherd was named Lu-kala (title given).[373] All four texts were from either month ten or month twelve of the year ŠS 3, and three out of four of these texts recorded only one ewe. The phrase "bartered for barley" occurs frequently in the Umma material, but only in recording reed and animals.[374]

When Dadaga, and before him A(ya)kala, sealed receipts concerning deliveries of dead animals from individual shepherds, it is credible that they too held the office as chief household administrator. However, no shepherds were called Dadaga or A(ya)kala, eliminating the need for ever using a title when recording these transactions. It is clear that the reason behind using the title of Lu-kala, son of Ur-E'e, in this particular text lies with an urge to avoid any misunderstanding of who was chief household administrator (*šabra (e$_2$)*) and who was the shepherd (*sipa*) in a record where both names were identical. However, we must consider the parallel text MVN 14, 389 (ŠS 3 xii), which also mentions Lu-kala, the shepherd, as the delivering agent of several dead animals, and Lu-kala as the sealing party. Although the text is sealed with the same seal of Lu-kala, the son of Ur-E'e, the text lacks any identification of Lu-kala as chief (household) administrator (*šabra*). There is other evidence, however, that suggests that Lu-kala held the office of chief household administrator, above all his involvement in the daily business of the province, the supply of the governor's household, and the *bala*-contribution of the governor.

Close to 300 texts have been published that record deliveries made by several shepherds and that

371 See, for example, NYPL 330 (Š 45), obv. 1: 3(barig) zi$_3$ lu$_2$-kal-la sipa, and MVN 15, 390 (Š 37 iii to vii), obv. i 30: lu$_2$-kal-la sipa.

372 See MVN 16, 1559 (ŠS 3 x) and MVN 14, 320 (ŠS 3 xii); both texts record one ewe.

373 See MVN 16, 1294 (ŠS 3 x), mentioned above, and MVN 14, 389 (ŠS 3 xii); both texts record one ewe, MVN 14, 389 adds a ram and one goat.

374 " Bartered for barley" can be compared to the phrase "bartered for silver" which is attested even more rarely and in an unqualified context. "Bartered for silver" is used in relation to all aspects of the economy, including man-days.

were sealed by either A(ya)kala, Dadaga, Lu-kala, or Gududu (some other Umma administrators also sealed similar tablets from the same shepherds but these transactions and their possible interpretation are noted under the respective persons).[375] The first of these texts in chronological order is Aleppo 368 (M 3609) (Š 37 iii). It records the delivery of one slaughtered ewe (*u*$_8$ *ba-uš*$_2$, further classified as foreign (*kur*)) from Ur-Ištaran, sealed by A(ya)kala. A(ya)kala sealed approximately sixteen such texts from Š 37, month 3, to Š 39, month 2,[376] with his regular seal (see above); all of these animals were classified as "slaughtered" (*ba-uš*$_2$), and all were delivered by either Ur-Ištaran or Urru, two well-known shepherds. Dadaga, who was mentioned as the sealing party in 34 texts, took over after A(ya)kala in Š 39 month 9.[377] Dadaga received the animals from the shepherds Ur-Ištaran and Urru. Dadaga is mentioned in this connection for the last time in the twelfth month of Šulgi's last year.[378] Dadaga, however, never used his own seal to seal these tablets. Rather, all of the texts that mention Dadaga as the sealing party had the seal of a person named Lu-duga rolled upon them. During the first half of the period when Dadaga held office as chief household administrator, the seal he used was that of Lu-duga, the son of Nigar-kidu. During the latter half he used the seal of Lu-duga, the son of Ur-nigar. No texts have been found dating to the first year of Amar-Suen. From AS 2 the same sort of deliveries were sealed by Lu-kala.[379] Lu-kala sealed more than 200 documents recording the delivery of one or several dead animals. Lu-kala was presumably followed by Gududu, in ŠS 9, as the Umma official sealing receipts of dead sheep and goats. The last text mentioning Lu-kala as the sealing party in this is from ŠS 6, month 13,[380] the first to mention Gududu is from ŠS 9, month 10.[381] I have no explanation for this break in the textual record. Only a few texts from this group sealed by Gududu have survived, perhaps due to the late date of his tenure and the corresponding decrease in records altogether. Below (figure 9) is a graphic representation of the sequence of people holding the office of governor and those holding the proposed office of chief household administrator of the governor. The administrators who occasionally acted as chief household administrators are also listed.

375 These texts should not be confused with other receipts for animals. See, for example, CST 781 (ŠS 2) recording animals for *siskur*-offerings received by Dadaga and sealed with Dadaga's own seal. This document falls within the period of Dadaga's nephew Lu-kala's tenure as chief household administrator.

376 MVN 14, 5 (Š 39 ii) and OrSP 47-49, 206 (Š 39 ii).

377 MVN 14, 66 (Š 39 ix). One text sealed by Dadaga; Akkadica 7 pl. 1 2, falls within the sequence of A(ya)kala.

378 Aleppo 395 (M 3534) (Š 48 xii).

379 See Ligabue 15 (AS 2 vii). No texts have been found from AS 3, but the sequence restarts with BM 107994 (AS 4 i).

380 SANTAG 6, 307 (ŠS 6 xiii); see also CST 793 (ŠS 7).

381 MVN 14, 493 (ŠS 9 x).

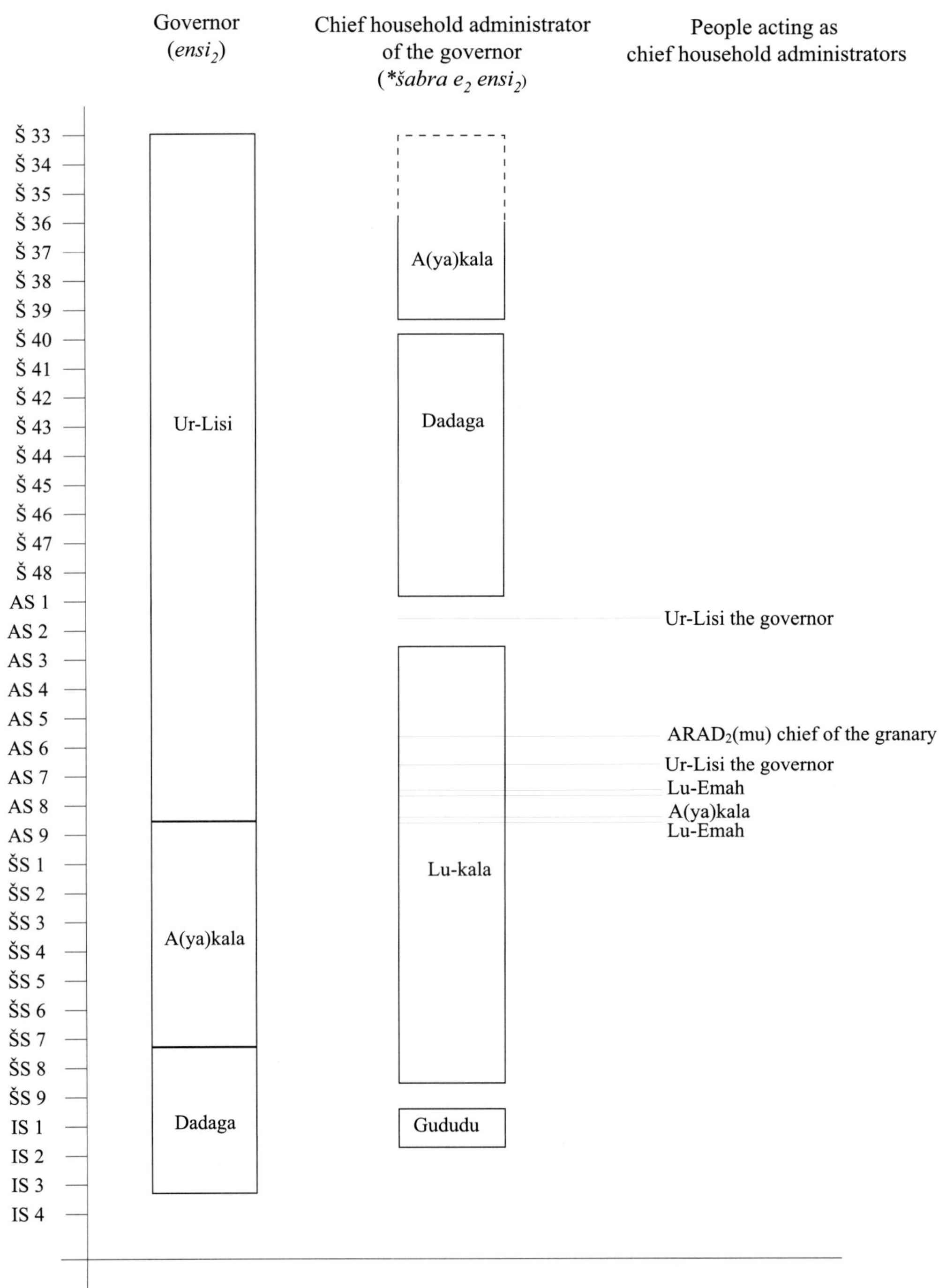

Figure 9: Sequence of persons holding the title of chief household administrator of the governor

It cannot be proven that Lu-kala, the son of Ur-E'e, was active in the administration of Umma prior to Š 48. A person named Lu-kala with the title of overseer appears in a number of texts from before this date, but there is no reason to believe that he is identical with the son of Ur-E'e by the same name.[382] Between Amar-Suen's first year and the end of Ur domination over Umma, only one person named Lu-kala carried a seal. Thus it is likely that all attestations of a high-ranking Lu-kala—a Lu-kala entitled scribe—referred to Lu-kala, son of Ur-E'e, the member of the ruling family of Umma. Nothing is known about Lu-kala's own family. Since he is never mentioned with a title specific to any office (save for the one example quoted here), it is impossible to ascertain whether any of the people claiming to be sons of Lu-kala were, indeed, sons of Lu-kala, chief household administrator.[383]

As long as Lu-kala is attested in the extant sources, he also held the office of chief household administrator of the governor. Lu-kala rarely sealed documents that seem to relate to the activities of a provincial administrator, and no certain use of a *nam-šatam* seal can be ascertained for Lu-kala.[384]

Lu-kala not only oversaw agricultural work done by teams of agricultural workers and workers from the workshops of the Umma households,[385] he also functioned as a foreman of large work-crews

---

382 Note, however, the dedicatory seal rolled on BIN 5, 232 (Š 37): ur-^{d}li$_{9}$-si$_{4}$ / ensi$_{2}$ umma^{ki} / lu$_{2}$-kal-la // ⸢x⸣-[x] / ARAD$_{2}$-[zu].

383 Among the other people in Umma called Lu-kala we find Lu-kala the cultivator (*engar*) (for example, AAS 83 [no date]). The text Aleppo 51 (M 3632) (no date), has a peculiar seal inscription mentioning Lu-kala, the son of Lugal-ezem. Compare this text to Aleppo 132 (M 3960) (no date), which is said to be sealed by Lu-kala, but carries the seal of Lugal-ezem, the well-known agricultural overseer and son of Lugal-Emah(e). This Lu-kala, son of Lugal-ezem is then likely to be identical with the cultivator by that name; he was perhaps a junior member of the family of Dada. See, in that regard, SAT 2, 77 (Š 33 vi), obv. ii 9, which offers conclusive evidence in support of this reconstruction. Among the other people named Lu-kala, we find Lu-kala, the son of Lugal-Suen (see, for example, Aleppo 62 (M 3759) [Š 35vii], with seal inscription); Lu-kala, son of Uludi (*ulu$_{3}$-di*) (see for example, UCT 3, 334 [no year, month 11], with seal inscription); Lu-kala, the shepherd (see, for example, NYPL 121 [AS 6]; MCS 1, 54, BM 106045 [ŠS 5] (title *na-gada*); MVN 15, 390 [Š 37 iii to vii] (title *sipa*)); Lu-kala the oil presser (for example, BIN 5, 277 [AS 8?]). Lu-kala, the forester (see, for example, BM 104774 (unpubl.)); Lu-kala, the police officer (see for example, MCS 7, 22 BM 105330 [Š 43]); Lu-kala, the overseer (*ugula*) (see, for example, MVN 13, 316 [Š 42 ii]; Rochester 173 [Š 37 v]); Lu-kala, the scribe of beer (for example, Nebraska 39 [no year, month 11]).

384 One text concerned with labor, SNAT 495 (ŠS 4), directly states that it has been sealed with the *nam-šatam* seal of Lu-kala; however the seal rolled on that document was published as: *lu$_{2}$-kal-la / dub-sar / dumu ur-nigar^{gar} šuš$_{3}$* (see also MVN 15, 83 [ŠS 4]). This unique reference might, however, be the result of a copying error. The text was unavailable to me, and the seal is not included in the catalogue of R. Mayr 1997. Note that the parallel text AAS 26 (ŠS 6 vii to viii), which failed to use the phrase *kišib$_{3}$ nam-ša$_{3}$-tam*, was sealed with a seal of Lu-kala where the patronym is illegible (collated J. L. Dahl, 2004).

385 See MVN 16, 1047 (ŠS 6 iii) recording laborers from Agu's basketry workshop working in the fields, sealed by Lu-kala, or Nik 2, 103 (ŠS 6) recording leather workers likewise doing field work sealed by Lu-kala, and credited to A(ya)kala (presumably the chief of the leather workers). Whereas one account concerning Agu

himself.[386]

Relatively few accounts of the work of female dependent workers (*nig$_2$-ka$_9$-ak a$_2$ geme$_2$*) have been recovered.[387] Three of these mention Lu-kala in the colophon: Aegyptus 21, 159 (AS 8 i to xi); MVN 21, 200 (AS 2); and MVN 21, 201 (AS 5).[388] The amount of work-days recorded in each of these three texts surpasses, by far, those of the other accounts of the work of female dependent workers. Only the account concerning Lu-dingira, the scribe of flour, rivals that of Lu-kala.

The first entry in the "debits" section of all three accounts (in MVN 21, 201 following a "remainder") is an artificial computation of the average number of female dependent workers available each day during the period of accounting. The calculation of the work-days of the crew was presumably aided by the work-crew inventories such as AAICAB 1, 1912-1141 (no date).[389] A normal work-crew of female dependent workers seems to have averaged thirty women in total,[390] Lu-kala's crew totaled more than one hundred dependent female workers.

It seems reasonable to assume that this work-crew was the permanent staff of the mill of the governor's household,[391] and produced for the governor and his *bala*-obligations.

Three large accounts have survived that closely tie Lu-kala and the household of the governor to the production of pottery.[392] Whereas the summary statement "pottery-worker-account concerning Lu-kala" is only attested in the recently published text MVN 21, 203 (AS 8), it can be suggested that at least one of the other texts contained such a statement, namely MVN 1, 231. This text is an exact parallel to MVN 21, 203, but from the year AS 4; the work crew of the two texts is largely identical

has been found (TCL 5, 6036 [AS 4]), no such text has ever been discovered concerning A(ya)kala.

386 It is possible that the work crew of Lu-kala was previously managed by Dadaga when he held the office of chief household administrator; see, in particular, CHEU 49 (Š 48 ii 1), where Dadaga is listed first among the well-known Umma milling foremen as being responsible for a work crew of his own.

387 JNES 50, 255-80 (ŠS 4), the name of the responsible person is broken; MVN 21, 204 (ŠS 7?), account concerning Lu-balasaga; STA 2 (AS 4), account concerning Lu-dingira, scribe of flour; TCL 5, 5669 (Š 48 i to xii), account concerning Lugal-inimgina.

388 In both texts, from MVN 21, almost the entire "credits" section is devoted to milling grain for the *bala*.

389 AAICAB 1, 1912-1141 recorded the total number of work days and the average number of female workers in a work crew during one year by totaling a progressively diminishing number of female workers actually available (according to different work categories), listed monthly. The work-crew listed in AAICAB 1, 1912-1141, was under the administrative control of Lu-kala.

390 See also AnOr 7, 226 (ŠS 6), recording a transfer of three female milling workers from the crew of Ur-Nintu to the crew of Ur-Suen and Dagu, sealed by Lu-kala (with regular seal of Lu-kala).

391 See, for example, YOS 18, 115 (no date), rev. i 2-3: 1(U$_c$) 7(DIŠ$_c$) geme$_2$ kikken-na 3(ban$_2$) 3(diš) ma-na-ta / ugula kikken$_2$ i$_3$-dab$_5$ and 14: gir$_3$-se$_3$-ga ensi$_2$, perhaps to be understood as an inventory of the female workers of the mill of the governor's household among other staff.

392 MVN 1, 232 (Š 43 iii); MVN 21, 203 (AS 8); and MVN 1, 231 (AS 4).

as is the production according to standing orders.[393]

The pottery workshop of the governor's household is the only such workshop attested in Umma. However, the production figures of that workshop suggest that it monopolized Umma pottery production. Contrary to what has been suggested in a recent study,[394] there is now evidence to suggest that the potter—like other work groups—worked full time for the state, with only a limited number of "days off" (*a_2 u_4-du_8-a*).[395]

Lu-kala did not personally manage the delivery of all the finished products (which were credited to his account); rather, a member of his work crew (presumably an overseer) was responsible for transferring most products from Lu-kala's workshop to other Umma households˙

Since Lu-kala appears very frequently as the contributor, or recipient, of large (as well as small) amounts of silver, and since the silver involved in the so-called balanced trade agent accounts have received enormous attention from historians of late third-millennium economic history, the office headed by Lu-kala was named the fiscal office of Umma, or the "irrigation office," and Lu-kala himself the "silver comptroller" of Umma.[396]

The amounts of silver debited or credited to the account of Lu-kala did not, as a rule, represent real metal, but rather obligations enumerated in terms of silver equivalencies. This can be inferred from the fact that it is impossible to trace any particular amount (representing a piece) of silver from one account to another, which would have happened had the metal been a physical commodity. The amounts of silver received by Lu-kala from a wide range of individuals represented mostly arrears from shepherds, cultivators or foremen.[397] Amounts of silver were also entered into the books as payments for the so-called "field interest" (*maš$_2$ a-ša$_3$-ga*).[398] It is likely, but not certain, that Lu-kala

---

393 For the term standing orders, see D. Snell 1982: 96–99 and appendix 2, 270–278. Snell did not describe standing orders within the production of household items. Both the workshops discussed here, as well as the basketry workshop documented in the account TCL 5, 6036, produced according to standing orders.

394 P. Steinkeller 1996: 232-253.

395 The work crew in MVN 1, 231, and MVN 21, 203, is almost identical. In both texts the foreman is debited with the full work-time of the workers, that is, all twelve month of the year. See the forthcoming study by the author (and paper by the author read at the 53rd RAI in St. Petersburg, the 27th of July, 2007). Compare this with V. V. Struve 1969: 139.

396 See P. Steinkeller 1981: 121. P. Steinkeller 1987b: 76 and fn. 17. T. Maeda 1996: 254-260. Snell gave Lu-kala the title "Comptroller," and devoted a section of his book on the 'balanced accounts' to his office, see, D. Snell 1982: 77–81.

397 See, for example, TSU 15 (ŠS 3 xi): 9(diš) 1/2(diš) gin$_2$ 1(u) 5(diš) še ku$_3$-babbar sag tuku / la$_2$-ia$_3$ su-ga ur-^{d}utu sipa / ki KAS$_4$-ta / gaba-ri kišib$_3$ lu$_2$-kal-la // iti [pa$_4$]-u$_2$-e / (blank space) / mu si-ma-num$_2$^{ki} ba-hul, "9 1/2 shekel and 15 *še* of silver, having '*saŋ*' (presumably a kind of tax), repaid arrear of Ur-Utu the shepherd. From EnKAS, copy of a sealed tablet of Lu-kala. Month Pau'e, year: 'Simanum was destroyed'."

398 There are only a few examples of "field interest" received directly by Lu-kala. See for example, AAICAB 1/1, pl. 18, 1911-148 or SANTAG 6, 242. Other members of the ruling family, in particular Dadaga, Gududu,

was transferring some of this metal into the "debits" section of the accounts of the trade-agents.

Lu-kala was presumably the overseer of the Umma colony of trade-agents, as suggested by TCL 5, 6037, the colophon of which is given here:

TCL 5, 6037 (ŠS 6):

Reverse column 10.

...

10. nig$_2$-ka$_9$-ak dam-gar$_3$-ne	Account of trade agents,
11. lu$_2$-kal-la	concerning Lu-kala.
12. mu ^{d}šu-^{d}suen lugal uri$_5$^{ki}-ma-ke$_4$	Year: "Šū-Suen, the king of Ur
na-ru$_2$-a mah [^{d}en]-lil$_2$ [^{d}nin]-lil$_2$-ra	erected the lofty stela for Enlil and
[mu-ne]-⸢ru$_2$⸣	Ninlil."

Although no such account has survived it is the hypothesis of this study that Lu-kala managed the flow of wealth from Umma to the imperial center, as is indicated by the tablet container Hirose 405 (ŠS 1? to 8):

1. pisan dub-ba	Tablet container:
2. nig$_2$-ka$_9$-ak bala-a	*bala*-accounts
3. lu$_2$-kal-la	(concerning) Lu-kala,
4. mu ma-da za-ab-ša-li^{ki}	from the year: "Zabšali (was destroyed),"
5. u$_3$ mu ma$_2$-⸢gur$_8$ mah⸣	and the year: "the lofty barge (was fashioned)."
Reverse	
1. i$_3$-⸢gal$_2$⸣	are present.

He certainly also managed the wealth of the governor, which is above all ascertained from the colophon of the short account Ledgers pl. 23 13 (ŠS 1 to 5):

Reverse

...

9. nig$_2$-ka$_9$-ak ku$_3$ ensi$_2$-ka	Silver account concerning the governor,
10. giri$_3$ lu$_2$-kal-la	conveyor: Lu-kala.

....

As a collector of arrears and field interest and a foreman of the Umma trade agent colony Lu-kala naturally transferred large amounts of silver, presumably in the form of obligations, from one account

and A(ya)kala are mentioned much more frequently as recipients of "field interest."

to another.[399] However, the economic importance of the production of the work crew he oversaw by far out-weighed that of the silver business.

Finally, the phrase "on the command of Lu-kala" (*inim* lu_2*-kal-la-ta*) is rather well attested, certifying his high-ranking position and his close relationship with the ruling clan.[400]

---

399 See, in particular, Ledgers, pl. 23 13, the 'silver account of the governor, via Lu-kala' (nig_2-ka_9-ak ku_3 $ensi_2$ / $giri_3$ lu_2-kal-la [rev. 9–10]).

400 The texts are: BIN 3, 549 (AS 9 viii); BPOA 2, 2591 (BM 105444) (ŠS 7 ii) rev. 2; MCS 3, 86 BM 105455 (AS 9 vii); MVN 16, 1516 (AS 8); Princeton 1, 150 (ŠS 1 viii); UTI 4, 2924 (AS 9 vii); and UTI 4, 2991 (ŠS 1).

4.11. $ARAD_2$(MU), CHIEF OF THE GRANARY

$ARAD_2$(mu),[401] the brother of the governor, held the office "chief of the granary" (*KA-guru*$_7$) from the middle of the reign of Šulgi (Š 33) until at least the end of Amar-Suen's reign, and perhaps considerably longer. I have already referred to the texts concerning $ARAD_2$(mu)'s accession to office when describing Ur-Lisi, $ARAD_2$(mu)'s predecessor as chief of the granary (p. 55 and fn. 204). In this section I will try to describe his office in greater detail.[402]

Little is known about $ARAD_2$(mu)'s own family; the few extant references to his wife do not reveal her name.[403] We only know for certain the name of one of his sons, Šara-izu, although he may have had more than one.[404] This Šara-izu was certainly identical with the person mentioned in the colophon of TCNU 468 (IS 3), a text which seems to be an almost exact parallel to an earlier account concerning $ARAD_2$(mu) (ASJ 19, 226 72 (no date), see below). If that observation is correct, then there is reason to believe that towards the end of Ur domination over Umma, $ARAD_2$(mu) was succeeded by his son, Šara-izu, as chief of the granary.[405]

From the end of Amar-Suen's reign, the name of the chief of the granary ceases to be recorded. The last explicit reference to $ARAD_2$(mu), holding the title of chief of the granary, is from AS 8, in a text mentioning his wife.[406] However, the absence of references to $ARAD_2$(mu)'s name together with the title of chief of the granary is not sufficient evidence to show that that office was not in his hands no longer, since throughout the history of Ur III, Umma references to the name of the chief of the granary were relatively rare, whereas the title was mentioned alone very frequently. Consequently, it has proven quite difficult to reconstruct the sequence of people holding that office. Here I will tentatively suggest that Ur-Lisi was chief of the granary until Š 33 when $ARAD_2$(mu) took over; he was in turn followed by his son Šara-izu some time after AS 8 and before IS 3.

It should be noted that Šara-izu is never mentioned with the title of chief of the granary—this

---

401 $ARAD_2$(mu)'s name is almost exclusively written $ARAD_2$ in the body of the texts, but always $ARAD_2$-mu in his seal inscription.

402 A *guru*$_7$ is both a very large unit of measurement in the capacity system (equal to 3,600 gur or approximately one million liters), as well as a word for the physical structure of a granary. The sign *KA* may refer to the opening (mouth) of the silo, analogous to the Sumerian word for the opening of a canal, *ka i*$_7$*-da*. Thus, the *KA-guru*$_7$ may be interpreted as the one who controls the opening of the granary.

403 See, for example, MVN 16, 908 (AS 8 iii), obv. 10: dam $ARAD_2$ KA-guru$_7$, and perhaps also MVN 2, 176 (Š 48 vii), rev. viii 9': dam $ARAD_2$-mu.

404 Seal of Šara-izu see, for example, MVN 2, 128 (ŠS 7): ^{d}šara$_2$-i$_3$-zu/ dub-sar / dumu $ARAD_2$ KA-guru$_7$.

405 There are other indications that Šara-izu did indeed follow in his father's footsteps as chief of the granary, notably the many primary documents from the time of Šū-Suen's reign until the end of Ur domination over Umma dealing with activities previously managed by $ARAD_2$(mu). The earliest certain references to Šara-izu are MVN 13, 353 and SAT 3, 1734, both from ŠS 6.

406 MVN 16, 908 (AS 8 iii), cited above (fn. 403).

resembles the situation at the time of the transfer of office between Ur-E'e and his son Lu-Haya, and perhaps even between Ur-E'e and his father Ur-nigar.

In his capacity as the chief of the Umma central granary, ARAD$_2$(mu) supplied a number of other institutions with barley for fodder and rations. Hence we find him supplying the fatteners (*kurušda*), the foremen of the mill (*ugula kikken$_2$*), and foremen of other work-crews. In addition we find ARAD$_2$(mu) supplying the trade-agents with barley for barter.[407] As a member of the ruling family of Umma, ARAD$_2$(mu) also partook in the agricultural administration and occasionally sealed documents as a provincial administrator.[408] In addition, ARAD$_2$(mu) sometimes sealed receipts for dead animals for the chief household administrator.

ARAD$_2$(mu) supplied the animal fatteners with barley on what seems to be a regular monthly basis. The four leading Umma fatteners were Ušmu, Inim-Šara, Bida, and Anahilibi.[409] The fattened oxen were controlled by several people, but ARAD$_2$(mu) seems to be the main supplier of fodder

---

407 See, in particular, SA 134 (ICP 1143) (AS 4), and OrSP 47-49, 411 (ŠS 3).

408 Only one text is sealed with the *nam-šatam* seal of ARAD$_2$(mu) (MVN 18, 543 [no date]). Some of ARAD$_2$(mu)'s sealed documents (which do not mention the use of a nam-šatam seal) do, however, resemble documents otherwise normally sealed by provincial administrators, suggesting that ARAD$_2$(mu) too held that position.

409 The most important Umma sheep and goat fattener during the latter part of Šulgi's reign, and presumably during the reign of Amar-Suen as well (and perhaps beyond), was Inim-Šara. See, for example, Syracuse 169 (Š 48 v 5), where Inim-Šara figures as the most important among the three well-known fatteners Inim-Šara, Bida, and Anahilibi:

Obverse	
1. 4(geš$_2$) 5(u) 3(diš) sa gi zi	293 bundles of *zi* reed;
2. inim-^{d}šara$_2$ kurušda	Inim-Šara, fattener.
3. 4(geš$_2$) 4(u) 4(diš) sa gi zi	284 bundles of *zi* reed;
4. bi$_2$-da kurušda	Bida, fattener.
5. 1(geš$_2$) 4(u) 5(diš) sa gi zi	105 bundles of *zi* reed;
6. an-na-hi-li-bi kurušda	Anahilibi, fattener.
Reverse	
1. u$_4$ 5(diš)-kam	On the fifth day.
2. gu-kilib-ba 6(diš) sa-ta	In each sheaf there are six bundles.
3. giri$_3$ igi-peš$_2$	Via Igipeš,
4. kišib$_3$ hu-wa-wa	Sealed by Huwawa.
5. iti RI mu-us$_2$-sa ki-maš^{ki} mu-us$_2$-sa-a-bi	Month *RI*, Year after: "Kimaš (was destroyed), the year after (that)."
Seal	
1. lu$_2$-eb-gal	Lu-Ebgal,
2. dub-sar	scribe,
3. dumu ur-gi$_6$-par$_4$	son of Ur-gipar.

for these animals as well.[410] The interaction between fattener and chief livestock administrator has been dealt with above. Ušmu and his circle perhaps operated at a higher level of the administrative hierarchy than the three fatteners mentioned here.[411]

Anahilibi's herd of approximately 100 animals supplied the provincial court and presumably also the imperial court with fattened animals. Anahilibi received the barley and bran for the fattening directly from the governor and his chief household administrator and not from ARAD$_2$(mu). On the other hand, Inim-Šara, perhaps the principal animal fattener of the Umma city-administration, received fodder for his animals directly from ARAD$_2$(mu).[412] Inim-Šara was perhaps connected with the household of Šara,[413] Bida—another fattener—with the Umma *bala* account.[414]

The chief of the granary also supplied the foremen of the workshops and the agricultural foremen (these are the foremen called "captains of (plow-)oxen" in some contexts and "foremen" in others) with barley rations for the dependent workers under their care and control.[415] Fodder (*ša$_3$-gal*) was also given to the draft donkeys (*anše kunga$_2$*),[416] other donkeys,[417] and plow oxen (*gu$_4$ apin*), and, not

---

410 Nigar-kidu, an important fattener of oxen in Umma, received fodder from ARAD$_2$(mu) in Aleppo 302 (M 3490) (Š 45 xii). Note that Atu the chief livestock administrator received fodder for calves from Ur-E'e in AnOr 1, 51 (Š 44).

411 Ušmu was perhaps the main Umma cattle fattener (MVN 2, 91 [AS 8]; MVN 16, 1094 [ŠS 5]; UTI 4, 2711 [AS 8]) in addition to being responsible for the regular fattening of sheep (MVN 14, 525 [IS 2]; etc.). He may also have operated as a *šatam* official (Georgica 5.08 [AS 7 iii]). Several texts testify to Ušmu's involment in the shipment of livestock to Ur (NYPL 111 [ŠS 5]; MVN 21, 72 [AS 9]; MVN 21, 126 [ŠS 7]; Nik 2, 116 [ŠS 5 x]).

412 See, for example, AnOr 7, 182 (no date); ASJ 19, 226 72 (no date), the account concerning ARAD$_2$(mu) discussed below (p. 118) (see rev. vii 2'-3': 1(u) 1(aš) gur / ša$_3$-gal udu niga / kišib$_3$ inim-^{d}šara$_2$); and CHEU 27 (Š 39 iv).

413 For the seal of Inim-Šara, see for example, MVN 21, 156 (Š 46 xiii): inim-^{d}šara$_2$ / dumu ur-dingir-ra / kurušda ^{d}šara$_2$. For the seal of Inim-Šara's son and successor as fattener, see CST 797 (IS 2): a-lu$_5$-lu$_5$ / dumu inim-^{d}šara$_2$ / kurušda ^{d}šara$_2$-ka.

414 See also the milling-accounts below, table 3 on p. 120, in which Bida contributes to the "debits" of three accounts.

415 Rations for humans were often called "barley-rations" (*še-ba*), but could be called "fodder" (*ša$_3$-gal*). See, for example, Orient 16, 71 96 (ŠS 1 x) concerning rations (*še-ba*; obv. 1); AAICAB 1, 1911-170 (ŠS 2 x to xi) concerning rations (*še-ba*; obv. 4); MVN 13, 276 (ŠS 6 i) concerning fodder (*ša$_3$-gal*; obv. 4); and MVN 16, 1272 (ŠS 3 xii) concerning fodder (*ša$_3$-gal*; obv. 2).

416 Delivery said to be from ARAD$_2$(mu). See, for example, AnOr 7, 174 (Š 44 xii; obv. 5) and AnOr 7, 179 (Š 38 x; obv. 4). Delivery said to be from the chief of the granary (no mention of personal name). See, for example, ArOr 25, 561 20 (ŠS 6 iv; obv. 4).

417 Delivery said to be from the chief of the granary (no mention of personal name); see, for example, ASJ 19, 220 58 (ŠS 5 xi; obv. 4); and BCT 2, 256 (ŠS 3 ix; obv. 4).

to be forgotten, the gods of the Mesopotamian pantheon.[418]

ARAD$_2$(mu) appears in numerous texts as the supplier of amounts of barley converted into work days at fixed rates, mostly at an equivalence of between six and eight *sila*$_3$ per day. These were the "wages" for the hirelings (*a*$_2$ *lu*$_2$*-hun-ga*$_2$).[419]

ASJ 19, 226 72, dating to the earliest part of Ur III Umma history,[420] is a ten-column account (column ten was perhaps blank), concerning ARAD$_2$(mu). The "debits" section recorded the deliveries of barley to the granary by temple-household administrators; the "credits" section, on the other hand, recorded the deliveries of barley and wheat to a number of administrators and foremen working for one or more households.[421] TCNU 468 is a shorter account recording a smaller amount of barley, but otherwise an exact parallel to ASJ 19, 226 72. Perhaps due to a separation of many years, very few persons were still in office when TCNU 468 was written.[422]

Barley was processed in the mill (*kikken*$_2$[423]). In the following I will briefly discuss the

---

418 Rations for the gods were mostly called *sa*$_2$*-du*$_{11}$, which seems to be the correct term for describing "rations" for deities. See, for example, ASJ 19, 220 56 (ŠS 5 iv) obv. 3-4: *sa*$_2$*-du*$_{11}$ for Nin-Egal; MVN 3, 269 (ŠS 5): *sa*$_2$*-du*$_{11}$ for the divine Amar-Suen; and Orient 16, 73 103 (ŠS 5): *sa*$_2$*-du*$_{11}$ for Šara. However, see AnOr 7, 309 (ŠS 9), rev. 3: ša$_3$-gal udu niga sa$_2$-du$_{11}$ ^{d}šara$_2$ u$_3$ dingir-re-ne, clearly advocating a distinction between *sa*$_2$*-du*$_{11}$ and *ša*$_3$*-gal*.

419 See, for example, the two accounts TCL 5, 5675, and TCL 5, 5676. In TCL 5, 5675 (AS 4 i to xii), ARAD$_2$(mu) delivered 5 *gur*, 2 *barig* and 4 *ban*$_2$ of barley to be converted at a rate of 7 *sila*$_3$ per day (= 237 work-days), and 7 *gur*, 4 *barig*, 1 *ban*$_2$ and 8 *sila*$_3$ of barley to be converted at a rate of 6 *sila*$_3$ per day (= 393 work-days) to the debit section of the account of Lugal-gu'e the captain of (plow-)oxen (obv. i 6–13). In TCL 5, 5676 (ŠS 2), the chief of the granary delivered 36 *gur* and 80 *sila*$_3$ of barley which was to be converted at a rate of six *sila*$_3$ per day (= 1813 1/3 work-days), to the account of Ur-Ninsu the captain of (plow-)oxen (obv. i 23-27). Primary documents were, as we have seen, used to draw up the accounts. However, none of the primary documents recording transfers to the "debits" of the two accounts cited above have been found. As an example of such a document, see AUCT 1, 681 (Š 45).

420 ARAD$_2$(mu) is mentioned in the colophon as Ur-Lisi's brother, and Ur-Lisi is not (yet?) called governor advocating an early date for this text.

421 See, for example, rev. vii 2'–14': 1(u) 1(aš) gur / ša$_3$-gal udu niga / kišib$_3$ inim-^{d}šara$_2$ / 8(aš) 2(ban$_2$) gur / kišib$_3$ uš-mu / 2(aš) gur / ša$_3$-gal anše / kišib$_3$ ur-dingir-ra / 3(barig) ša$_3$-gal mušen / kišib$_3$ ha-lu$_5$-lu$_5$ / 1(u) 4(aš) 2(barig) gur / še-ba-še$_3$ / kišib$_3$ lugal-nig$_2$-lagar-e ugula uš-bar, "11 *gur* as fodder for the fattened sheep, sealed by Inim-Šara, 8 *gur* and 2 *ban*$_2$, sealed by Ušmu, 2 *gur* as fodder for the donkeys, sealed by Ur-dingira, 3 *barig* as fodder for the birds, sealed by Halulu, 14 *gur* and 2 *barig* as rations, sealed by Lugal-niglagar'e, foreman of the weaving mill."

422 See, for example, Ušmu: ASJ 19, 226 72, rev. vii 6' // TCNU 468, rev. ii 8.

423 A reading *kikken*$_2$ of *HAR.HAR* is supported by numerous Ur III attestations of *kikken*$_{1\text{-}2}$*-na*, a reading *har-har-ra*, or perhaps *ar*$_3$*-ar*$_3$*-ra* cannot be excluded for the title of the foreman of the mill. See MVN 6, 84 (Š 46), obv. 5; ab-ba-mu HAR-HAR-ra, as well as for the verb "to mill, grind, etc." Note that *ar*$_3$*-ra* is *hamṭu*, and *ar*$_3$*-ar*$_3$*-ra marû*.

administration of the work and products of the mill. One group of six foremen of the mill (*ugula kikken$_2$*) seems to have operated together as one unit. They were perhaps all associated with the same household. The summary document AAICAB 1, 1911-485 (AS 1) records the "arrears" from the accounts of these foremen. The colophon of that text reads:

Reverse	
(blank space)	
1. ŠU+NIGIN$_2$ la$_2$-ia$_3$ 5(geš'u) 1(geš$_2$) 1/3(diš) geme$_2$ u$_4$ 1(diš)-še$_3$	Total deficits: 3060 1/3 work-days,
2. ŠU+NIGIN$_2$ diri 4(geš$_2$) 1(u) gin$_2$ geme$_2$ u$_4$ 1(diš)-še$_3$	Total surplus: 240 1/6 work-days,
3. diri la$_2$-ia$_3$ a$_2$ geme$_2$-ka	(It is) the surplus and the deficits of the work of female dependent workers,
4. ugula kikken$_2$-na-ke$_4$-ne	of the foremen of the mill.
5. mu ^{d}amar-^{d}suen lugal	Year: "Amar-Suen (became) king."
(blank space)	

From the same text we are able to produce this table:

Foreman	Lu-sa'izu	Ur-Nintu	Ur-Šara	Lu-balasag	Dingira	Šara-zame
"remainder" (in work days)	- 240 1/6	- 506 1/6	- 620 1/6	- 971	- 959 1/2	- 3 1/2

Table 2: Foremen of the mill (from AAICAB 1, 1911-485)[424]

Four of the same foremen are also known to us from their own "milling-accounts," recording a "debits" and a "credits" of both female dependent workers and grain (except for Šara-zame's account MVN 21, 204, which does not include grain).

The regularity of the production, visible from following table (3), suggests that the same foremen participated in a "planned" economy, where grain as well as labor was distributed to the mill-foremen centrally, and according to fixed rates:

424 Dingira, Ur-Nintu, Šara-zame, and Lu-balasag are also known from CHEU 49 (Š 48 iii 1) (obv. 2; 3; 4; and 5). Lugal-Emah(e), Lu-balasag, Šara-zame, Ur-Šulpa'e, Adu, and Ur-Nintu are also attested in TCL 5, 6039 (AS 5 ii) (obv. i 28; obv. ii 14; obv. Ii 36; obv. iii 15; obv. iii 30; rev. iii 3).

Foreman / Supplier	Lu-sa'izu Erlangen 1 Š 48 to AS 1	Ur-Nintu	Ur-Šara TCL 5, 5670 [a] AS 1	Lu-balasag	Dingira TCL 5, 5668 Š 48	Šara-zame MVN 21, 204 ŠS 6 to 7
ARAD$_2$(mu)	216 *gur* 230 *sila$_3$* of barley, 35 *gur* of emmer?, 16 *gur* of wheat		193 *gur* 25 *sila$_3$* of barley 38 *gur* of emmer, 33 *gur* 40 *sila$_3$* of wheat		184 *gur* 280 *sila$_3$* of barley 35 *gur* of emmer, 16 *gur* 110 *sila$_3$* of wheat	
Bida [b]	3 *gur* of barley		3 *gur* of barley		3 *gur* of barley	
Work-crew [c]	36 females	[d]	36 females		36 females	

[a] R. K. Englund 1990: 79-90.

[b] Other people contributed to the "debits" as well.

[c] The work-crews did not work all year in this institution, but rather between eight and ten months.

[d] See MVN 21, 212 (Š 42 i to xiii) for a calculation of Ur-Nintu's work crew of female dependent workers. See also Nebraska 42 (AS 7).

Table 3: Foremen of the mill; the "debits"[425]

It seems appropriate to interpret the data presented above as describing the mill of one administrative unit, perhaps one household. All four, and perhaps even all six, foremen mentioned in table 2 worked in close cooperation with the chief of the granary, who supplied them with the grain to be processed. Further, it seems likely that they all worked closely together with, and perhaps directly under the administrative control of the chief household administrator of the governor. Bida, who is mentioned in three of the accounts presented in table 3, was, as we have suggested, connected with the Umma *bala*, and it would be interesting to see this group of millers as connected with the Umma *bala* as well. It is, however, also possible to see these six overseers as connected directly with the household of the governor.

Some texts indicate that ARAD$_2$(mu) too, from time to time received dead animals following the pattern defined above. Further, it can be shown that ARAD$_2$(mu) sealed these documents almost exclusively when Lu-kala was not available to do so. That is, in particular, during the tenth month

425 The interaction between the three accounts cited above was discussed by R. K. Englund 1990: 78 and fn. 263.

of Amar-Suen 5.[426] The texts are entirely similar to the texts described above under Lu-kala, and the shepherds delivering the animals were the same.

426 One of these texts (Aleppo 381 (M 3601) [Š 39 v]) falls right in between the tenure of A(ya)kala and Dadaga, the next two texts (Aleppo 391 (M 4153) [Š 47 i]; and MVN 14, 62 [Š 48 ii]), are from within the tenure of Dadaga. One text is from month 9 of AS 5 (Syracuse 85), contemporary with several documents sealed by Lu-kala. Six texts date to month 10 of AS 5, when Lu-kala sealed no records (BPOA 2, 2576 (BM 105419); MVN 5, 36; MVN 18, 471; MVN 18, 474; SNAT 361; and SNAT 362. Although Lu-kala began sealing these documents again in the eleventh month of AS 5, $ARAD_2$(mu) still sealed two more texts (MVN 4, 85, and Syracuse 86).

4.12. THE OTHER SONS OF UR-NIGAR

At least two high-level administrators in the Ur III empire were called Ur-nigar: Ur-nigar, the chief livestock administrator of Umma, and the prince Ur-nigar, a son of Šulgi. Early Umma texts mentions Ur-nigar, the fattener (*kurušda*), who is also attested in the seals of his three sons.[427] The best-known sons of Ur-nigar, the Umma chief livestock administrator, have been mentioned above. However in the following I will try to list and discuss the remaining sons of Ur-nigar.[428]

It is important to try and understand the career of these members of the ruling family since they seem to have been by-passed in the line of succession for the four leading offices in the Umma central administration. This chapter will therefore seek to answer what became of these family members.

The following five persons were all called "son of Ur-nigar, the chief livestock administrator": Lu-duga, Lugal-kuzu, Inim-Šara, Lu-Šulgi(ra), and Gudea. The following four persons were all

---

427 The seal rolled on AAICAB 1, 1912-1148 (AS 5), probably reads: ur-^{d}dumu-zi-da / dub-sar / ur-nigar^{gar} ⸢kurušda⸣; compare with Torino 2, 645 (ŠS 2), and TIM 6, 55 (IS 2 ix), rev. v 12: ur-^{d}dumu-zi-da engar dumu ur-⸢nigar⸣^{gar} kurušda. Two other sons of Ur-nigar, the fattener, are known from their seals; Lu-Suen and Ur-Halmutum. For the seal of Lu-Suen; see, for example, MVN 14, 453 (ŠS 1). For the seal of Ur-Halmutum; see, for example, MVN 16, 1201 (ŠS 1). The majority of the documents that mention Ur-nigar, the fattener, date from the ten year span between Š 34 and Š 44. Ur-nigar seems to have been in a position with direct responsibilities to both the (Drehem-based) imperial administration (of livestock), as well as the local court in Umma. Two interesting documents describe his interaction with a certain Basa and the *bala* account of Umma: BIN 5, 80 (Š 43): 1(geš$_2$) 2(u) 3(diš) udu bar su-ga / 1(geš$_2$) 7(diš) sila$_4$ bar gal$_2$ / 4(u) 6(diš) maš$_2$ / zi-ga bala-a / ša$_3$ nibru^{ki} // ki ba-sa$_6$-ta / giri$_3$ ur-nigar^{gar} kurušda / mu en ^{d}nanna maš-e i$_3$-pa$_3$, "83 sheep without fleece, 67 lambs with fleece, 46 goats, booked out of the *bala*, in Nippur, from Basa, via Ur-nigar the fattener. Year: the En-priest of Nanna was installed." MVN 2, 301 (Š 35 xi): 1(geš$_2$) 3 (u) 2(diš) [udu] bar su-⸢ga⸣ / 1(geš$_2$) 3(diš) maš$_2$ / udu didli u$_3$ udu a-[x]-ra u$_3$ udu bala-a / ki ur-nigar^{gar} kurušda-ta // ba-sa$_6$ i$_3$-dab$_5$ / iti pa$_5^{?}$-u$_2$-⸢e⸣ / mu-us$_2$-sa an-ša^{ki} ba-hul, "92 sheep without fleece, 63 goats, they are the mixed sheep, and the x sheep, and the *bala* sheep, from Ur-nigar, the fattener, Basa seized. Month Pau'e. Year after: Anšan was destroyed." See also Nik 2, 371 (Š 41) and SACT 2, 242 (Š 43) recording the fulfillment of the "debits" (rev. iv: sag-nig$_2$-gur$_{11}$-ra-kam ša$_3$-bi su-ga) of Ur-nigar, the fattener; and TLB 3, 37 (Š 42), a record of the "debits" of Basa, in which Ur-nigar, the fattener, figures among the people contributing to the "debits."

428 Two texts included in the unpublished French dissertation of M. Touzalin (1982) mention additional sons of Ur-nigar the chief livestock administrator (*šuš$_3$*). However, collations of these texts housed in the Archaeological Museum of Aleppo (by J. L. Dahl and B. Lafont September 2006), have shown that these texts were wrongly transliterated. Aleppo 371 (M 3561) (Š 37 viii) has an impression of a seal with the following inscription *a-kal-la / dub-sar / dumu ur-nigar^{gar} šuš$_3$*, and not *lugal-ezem / dumu ur-nigar^{gar} šuš$_3$*. The seal rolled on Aleppo 176 (M 4075) (AS 3) text reads *a-tu / dub-sar / dumu ⸢šeš-kal⸣ -[la]*, and not *dumu ur-nigar^{gar} šuš$_3$*. This in turn highlights the need for caution when using any text published without a photo or hand-copy, in particular, as the sole foundation for an argument. Furthermore, the Touzalin texts are known to most Assyriologists only through the electronic copies posted on the web first by the Dutch group of Remco de Maaijer, and later the CDLI. These texts are in dire need of collation, and should be used with care until the immanent publication of collations by Dahl and Lafont.

called "son of Ur-nigar" without any mention of his title: Lu-dingira, Mansum, Lugal-hegal,[429] and Ur-Nisaba.

Lu-duga:

The seal of Lu-duga; *lu$_2$-du$_{10}$-ga / dub-sar / dumu ur-nigar^{gar} šuš$_3$*, was used exclusively on tablets said to be sealed by Dadaga, Lu-duga's brother. This paradox is not easily resolved; the suggestion that Dadaga was another name for Lu-duga is not convincing.[430] Although the names of Dadaga and his son Gududu are the only names of members of the Umma ruling family which are not readily explicable according to our understanding of Sumerian, they still conform nicely with third millennium naming practices.[431] The explanation that Lu-duga rolled his seal on tablets for a minor brother, fails to account for why no single tablet bears both the information "sealed by Lu-duga" (*kišib$_3$ lu$_2$-du$_{10}$-ga*) and the seal of Lu-duga.

However, after scrutinizing the approximately thirty-four texts that contained the seal of Lu-duga, the following picture emerges: twenty-two texts are receipts of dead animals of the type mentioned several times before. The first text is from Š 36 and the last from Š 48; a majority of the texts are from Š 48 (twelve). The names of the shepherds and the number of dead animals are similar to all the other texts from the same group. These texts were used above (pp. 69 ff. and 104 ff. and figure 9) in defining the time frame for Dadaga's tenure as chief household administrator.

Four texts, from Š 45 (1 text), 46 (two texts), and 48 (one text), were concerned with work and resemble other texts from the same period sealed by Dadaga. The remaining twelve texts record various minor transactions, with one exception: Ontario 2, 219 (ROM 925.62.306) (AS 2 or Š 45), which is an administrative document referring to the fulfillment of the "debits" of a silver account concerning the trade agents.[432] This suggests that Lu-duga was not active in the state administration, but that he occasionally sealed tablets for his brother Dadaga. He may have served as a sort of assistant or adjunct during Dadaga's tenure as chief administrator of the household of the governor (*šabra e$_2$ ensi$_2$*). See p. 48 above for a brief discussion of Lu-duga, the son of Nigar-kidu, whose career in many ways resembled that of his cousin and name sake, Lu-duga, the son of Ur-nigar.

Lugal-kuzu:

429 Only the text MCS 3, 91, BM 112993 (ŠS 3) is said to be sealed with a seal including the title of Ur-nigar, the father of Lugal-hegal. Note in this regard also SAT 2, 315 (Š 43 iv), which has the title *mu$_6$-sub$_3$ ^{d}šara$_2$* for Ur-nigar, the father of Lugal-hegal.

430 Although no conclusive evidence from the Third Dynasty of Ur in favor of this theory can be offered, it remains a topic for further investigation. The theory in question here was put forward by R. Mayr 1997: 141–143. The use of double names is, as far as I know, only attested for Neo-Babylonian Sippar (see most recently M. P. Streck 2001: 110–111).

431 See H. Limet 1968: 61–112.

Lugal-kuzu was active from Š 44 to ŠS 9, exclusively sealing documents relating to the agricultural administration. He operated at the level above the captains of (plow-)oxen, perhaps with the title provincial administrator. Lugal-kuzu sealed more than thirty documents after AS 6, all relating to the district of Gu(e)dena and Mušbiana, a district that was managed by a number of agricultural overseers mentioned earlier in this study (fn. 248). It may be appropriate to compare UTI 4, 2569 (ŠS 2), MVN 11, 164 (ŠS 4), AnOr 7, 313 (no date), UTI 4, 2864 (ŠS 2), and UTI 3, 2126 (ŠS 4 iv), four texts concerned with Gu(e)dena and Mušbiana.

UTI 4, 2399,[432] is a list of work-days expended weeding (*^{u2}kiši$_{17}$ ku$_5$-a*) six different units in the Gu(e)dena and Mušbiana area. The fields, here termed *GAN$_2$*,[433] were each qualified according to a personal name; the majority of these names correspond to the names in the other texts to be discussed here (see table 4, p. 123). The next text, MVN 11, 164 is a list of amounts of barley levied from the threshing floor of Gu(e)dena (reverse lines 6–7; še geš e$_3$-a$^!$ / ki-su$_7$ gu$_2$-eden-na). The personal names in MVN 11, 164 are almost identical with the ones from the first text. The same group of people were, however, in this text referred to as captains of (plow-)oxen (*nu-banda$_3$ gu$_4$*). MVN 11, 164, should be compared to AnOr 7, 313 (no date), a much more detailed record with the same subscript as MVN 11, 164. In AnOR 7, 313 the same persons were again listed, but the amounts of grain recorded for each person was approximately twenty times larger than the amounts recorded in MVN 11, 164, which therefore might only be a partial record of the product of the fields. In AnOr 7, 313 the farmers who worked on the different units were also listed. Some of the people in this text were called (agricultural) administrators (*šabra*). UTI 4, 2864 records the disbursement of wool and hides for the cultivators of the same units—the same people previously called "captains of (plow-)oxen" were here called "foremen" (*ugula*). It is likely that the reason behind this change in titles reflected the different functions of the same persons. In UTI 4, 2864, the captains of (plow-)oxen acted as foremen in relation to the cultivators who were to receive the wool and hides. The titles given in AnOr 7, 313 might reflect the actual hierarchical standing of the persons.

The reason for this change of title, which seems to be determined by the function of the person, is even more confusing when studied chronologically and interregionally. It appears that the original title for the same official might have been scribe of ten oxen (*dub-sar gu$_4$ 1(u)*).[434] The last text to

432 Compare to the parallel text UTI 4, 2569.

433 A brief investigation of the domain units worked by the individuals in this text shows that these were not static; rather, each person worked on a number of different fields within the greater area of Gu(e)dena and Mušbiana.

434 See, in particular, Syracuse 356 (Š 35 iv), a text which has the same format as UTI 3, 2126, mentioned here, and according to which the foremen were referred to as follows: "foreman: Lugal-kugani, scribe of ten oxen" (obv. 9: ugula lugal-ku$_3$-ga-ni dub-sar gu$_4$ 1(u)); "foreman: Dada, scribe of ten oxen" (rev. 2: ugula da-da dub-sar gu$_4$ 1(u)); and "foreman: Lu-gina, scribe of ten oxen" (rev. 11: ugula lu$_2$-gi-na dub-sar gu$_4$ 1(u)). These three foremen were all attested with the title captain of (plow-)oxen (*nu-banda$_3$ gu$_4$*), and it is entirely possible that the title scribe of ten oxen became obsolete during the later years of Šulgi.

be mentioned here, UTI 3, 2126, is a list of ox-carcasses, hides, and barley. The animals, which were referred to as "fallen" (*gu*$_4$ *ri-ri-ga*) were presumably the plow-oxen used on the same units as described above; the barley recorded here is likely to be the barley that these creatures had not eaten. The fact that the number of hides does not reflect the number of dead animals may indicate that they died an untimely death, which could have left some hides useless.[435] In this text the persons are once again referred to as captains of (plow-)oxen.[436]

UTI 4, 2399 [a] record of work-days weeding plots in Gu(e)dena and Mušbiana ŠS 2	MVN 11, 164 record of levied? barley from Gu(e)dena ŠS 4	AnOr 7, 313 account of total out-put of grain from Gu(e)dena and Mušbiana no date	UTI 4, 2864 disbursements of wool and hides for the cultivators of Gu(e)dena and Mušbiana ŠS 2	UTI 3, 2126 record of fallen oxen and their fodder ŠS 4 iv
Ur-Abzu	Ur-Ninsu (*nu-banda*$_3$ *gu*$_4$)	x	Ipa'e (*ugula*)	Ur-Enun(a) (*nu-banda*$_3$ *gu*$_4$)
Ur-Enun(a)	Dada (*nu-banda*$_3$ *gu*$_4$)	Dada (*nu-banda*$_3$ *gu*$_4$)	Ur-Ninsu (*ugula*)	GuTAR (*nu-banda*$_3$ *gu*$_4$)
Lu-dingira	GuTAR (*nu-banda*$_3$ *gu*$_4$)	Lu-duga (*šabra*)	GuTAR (*ugula*)	Ur-Ninsu (*nu-banda*$_3$ *gu*$_4$)
GuTAR	Ur-Enun(a) (*nu-banda*$_3$ *gu*$_4$)	Ur-Enun(a) (*šabra*)		Ipa'e (*nu-banda*$_3$ *gu*$_4$)
Ur-Ninsu	Lu-dingira (*nu-banda*$_3$ *gu*$_4$)	Ur-Enlila (*šabra*)		
Dada		GuTAR (*ugula*)		
		x		

[a] Compare to UTI 4, 2569, a parallel text where the sequence of persons is Ur-Abzu, Lu-Utu, Ur-Enun(a), Lu-dingira, GuTAR, Ur-Ninsu.

Table 4: Captains of (plow-)oxen under the command of Lugal-kuzu

Several of the persons in the table above may be related to one another. Egalesi a member of the family of Lu-Šara, the land-surveyor (*sa*$_{12}$-*sug*$_5$), sealed documents very similar to those sealed by Lugal-kuzu concerning the fields Gu(e)dena and Mušbiana.[437]

It seems that Lugal-kuzu operated as a provincial administrator supervising a group of approximately six captains of (plow-)oxen, perhaps making up an entire district. The following text supports this interpretation:

435 *ri-ri-ga* is always contrasted to *ba-uš*$_2$, which is understood as "slaughtered."

436 Compare this text to MCS 1, 54, BM 106045, obv. iv 14 (24) to v 9 (24), where the same units are listed. It is entirely possible that UTI 3, 2126, mentioned here was the actual receipt used when composing the account MCS 1, 54, BM 106045. However, due to minor discrepancies, this cannot be proven at present.

437 Compare to P. Steinkeller 1981: 116–119.

CHEU 46 (Š 47 ix):

Obverse	
1. 8(geš$_2$) še gur lugal	480 *gur* of barley, according to the royal measure,
2. ma$_2$-a si-ga	loaded in the boat,
3. nibru^{ki}-še$_3$	for Nippur.
4. guru$_7$ i$_7$ lugal-ka-ta	From the granary of "the canal of the king,"
5. ki lugal-ku$_3$-zu-ta	From Lugal-kuzu
6. še gu$_2$-na šabra-e-ne	(it is the) *gun*[438] barley of the *šabra*-administrators
Reverse	
1. kišib$_3$ lugal-ušur$_x$(LAL$_2$.TUG$_2$)-ra	Sealed by Lugal-ušur.
2. iti ^{d}li$_9$-si$_4$	Month "Lisi."
3. mu-us$_2$-sa ki-maš^{ki} ba-hul	Year after: "Kimaš was destroyed."
(blank space)	

From this text we can infer that Lugal-kuzu was supervising a large area, managed by *šabra* administrators (perhaps also referred to as captains of (plow-)oxen (*nu-banda$_3$ gu$_4$*) in other circumstances). This corresponds nicely to what we saw above.

Most of the sealed documents of Lugal-kuzu contained the phrase "sealed with the *nam-šatam* seal of Lugal-kuzu," in the body of the text. It is uncertain whether this expression referred to a specific seal of the person, or to an act of sealing as someone else, or even to the specific tablet being "of the *šatam*." However, the most likely option seems to be that *kišib$_3$ nam-šatam* implied that the sealing party sealed in his capacity as a provincial administrator, as suggested throughout this study. There is no consensus as to how to translate *šatam*, nor how to understand the office of the *šatam*,[439] and it is still too premature to directly connect the office of Lugal-kuzu (here tentatively designated as a provincial administrator) with the title *šatam*.

Inim-Šara:

Inim-Šara is well attested in the Umma records, having sealed close to one hundred tablets. The

438 The "*gun*" tax was paid by the agricultural overseers in both barley and livestock.

439 The corresponding Akkadian *šatammu(m)* is apparently a loan from the Sumerian. AhW (p. 1199) translates, "Verwalter; Verwaltungsdirektor." Neither the office of the *ša$_3$-tam*, nor its Akkadian equivalent, the *šatammu*, has to my knowledge been discussed in the literature: M. Sigrist 1992: 66, 68, and 122 does not translate the term, nor does he give any suggestions for its functions. W. Sallaberger 1999: 266, translates "Verwalter" without further comment. See also M. Gallery 1975 (for example p. 63) and 1980: 1–36.

majority of these tablets were sealed with a regular "*dub-sar*" seal, and a smaller number were sealed with a seal with a simple two line inscription naming the holder of the seal and the name of the father of the seal holder.[440] There seems to be only a very minor difference between texts sealed with either seal, and in fact several texts are almost identical, although they are not duplicates.[441] It is therefore likely that both seals referred to the same person. Inim-Šara's regular seal was used from Š 47 to ŠS 5. This seal was rolled on several tablets said to be sealed by Gududu, whereas his simple seal (used from AS 7[442] (5?)[443] to ŠS 1) was rolled exclusively on tablets said to be sealed by Inim-Šara himself. Eight texts were rolled with the seal of Inim-Šara, the son of Dadaga (all dated to ŠS 4 xi and ŠS 6 xii)—all were said to have been sealed by Gududu.[444] The frequency with which Inim-Šara sealed for Gududu increased over time and peaked around AS 8. The first occurrence of the second, simpler seal belonging to Inim-Šara coincides with this development.

The activities recorded in texts sealed with either seal are, as already stated, almost identical. The overwhelming majority of the texts record agricultural activities at a particular set of fields.[445] Six texts, all sealed with Inim-Šara's regular seal but said to have been sealed by Gududu mention the Apisal granary and the work of bringing barley to the granary from the threshing floors of the province, etc. The rest of the sixteen texts sealed by Inim-Šara rather than Gududu are also concerned with granaries or barley for the *bala* contribution of the province.

There is compelling circumstantial evidence then to suggest that Inim-Šara sealed, using a distinct seal, instead of Gududu only insofar as certain particular administrative functions were concerned, primarily those restricted to the provincial district of Apisal. In fact Gududu rarely sealed documents relating to field work. Rather, the seal of Inim-Šara rolled on the tablets was said to have the seal of Gududu. Gududu never sealed any documents during the reign of Amar-Suen, although he was active at that time. Gududu was active during the same years as an administrator (perhaps based in Umma), receiving animals and silver (from field interest) among other things.

All of the foremen and captains of (plow-)oxen appearing in the texts sealed by Inim-Šara were

---

440 See, for example, ASJ 19, 214 39 (Š 48 xi) with the seal-inscription: inim-^{d}šara$_2$ / dub-sar / dumu ur-nigar^{gar}. See also, for example, MVN 16, 866 (ŠS 1) with the seal-inscription: inim-^{d}šara$_2$ / dumu ur-nigar^{gar}.

441 Compare UTI 3, 2099 (AS 7) to Princeton 1, 516 (AS 7); and UTI 3, 1785 (AS 7 v) to UTI 4, 2912 (AS 7).

442 UTI 4, 2912 (AS 7).

443 UTI 3, 2094 (AS 5).

444 BCT 2, 39 (ŠS 5), seal: inim-^{d}šara$_2$ / dub-sar / dumu da-da-ga. See also MVN 16, 1532 (ŠS 5); NYPL 364 (ŠS 6 1 to xii); OrSP 47-49, 429 (ŠS 5); SAT 3,1525 (ŠS 4 xi); SAT 3, 1718 (ŠS 6 xi to xii); SNAT 501 (ŠS 5); and UTI 4, 2927 (ŠS 5).

445 For example the A'uda (*a-u$_2$-da*) field (e.g., Princeton 1, 516 [AS 7]), the Ninudu (*nin$_{10}$-nu-du$_3$*) field (e.g., UTI 3, 2099 [AS 7]; Princeton 1, 473 [AS 6]), and the Nagabtum (*na-ga-ab-tum*) field (e.g., MVN 16, 1378 [AS 7]; UTI 3, 1785 [AS 7 v]).

known members of the same group of agricultural overseers, and there is therefore good reason to assume that also Inim-Šara as well as perhaps Gududu held the position of a provincial administrator, with Gududu having his uncle (and cousin?) seal the documents relating to his office.

Lu-Šulgi(ra):

Lu-Šulgi(ra) has been mentioned several times above (see in particular pp. 78 ff.); two members of the ruling family of Umma were named Lu-Šulgi(ra), a son of Dadaga, and a son of Ur-nigar. Both were active primarily outside of the state-administration retaining, however, certain privileges or obligations for which they deposited a seal with a close relative or did in fact seal in person, either as an aid to this relative or fulfilling an obligation.

Gudea:

Gudea, the son of Ur-nigar, was briefly mentioned in footnote 37 of this study. There is no indication that Gudea ever participated in the state adminstration.[446]

A number of other persons attested in the Umma material appear as descendants of a person called Ur-nigar. They are listed here although their affiliation with the ruling family cannot be proven since they do not record the title of their father or any other indication of their familial relationship.

Lugal-hegal:

Twenty of the texts that have the subscription "sealed by Lugal-hegal" were receipts of work done mostly by male workers (both guruš and ug_3-ga_6). All of the recorded work was agricultural field-work.[447] One text (MVN 16, 1500 [ŠS 1 vi]) was a receipt of three reed-mats from Lu-Ebgal. Three texts mention the granary of Apisal,[448] two texts mention a canal outlet (*kun-zida*) at Apisal,[449] and three texts mention the field APIN-bazi located in the Apisal district.[450] There appears to be some substance to the claim that Lugal-hegal was indeed associated with one area in particular: the granary of Apisal, and the field APIN-bazi. Therefore, it may be argued that Lugal-hegal was a member of the ruling family of Umma who was not active in the state-run administration, but rather in the private sector of the economy, while retaining certain ties to the state. In this regard he can be said to have

446 Princeton 1, 414 (AS 3); SAT 2, 665 (AS 1); and YOS 4, 84 (Š 48 v), without the title chief livestock administrator in the seal.

447 Add Aleppo 257 (M 3659) (AS 1 v), wrongly transliterated by M. Touzalin as sealed by a lu_2-he_2-gal_2 (reverse line1, and seal inscription). Note also that obverse line 4 reads *ugula lugal-^{geš}gigir* and not *ugula ur-^{geš}gigir* (the text was collated by the author and B. Lafont in September 2006).

448 MVN 14, 65 (AS 1 ix); MVN 16, 1427 (AS 7 iii); and UTI 3, 1777 (AS 7).

449 UTI 3, 1669 (ŠS 4), obv. 2; kun-zi-da a-pi_4-sal_4^{ki}; MVN 16, 775 (ŠS 4), obv. 2; kun-zi-da a-pi_4-sal_4^{ki}.

450 MVN 21, 152 (ŠS 6); SAT 3, 1696 (ŠS 6); UTI 4, 2509 (ŠS 7 i). For the location of this field within the Apisal district, see CST 539 (IS 3).

had a career analogous to Inim-Šara and several other well-known members of the ruling family.

Lu-dingira, Mansum, and Ur-Nisaba:

Lu-dingira's seal (lu_2-dingir-ra / dub-sar / dumu ur-nigar^{gar}) appears on very few texts; Lu-dingira is always mentioned as the sealing party in these texts. They deal mainly with labor, a few with household items, and one six-column text concerns a multitude of commodities, which Lu-dingira sealed instead of Ur-gipar, the išib-mah priest (AAICAB 1, 1911-240 [ŠS 5]). All the texts sealed by Lu-dingira fall between AS 9 and SS 7. Lu-dingira cannot be included, for certain, in the family of Ur-nigar; he remains almost entirely outside the state-administrative records.

Mansum, the son of Ur-nigar, is known from his seal-inscription found on one, possibly two, tablets.[451] Mansum's seal had a dedication to Ur-Lisi, and we can speculate that he was active very early, before the administrative expansion following the construction of Drehem.

Ur-Nisaba's seal (ur-^{d}nisaba / dub-sar / dumu ur-nigar^{gar}) was rolled on very few tablets. The majority of these documents recorded the production of simple household items.[452] Ur-Nisaba was active between Š 38 and Š 44. There seems to be no particular reason to include or to exclude Ur-Nisaba from among the members of the ruling family of Ur III Umma.

451 Nik 2, 188 (Š 35 vii), and BIN 5, 183 (no date).

452 See Aleppo 54 (M 3596) (no date); Aleppo 153 (M 4028) (Š 38 vii); MVN 18, 462 (Š 38 ix); SAT 2, 201 (Š 38). Some other texts may refer to the same person; see SANTAG 6, 33 (Š 37); BCT 2, 101 (Š 34 vii); Syracuse 265 (Š 34 vii); Syracuse 266 (Š 44 ix); Syracuse 267 (Š 43 x); and MVN 18, 400 (Š 44 viii).

CHAPTER 5. CONCLUSIONS

This study has investigated the system(s) of succession during the late third millennium BC in southern Mesopotamia, and in particular sought to describe a provincial elite family. Certain problems were isolated and it is now possible to paraphrase these as questions:

1. Did a common "law" of succession exist in late third millennium BC Mesopotamian society?
2. Did the ruling family of Umma imitate the royal family?
3. Can we modify the current understanding of the public and private spheres of the Ur III society?

The answer to the first question is probably no. Late third millennium BC Mesopotamian society did not witness the formulation of a codified law of succession, nor the evolution of a set of commonly accepted social practices comparable to a law.

We have looked at several families in this study, some of which relied on fraternal succession when choosing an heir—others favored primogeniture. It is possible that two traditions existed, for example the clan of Ur-Nammu, bound by custom, favored fraternal succession, while other families, perhaps based on ethnicity, advocated primogeniture. However, one succession scheme may have been deemed more prominent or correct. The absence of written inheritance laws is not limited to ancient societies. The Saudi royal family (described in Excursus 1), to quote only one modern example, also lacks a codified plan for succession.

Two offices held by members of the ruling family of Umma were handed down laterally, but two other offices were inherited vertically within that very same family, suggesting that the system of succession was more complex than a simple opposition between fratrilineal or non-fratrilineal might suggest. Although it is impossible to determine the exact sequence of the sons of, for example, Ur-nigar—head of the Umma ruling family—and therefore impossible to determine whether Ur-Lisi was his oldest son, it remains certain that primogeniture did not determine the line of succession since we know that both Ur-Lisi and A(ya)kala, his successor, had sons who were by-passed in succession. However, it may be correct to describe the system of succession as patrilineal since, as we shall see, inclusion in succession was based on patrilineal decent only.

In our analysis of the ruling family of Ur III Umma (Chapter 4) we began by investigating the earliest generations (Sections 2 and 3). This investigation was in some regards unproductive since it is impossible at present to connect the earliest rulers of Ur III Umma with the clan of Ur-nigar, although this family was clearly involved in the management of the province from the time of the earliest documentation. The next sections (4 to 6) dealt with the three well-known governors of Umma, Ur-Lisi, A(ya)kala, and Dadaga, who were shown to be brothers. Succession to the highest of offices in Umma thus remained within one generation of brothers, and succession can be described as fratrilineal. This was exactly the basis for the question posed in the beginning of the next section (7). Why did the brother of the governor succeed him and not his own son? Only Gududu, the son of

Dadaga, seems to have aligned himself in the line of succession; his cousin Lu-kala, however, may have done the same. The many sons of the three Umma governors Ur-Lisi, A(ya)kala, and Dadaga, who have left little trace in the public records of the period must have all been by-passed, either willingly or otherwise, in the line of succession so as to allow for the fratrilineal succession. Whether this was out of concern for tradition or due to a desire to follow a quasi-imperial ideology will be discussed below. The following sections (8 to 10) concerning Ur-E'e and his sons were aimed at connecting this group with the ruling family. This was successfully carried out based on the existing evidence associating Ur-E'e and his sons with the ruling family, as well as on the basis of the strong circumstantial evidence showing that the careers of Ur-E'e and his sons were closely connected to the ruling family. Section 11 which dealt with $ARAD_2$(mu) and his son shows that the patterns of office succession in these two family-lines were identical; that both Lu-Haya, Ur-E'e's son, and Šara-izu, $ARAD_2$(mu)'s son, inherited their father's office without using his title. Based on this analogy it is strongly suggested that the rules of office inheritance were more complex than hitherto believed. In the last section (12) the remaining sons of Ur-nigar were surveyed, and their careers described. The fact that only very few of the many remaining sons of Ur-nigar ever pursued a career within the state administration is indicative of the fact that succession was limited to a restricted sequence of candidates.

The result is a system not unlike that of Saudi Arabia, where the succession pattern within the royal family is largely fratrilineal but not systematized, and where, generally speaking, seniority seems to be the dominant pattern. A member of that family described succession as a system in which an heir is chosen among the most fit senior princes by means of a set of unspecified "coincidences."[453]

Even if a law of succession is defined as a common set of rules adhered to by a majority of the population, we are still forced to admit that we do not know of any such law. We note, in passing, the results of Steinkeller's investigation of the social structure of the family groupings making up the forester work-crews—similar to our results concerning the ruling elite—and suggest that even the much larger groupings working the domain lands of Umma were arranged in a similar way.[454]

Figure 10 below demonstrates the sequence of persons holding the four most important offices in Umma (it should be compared to the preliminary survey of the ruling family of Nippur presented elsewhere in this study [Figure 3]). Here it is worthwhile to note, in particular, three different

---

453 See fn. 481.

454 See, in particular, P. Steinkeller 1987b: 80–81, and figures 2–5. The family of Dada was mentioned above (fn. 293). SAT 2, 77 (Š 33 vi), which is a summary of the work-force associated with the ca. ten domain units controlled by Dada (who in this text is given the title scribe of ten oxen (*dub-sar* gu_4 *1(u)*), clearly advocates that this group (consisting of nine administrators and forty permanent workers plus ca. twenty additional workers) was made up of an extended family. Four generations are mentioned in this text. Note, for example, the following: Lu-kala the cultivator (obv. ii 9) was the son of Lugal-ezem (obv. i 2), who is mentioned here as the assistant to his father Dada (obv. i 1). Moreover, Lu-kala's own son, Ur-Ninpirig, is mentioned immediately after Lu-kala as a member of his work-team (as ox-driver, *ša*$_3$-*gu*$_4$).

developments. First, at the time of the take-over by the clan of Ur-nigar in Šulgi 33 the family went from controlling only the offices of the chief of the granary and that of the chief livestock administrator, to having full control over the city of Umma.[455] Second, after the take-over, it appears that succession within those two offices became entirely lineal, passing from father to son. It is unclear whether the power of the two offices also diminished after the take-over; Lu-kala's high-ranking position within the local hierarchy seems to counter this suspicion. Likewise, it is probable but impossible to prove that the office of the chief livestock administrator and that of the chief of the granary were in some way closely related to the imperial court. Therefore we might see the events of Š 33 as a take-over by a family of imperial administrators. Lastly, it is important to note that four sons of Ur-nigar simultaneously took over the four most important offices in Umma in that same year, Š 33.

The historical sources do not relate any events dating to Š 33 which could be seen as an external reason for a hypothesized "take-over" by a clan of imperial administrators. Drehem, the administrative center of the empire, was supposedly not founded until Š 39 coinciding with the wide-spread, if not universal change in the dedications of seal-inscriptions away from the local governor and to the king. Šulgi was already deified around his twenty-first year, almost contemporary with the so-called reforms of Šulgi. In Š 34 we learn about the sack of Anšan, a city in Iran where Šulgi had sent his daughter (otherwise unknown) only four years earlier to become the "consort" of the ruler of that political entity (the ruler of Anšan was subsequently bequeathed with the title "governor" (*ensi*$_2$) by Šulgi). This campaign is hardly the reason for the "take-over" by the clan of Ur-nigar, but it may be possible to reconstruct the period as one of contraction and consolidation.[456] As such it may be possible to understand the "take-over" in the light of long-term trends in the political history of the Ur III period. It is equally difficult to find any internal reason for the take-over, although absence of the name of the governor of Umma prior to Š 33 is perhaps indicative of a very weak governorship prior to that date. Although it may be possible to speculate about several reasons for the situation in Š 33, it is better to await the publication of further records and perhaps even renewed excavations at the city of Umma before any further suggestions are made.

455 Of course, we do not know if the governor prior to Ur-Lisi (perhaps Abbamu) was a member of the same family that we have called the ruling family of Umma. The fact, however, that no reference exists to a familial relationship of the clan of Ur-nigar with the governor of Umma prior to Š 33 is indicative of the fact that that office was not yet in their hands. Note also that the important office of "archivist" (*ša*$_{13}$*-dub-ba*) was not in the hands of the ruling family.

456 See M. Stolper 1982: 52–53.

	Governor (*ensi*$_2$)	Chief household administrator of the governor (**šabra e*$_2$ *ensi*$_2$)	Chief of the granary (*KA-guru*$_7$)	Chief cattle administrator (*šuš*$_3$)
				GIRI$_3$.NI
	?	?	Ur-Lisi	Ur-nigar
Šulgi 33	- - - - - -	- - - - - -	- - - - - -	- - - - - -
	Ur-Lisi	A(ya)kala	ARAD$_2$(mu)	Ur-E'e
		Dadaga		
		Lu-kala		
	A(ya)kala			
			Šara-izu	
				Lu-Haya
	Dadaga			
		Gududu		

Figure 10: The succession of office in Ur III Umma

The fact that the son of the chief livestock administrator as well as the son of the chief of the granary rarely mentioned themselves with the titles of their predecessors has been noted above. In particular on pp. 83 ff. and pp. 113–114, it was suggested that the absence of the title of Ur-nigar in the seal of his son Ur-E'e was indeed not an accident, but rather inspired by a social practice "forbidding" the mention of the title of one's father when inheriting his office. Whether this has any importance for our understanding of the system of succession is not certain, but it could indicate that fratrilineal succession was more accepted within the ruling elite than primogeniture. This remains, however, largely speculative.

This of course leads us to the second question of whether the provincial ruling family mimicked the royal court. Since we initially investigated the Umma family as a comparative case in order to help us understand succession within the royal family, it appears unreasonable to ask whether the Umma ruling family mimicked the royal family. However, the fact that the patterns of succession observed within the Umma ruling family seem to be restricted to that family and perhaps only to a limited extent influenced the lower strata of society means that it may still be possible to suggest that the ruling family of Umma imitated the clan of Ur-Nammu when emulating their practice of lateral succession.

In other areas as well it seems likely that the Umma followed the example of the royal court, and we see that concubinage became (or was) an institution in Umma as well as at the court. The governor of Umma was, however, completely subordinate to the king of Ur.[457] Unfortunately, very few

457 This relationship is seen clearly in the documents describing the yearly visits of the "queen-dowager" Abī-simtī to Zabala (see pp. 38 ff.). It is documented that the household of the governor of Umma supported

documents provide evidence for direct correspondence between the royal and the provincial court, although two letters testify to its existence (see pp. 56–57 in this study). The accounts concerning the governor, as well as the military presence in the Umma province clearly show the degree of royal control.

It is, of course, peculiar that the fratrilineal kinship terms *(šeš / nin$_9$)* were used very infrequently in the Ur III administrative records since we have shown that fraternal lineage was indeed very important for succession.[458] The distribution of this term, as shown in Excursus 2, suggests that it was primarily used by the brothers of women connected through marriage or marriage-like liaisons with members of the ruling elite. This, of course, has a bearing on our understanding of neo-Sumerian system of succession since it is clear that paternal descent was considered the most important factor for success in society, whereas fraternal affiliation would have been useful only to people for whom this proved the only way to affiliate themselves with the ruling elite. Babati may be the best example of this. He had no other way of associating himself with the royal family than by claiming to be the in-law of the king, and later the maternal uncle of the new king. The *sukkalmah*, on the other hand, may have belonged to an important cadet branch co-opted into the ruling family through marriage with a royal daughter. His familial relations to the royal family are rarely mentioned in the extant documents.

It is unknown at present whether the system described here applies to all of Babylonia during

---

her visits in every way.

458 According to Yu. Yusifov 1976: 321–331, a fratrilineal order of succession is not present when the successor does not base his claim to the throne on a fratrilineal affiliation with the previous ruler (p. 327). Yusifov claims that the order of succession in Elam was not fratrilineal, as previously thought, but rather, "that in the history of Elam there existed more than one order of succession to the throne. At first there predominated the order of succession to the throne through the female side which subsequently gave place to the patrilineal principle of succession." (p. 331) The cases surveyed by Yusifov of brother succeeding brother all seem to have related to extreme situations and nowhere but once did the new king use the "title" brother of the king. However, it is my interpretation of the evidence put forward by Yusifov that the system of succession in Elam might have changed from matrilineal to patrilineal, but that primogeniture was hardly the rule. Yusifov does point out that the title "beloved son" (šak hanek) perhaps functioned as a title comparable to "heir apparent," whereby, as he writes, "this fact in its turn excludes succession to the throne in the order of seniority" (p. 328). The only example (according to Yusifov) for the use of the title "beloved brother" used by a successor to the throne, about his brother, a preceding ruler, was Šilhak-Inšušinak the brother of Kutir-Nahhunte. The titles used by Šilhak-Inšušinak were *i-ke ha-ne-ek kuti-ir-napnah-hu-un-te*, "beloved brother (of) Kutir-Nahhunte, and *i-ke ha-ne-ek u$_2$-ri-me*, "my beloved brother" used about Kutir-Nahhunte. Šilhak-Inšušinak was in time followed by Kutir-Nahhunte's son Huteleduš-Inšušinak who claimed to be the son of both his father and his uncle. Yusifov explains the usage of this title, as well as Šilhak-Inšušinak's use of a matrilineal claim to succession as the claims of an usurper (p. 325), and concludes that, "in that period the succession from the father to the son was a firmly established rule" (p. 325). Although the overall structure of Elamite succession seems clarified by the article of Yusifov, much still remains to be done (compare F. W. König 1964: 224–231), particularly with regard to the theoretical issues raised by the definitions of Yusifov.

the period in question, or whether regional differences existed. It may be opportune at a later date to extend this investigation in both time and space in order to uncover whether inheritance patterns were in any way connected to ethnicity. No such study is yet available, nor is the primary data necessary for such an investigation similar to the one conducted here available.

Based on what we know about other powerful patriarchs, such as Šulgi—or Abd al-Aziz, a more contemporary example—it seems very plausible that Ur-nigar, the head of the Umma clan, fathered multiple male heirs. Furthermore, it is very likely that only a handful of these sons embarked on a career in the state-administration, whereas the rest would have been able to profit from their connection with the powerful family of Ur-nigar and venture into the private sphere of the economy, leaving no traces behind them in the official record. It is only affirming to see these persons on an occasional basis fulfilling certain obligations within the state-administration. Another reason for the irregular, rather peculiar, and seemingly infrequent, appearance of the sealings of several high-ranking members of society is presumably connected to the familial structures of the clan of Ur-nigar. Some members perhaps fulfilled obligations for others. Therefore, it is both possible and likely that people would deposit their seal with other administrators or perhaps households for extended periods of time.

The relation between the members of the ruling family and the agricultural lands have been mentioned several times in this study. MVN 21, 343 (ŠS 3), a text recording the yield and field interest of various plots in different fields, gives interesting clues as to the administration of land. It can be suggested, on the basis of this text, that individuals had certain rights (or obligations depending on the point of view) to tracts of land in different fields, sometimes corresponding to the same plots of land mentioned in their sealed documents concerning labor.[459]

Therefore, it is safe to say, in answer to the third question, that we have modified the understanding of public and private Mesopotamia, since we have demonstrated (with numerous examples from the primary sources) the likelihood that some members of the most prominent family of Ur III Umma were not present in the public domain pursuing a career, but that they remained liable for some service to the state, and therefore were present in the records. And we have also suggested that the relations between high-ranking members of society and the estate land of Umma be reconsidered.[460] Finally, while describing the activities of Ur-E'e and his two sons Lu-Haya and Lu-kala (p. 88) it was stated, rhetorically, "that we can only speculate about the opportunities the members of this favored family may have had when controlling all of the important offices in the local administration." This seems to be true regardless of the fact that no private economy has ever been attested in the documents from the Ur III period. It is not the suggestion here that a high-risk, elite

459 See in this regard the field Abagal-Enlila and EnKAS mentioned above (see p. 87, above).

460 See also P. Steinkeller 1981: 118–119. Steinkeller associates some of the same persons which I have identified with the title provincial administrator, with individual temple households. However, aside from the fact that Steinkeller describes the Umma domain land as essentially tenant land, his outline of the administrative command structures is not far from the one suggested in this study.

economy, independent of the state, existed. Rather, private is here used only in opposition to official and may refer to the lack of any career as well.[461462]

However, it is evident that the Ur III state was neither feudal, nor bureaucratic, since power was dependent on the tribal or clan-like background of each individual. Estates were perhaps given to high-ranking officials, but the basis for these grants is not well understood. A bureaucratic class entirely dependent on education for office did not exist during the Ur III period either (except perhaps for the Drehem elite which however, cannot be proven at present). Rather, offices were passed down through and were dependent on family lines.

461 I. Gelb, as is well known, argued for the existence of a private economy coexisting with the state-sponsored economy. This cannot at present be proven or disproven. See I. Gelb 1971: 138-154.

EXCURSUS 1. THE HOUSE OF SAUD

In 1926 after he had conquered most of the Arabian Peninsula and secured his own rule, Abd al-Aziz ibn Abd al-Rahman (c. 1880 - 1953), head of the House of Saud (from 1902 to 1953),[462] assumed the title "king of the Hijaz and sultan of Najd and its dependencies" (*Malik al-Hijaz wa-sultan Najd wa-mulhaqatihah*) at a ceremony in Mecca — the most important city of Saudi-Arabia.[463] Although "ibn Saud," as he was often referred to by Westerners, had accumulated immense respect and an irrefutable reputation as a strong and charismatic ruler, he had not secured the line of succession. After his death, sovereignty over the House of Saud could have easily passed to his brother Muhammad ibn Abd al-Rahman, born almost at the same time as Abd al-Aziz.[464] Muhammad's son Khalid ibn Muhammad, almost the same age as Saud, the oldest surviving son of Abd al-Aziz, was also a contestant to the throne. Shortly after the proclamation of the kingdom of Saudi Arabia (1932), the king Abd al-Aziz challenged his own generation and nominated Saud his heir.[465]

The House of Saud had risen twice before to rule the Arabian Peninsula. The first great Saud leader, Muhammad ibn Saud (1742 - 1765), was able to secure succession for his own son, and lineal succession lasted for two generations before the House of Saud again collapsed due to internal rivalries. The second rise of the Al Saud, under Turki ibn Abd al-Allah (1824 - 1834), was even less successful in establishing lineal succession. Turki's son was deposed by the Ottoman Sultan and his Egyptian allies and imprisoned in Cairo. He was later to return to Riyadh and regain power over central Arabia but he was unable to secure succession. In sum, lateral succession was as common as lineal succession in the House of Saud, as it was among their immediate competitors on the Arabian Peninsula, the Al Rashid.[466]

Abd al-Aziz, being the strong charismatic ruler that he was, fathered at least thirty-five sons with

---

462 The House of Saud is named after Saud ibn Muhammad, who was a local Shaykh in the central Arabian province of Najd (1742–1765). Abd al-Aziz was the true head of the clan following his father's 1900 abdication, although his father (Abd al-Rahman) kept the title *imam* (a primarily religious title) for himself, and left Abd al-Aziz with the title *hakim* (arbitrator). Following Abd al-Aziz's successful conquest of Riyadh in 1902, he was granted the title *amir* by his father. Abd al-Rahman died in 1928. Note that this excursus was written prior to June 2003, it is therefore not up-to-date with respect to the most current developments in Saudi Arabia.

463 Abd al-Aziz was not crowned king of (unified) Saudi Arabia until 1932.

464 Both Abd al-Allah ibn Abd al-Rahman and Muhammad ibn Abd al-Rahman presented a challenge to the lineal succession when this was first introduced by Abd al-Aziz ibn abd al-Rahman in the 30's. The importance of the decendants of the brothers of Abd al-Aziz and the other cadet branches of the House of Saud is now dying out (J. Kechechian 2001: 32).

465 Saud was announced "heir apparent" in 1933 (not by public statement). Oil was discovered in Saudi Arabia for the first time in 1937. However, large oil-revenues were unknown before the Second World War.

466 Internal rivalry was one of the primary reasons for the final fall of the Al Rashidi (J. Kechechian 2001: 14-15).

numerous wives and concubines. However, following the example of hte prophet he never had more than four legally married wives at the same time.[467] Abd al-Aziz's first son was born in 1900, his last in 1947, resulting in a generation stretching an entire century. The oldest sons of Abd al-Aziz—some of whom rode with the *Ikhwan*,[468] uniting the Arabian Peninsula—had a vested interest in the creation of the kingdom of Saudi Arabia. The House of Saud faced widespread rebellion when they were rethinking succession, and confronted the cadet-branches of the House of Saud with the new centralization of power within one line of the family. Subsequently, Abd al-Aziz was forced to fight members of his own family who were to be known as the "*araif*" (an Arabic word used for redeemed camels, applied to this family faction since Abd al-Aziz had pardoned them after their first defeat). Abd al-Aziz managed the problem caused by the rebels, first by co-opting these cadet branches in his rule and finally by executing those who continued their rebellion.[469]

Rather than any legal claim the basis of Saudi rulership over the larger part of the Arabian Peninsula was military power and the religious fanaticism of the Beduin soldiers assembled by Abd al-Aziz. The Saudi theological claims of religious supremacy and custodianship of the holiest places in Islam negotiated with their allies, the Al Shaykh (descendants of the reformer Muhammad ibn Abd al-Wahhab), are easily contested from within Islamic circles. These theological claims are not founded on any genealogical claims, as was the case when the Hashemonites ruled the Hijaz, but exclusively on reformist, puritan arguments of the Wahhabi branch of Sunni Islam. This schism remains the Achilles heel of the Al Saud who have failed to eliminate all opposition to their religious claims.

The rulers of central Arabia prior to the successful conquest of Abd al-Aziz, the Al Rashid, were only one of the tribes of the Arabian Peninsula. Abd al-Aziz incorporated many of these tribes into his realm either by making them join his family (co-opting them in the rule of Al Saud) or by vanquishing them. Other tribes formed smaller "nation states" bordering the Persian Gulf, some of which relied on primogeniture for the selection of heirs.[470] The rulers of Saudi Arabia have tried several times to expand their territory at the expense of these states.

After the premature death of his first son Turki, the head of the Al Saud, King Abd al-Aziz, named his second son, Saud, "heir apparent" and his third son, Faysal, number two in the line of

---

467 Abd al-Aziz would take full advantage of the possibilities of divorce sanctioned by the Quran; however, he would continue to support his divorced wives, and those of them who had borne him children would remain living at the court. The exact number of Abd al-Aziz's sons remains unknown as does the number of wives he married over time.

468 The *Ikhwan*, or brotherhood, was Abd al-Aziz's creation: a Bedouin army fueled by a desire for plunder and religious fanaticism.

469 A. Bligh 1984: 17–18.

470 The rulers of both Yemen and Oman have been chosen according to the system of primogeniture, whereas the ruling families of Kuwait, Abu Dhabi, and Umm al-Quwayn all seem to have relied on seniority (A. Bligh 1984: 9-10).

succession.[471] Saud has been described as everything, ranging from the flattering image of a true son of the desert, a replica of his father, to being denounced as a dilettante without vision.[472] Whatever the viewpoint, it remains a fact that Saud ibn Abd al-Aziz had little training in foreign affairs and only limited official schooling.[473] His traditional education, unlike the more westernized education of his brother Faysal, centered around the virtues of a Bedouin sheikh more than those of a ruler of a rich oil-state. Saud therefore seemed utterly unprepared to take over at the time of his father's death in 1953. His reign became one of the most troubled in modern Saudi history. He was de-facto deposed after six years (in 1958), and was finally forced to sign a letter of abdication in 1964 (actually Faysal ibn Abd al-Aziz signed in his place, but the take-over remained peaceful).[474] Faysal, supported by a large number of senior Saudi princes, in turn nominated his younger brother Khalid as "heir apparent." A cousin, Faysal ibn Musaid ibn Abd al-Aziz, assassinated Faysal after only nine years as king of Saudi Arabia.

When Faysal replaced Saud he had to deal with the many grown sons of Saud, some of whom saw a potential spot in the line of succession slip out of their hands with the dethronement of their father Saud.[475] To this end Faysal could rely on the support of not only his own sons, but also his younger brothers and to some extent their sons.[476] Faysal managed to built considerable support

---

471 No public statement was issued in 1933 announcing the appointment of Saud as "heir apparent." The first such statement on the order of succession was issued in 1992, during King Fahd's rule, when it was then explicitely stated that Abd al-Allah was the "heir apparent," and implicitly that Sultan was number two to the throne. This is seen as a bargain between the powerful faction of princes known as the Sudayri Seven, after their maternal descent, and the other senior princes. The Sudayri Seven are: the present king (Fahd), Sultan, the minister of defence and civil aviation (number two to the throne), Nayif, the minister of the interior, Ahmad, the deputy minister of the interior, Salman, the governor of Riyadh, Turki, Sultan's deputy defence minister, and Abd al-Rahman, a successful business leader (see J. Kechechian 2001: 5ff.). The statement of 1992 is not a law of succession. However, even if it was considered a rule of succession, it is limited by physical conditions such as the longevity of the first generation following Abd al-Aziz. It follows that the question of succession will have to be addressed more seriously in the near future.

472 See, for example, D. Holden and R. Johns 1981: 176ff., W. Powell 1982: 222ff.

473 A. Bligh 1984: 58-59.

474 The struggle between the two brothers was seen by J. Kechechian 2001: 40ff. as amounting to a family feud lasting most of Saud's reign, in particular, picking up momentum after Saud's involuntary funnelling of executive power to Faysal in 1958. Saud regained power in 1960 and threw the country into one of the worst conflicts in its history.

475 J. Kechechian 2001: 41, 42 and again 43, suggested that Saud had tried to secure succession for his own progeny. See also A. Bligh 1984: 58.

476 The alliances between the more than 300 sons and grandsons of Abd al-Aziz are, of course, much more complex than this simplistic outline suggests.

for his rule, and it was he who finally secured lateral succession.[477] Following the death of Faysal, Khalid took over. He nominated prince Fahd as crown prince and Abd al-Allah as number two to the throne. King Fahd died in 2005, he was followed on the throne by his younger brother Fahd. The age of the king, as well as that of the remaining sons of Abd al-Aziz, today more than ever promotes speculations over the future of the Saudi monarchy.[478]

This particular system of succession, plotted by the old King Abd al-Aziz to prevent fraticide, has so far been successful, discounting of course the deposing of king Saud and the seemingly unconnected assassination of King Faysal.[479]

As the charismatic leader of the House of Saud for almost fifty years and a successful leader in war and politics, Abd al-Aziz managed to concentrate power within his branch of the family. From the middle of his reign he began securing the succession of power for his own line only, excluding the line of his brothers and their families. When Abd al-Aziz nominated Saud and Faysal as numbers one and two to the throne, he did not change any traditional Arabic rules of succession, for no such rules exist. Rather he did what any strong Arab leader would try to do, and secured his own line over that of his brothers.[480]

Primogeniture exists along with seniority as a system of succession among the ruling families of the post-Hijrat Arab world, but seniority has been traditionally by far the most common

---

477 J. Kechechian (2001) 47.

478 Decendents of Abd al-Aziz on the Saudi Arabian throne are, Saud (1902–1969, ruled 1953–1964 (deposed)), Faysal (1906–1975, ruled 1964–1975 (assassinated by nephew)), Khalid (1912–1982, ruled 1975–1982), and Fahd (born 1921, ruler since 1982). Abd al-Allah (born 1923) is the designated heir, and Sultan (born 1924) is considered second in line to the throne. Fahd was the real ruler during most of his brother Khalid's reign, Khalid himself had apparently little interest in the duties of the throne; his reign has been seen as part of a deal between two powerful factions within the royal family. The succession paradigm of the Saudi royal family is by Western observers often described as a nest for future troubles. With gradualy aging heirs waiting for their bid at the throne, this could result in a long list of elderly rulers in office for only a few years prior to their death, unless a generational change takes place.

479 Faysal's assassin seems not to have been motivated by a quest for the throne. It was perhaps an act of revenge by a young man following the execution of his brother and removal of his father from the line of succession.

480 "For a variety of reasons, chiefly because of religious and tribal traditions, primogeniture has not developed among Arabian dynasties in quite the same way [as in Europe], because under Shariah law, all sons of a man are equal and legitimate, even if they were born from illegitimate marriages. Moreover, in pre-Islamic tribal norms, while the throne could have passed from one generation to the next within a particular family, it was not necessarily passed from father to son. Rather, authority fell to a ruler's brother, uncle, or cousin, depending on which of these oldest male relatives was seen to possess "the qualities of nobility; skill in the arbitration; *hazz* or 'good fortune'; and leadership" [quoted from an interview with prince Sultan bin Salman, quoted in J. Kechechian 2001 see fn. 23], p. 10 in J. Kechechian 2001. Compare this autobiographical statement from a member of the royal family with the theoretical writings on the charismatic leader by M. Weber, see fn. 26.

of the two.[481] Looking to the Qur'an and the examples of the prophet Muhammad (*hadith*), even within the first four generations after Muhammad, Arab leaders are without any set of rules guiding succession.[482] During the early generations of the House of Saud (ca. 1700 to ca. 1900) all succession was presumably determined through the principle of seniority, and it was not before Abd al-Aziz that any ruler was able to favor his own line as decisively as he did.[483] So far Abd al-Aziz has been followed on the throne by four sons, and several well-educated aspirants to the throne follow the "heir apparent," Sultan, in seniority, but in a system such as that found in Saudi Arabia, where the ruler propagates heirs over a period of fifty years, it is likely that succession will pass some younger brothers by and eventually pass on to the next generation, the "grandson generation," where the most senior member suddenly is to be found.[484]

Abd al-Aziz seems to have been a strong and charismatic ruler, to use the terminology of M. Weber, whose decisions were not contested.[485] It is interesting, however, to note that not even Abd al-Aziz's plans for succession were adhered to for very long, and that his heir Saud was deposed only nine years after his death. Internally, the House of Saud is divided into competing factions

481 See A. Bligh 1984: 9–10.

482 See A. Bligh 1984: 6, and J. Kechechian 2001: 11-12. Harun al-Rashid, the calif of Baghdad, revealed his plans for succession inside the Ka'ba in 802. Al-Rashid decided, late in his reign, to nominate his son al-Amin as his first successor, and another son, al-Ma'mun, his second successor. Following the death of al-Rashid in 809, al-Amin perhaps tried to form his own line of succession. However, soon after their father's death, al-Ma'mun succeeded in forming his own power-base in a distant province and finally in 812 to take Baghdad and have al-Amin excecuted. T. El-Hibri writes (p. 463) ; "Al-Amin's execution, the first regicide in the Abbasid house, shook the caliphate's legitimacy ... In time it also gave rise to an apologetic historiography that sought to legitimate al-Ma'mun's overthrow of an incumbent caliph." According to the decree of 802, al-Amin was supposed to nominate the successor of al-Ma'mun, but in 805 al-Rashid nominated a third son, al-Mu'tamin, the successor of al-Ma'mun. The nomination of both al-Ma'mun and al-Mu'tamin were accompaigned by land allotments, or rather gubernatorial posts in border regions. T. El-Hibri (p. 475) concluded that "the caliph's purpose on the pilgrimage of 802 was simple. Having nominated al-Amin (in 792) and al-Ma'mun (in 799) during their minority [al-Amin's nomination of a minor as heir following the death of al-Rashid was used by al-Ma'mun as the juridical reason for the war], it was timely in 802 to confirm the succession with binding oaths on the princes in their majority." (T. El-Hibri 1992: 461-480).

483 Nineteenth century Ottoman tradition of succession, although far removed in space from the Arabian Penninsula, favored linial succession, passing the office from father to son. Traditionally the Ottoman ruling family did not enforce strict primogeniture, rather, the strongest and most cunning of the sultans' sons would take the throne, eliminating all of his rivals. Fraticide became institutionalized early on at the Ottoman court. Among the Arab rulers from the House of Saud there were those who had first-hand knowledge of the Ottoman traditions from their "imprisonment" in Istanbul. See J. Kechechian 2001: 12-13, and A. Bligh 1984: 9.

484 A. Bligh 1984: 53.

485 See A. Bligh 1984: 103. We exclude, of course, the above-mentioned contestants to succession who, ironically, in their defeat eventually contributed to the unrivaled position of Abd al-Aziz.

and the balance of power is very fine. Thus, the danger of relapsing into a system of fraticide is never far away and in every designation to a high office a number of political factors are taken into consideration.

The prospective heirs to the Saudi throne are chosen at present exclusively from among the sons of the late King Abd al-Aziz.[486] Maternal descent as well as the career and education of the individual princes are of importance for the selection. On the other hand, it is imperative for the brothers never to delegate too much power to one of their brothers, a faction of full brothers, or to anyone from the next generation.[487] It might be beneficial for our investigation of the system of succession within the elite families of late third millennium BC Mesopotamia to look at the credentials that may help a prospective heir within the House of Saud.

Succession within the House of Saud has bypassed several sons of Abd al-Aziz, either with the consent of the neglected (perhaps as an act of support for a full brother (brothers with the same mother) more fit for government) or for reasons such as mental disabilities or weak health. Several of the sons of Abd al-Aziz have not taken part in any aspects of the administration of the kingdom, a fact that would disqualify them at once in the struggle for succession. Most of these sons have ventured into the sphere of private enterprises, heavily subsidized by their affiliation to the ruling family, where they have become very wealthy.

The use of dynastic marriages—the co-optation of rivaling families by the ruling house—is widely employed in Saudi Arabia.[488] Abd al-Aziz would marry the daughters of opponents, or even rebels, as well as the daughters of his allies, to secure the line of ibn Saud.[489]

Among the many children of Abd al-Aziz, the sons from the political or dynastic marriages as well as sons from marriages within the extended clan of Saud have been the most successful. The children of his concubines have been successful too, albeit not ascending to the highest offices. This is perhaps only by chance since according to Shariah law all the sons of a man are equal. It is debated whether the tribal background of the mother is important for the success of her son. For example, the mother of the present "heir apparent," Abd al-Allah ibn Abd al-Aziz, is from the Shammar tribe, an influential tribe from the central Najd, supplying many Bedouin-conscripts for the national security forces, which also has Abd al-Allah as their chief.[490] In addition,

486 This was the topic of a paragraph in a royal decree, see J. Kechechian 2001: 210, quoting "Royal Decree Number A/90, Dated 27 Shaaban 1412H/1 March 1992" Chapter 2, article 5b. See also A. Bligh 1984: 53-55, who attempted to group the heirs according to their prospects of succession.

487 This can be seen, for example, in the Al Saud management of oil production and the government of the oil-producing eastern provinces that are never concentrated in the hands of one heir alone. J. Kechechian 2001: 87.

488 J. Kechechian 2001: 4.

489 R. Burling 1974 has pointed out some of the possible problems related to dynastic marriages, see p. 68.

490 However, precisely the fact that the familial structures of the Al Saud were so intricate perhaps weakens

it is likely that the mother's relationship to the king is important when the son later makes his bid for power.[491] The number of full brothers is another very important factor determining the standing of a Saudi prince, since brothers with the same mother tend to support each other.[492] Members of the grandson generation (grandsons of Abd al-Aziz) have also formed factions, mainly based on father - son relations, and largely dependent on the success of their fathers.[493] Saud ibn Abd al-Aziz had fifty-three sons many of whom ascended to high offices in the state when their father became king. Precisely the fact that Saud had multiple successful sons is a possible reason for his relative success, being as he was an otherwise unlikely candidate for the throne of Saudia Arabia. When Saud fell from power his sons fell with him; when Faysal ibn Abd al-Aziz rose to power his sons too assumed high offices. However, two of them remained in power after the assassination of their father, perhaps because of their long and sound bureaucratic training.[494]

Since succession in the House of Saud is based on seniority and restricted to the descendants of Abd al-Aziz, rulership will, at some point, be transferred to the grandson generation following a non-legalized scheme where both the individuality and familial connections of the contestants are likely to play a role. The education and offices of the sons and grandsons of Abd al-Aziz, which have been studied by J. Kechichian and others,[495] might point to any one descendant of Abd al-Aziz as the next in line for the throne, but with the large number of princes and the constant formation of factions the hierarchy of the House of Saud seems fluid.

During any struggle for succession, the contestant must delegate power to supporters in exchange for their support, endangering his future position. Is it possible for the new ruler to maintain dynastic power? Will his dynasty slowly disintegrate? Centralized power is perhaps at its peak in present day Saudi Arabia, with a minimum of cadet branches competing for the throne. But when power passes to the next generation it might result in the loss of control recoverable only through another strong leader.

The many similarities between the ancient ruling family of the Ur III empire and the

---

the argument that the tribal maternal affiliation of an heir is of much importance. See fn. 472. The sister of Abd al-Allah's mother was the wife of his own brother Saud.

491 A. Bligh 1984: 40–41. This is an interesting point with regard to the Ur III royal family. As seen above (pp. 104–105) the concubines of the Ur III ruler often employed a terminology invoking their closeness to the king.

492 J. Kechechian 2001: 26–28.

493 J. Kechechian 2001: 28-30.

494 For the careers of the sons of Faysal, see J. Kechechian 2001: 29. Note that Saud al Faysal was co-opted in the reign of Khalid as a minister of foreign affairs (A. Bligh 1984: 90).

495 Data concerning the political history of the House of Saud, from the early eighteenth century until today is not always readily available and many studies have been based, in part, on interviews with anonymous Saudi personalities.

contemporary royal family of Saudi Arabia has made this modern example a valuable model for studying patterns of succession during the time of Ur III. Many post-Islamic Arab ruling houses could be cited as useful comparative material for our study, but the House of Saud is more applicable for our case due to its unprecedented success and richness. Consider the following complex family structure: "Abd Allah was born in 1921, when his father was about fifteen years old. His mother, Faysal's first wife, was Sultanah bint Ahmad al-Sudayri, whose older sister Hassah was married to Abd al-Aziz. Hassah gave birth to the first of her seven sons, Fahd, at about the time Abd Allah was born. The oldest of the Sudayri Seven, Fahd, was thus both uncle and cousin to Abd Allah al-Faysal." (A. Bligh 1984: 66).[496] Earlier generations of the Al Saud had not yet generated such complex family structures since the rulers produced fewer heirs. The high number of surviving heirs of Abd al-Aziz seems to be the result of not so much the extraordinary richness which befell Saudi Arabia following the large-scale exploitation of natural resources; rather, Abd al-Aziz himself must be given credit for having created a power-base as powerful as that of his sons.

496 Note that Saud was married to a sister of Abd al-Aziz's *Shammar* bride (the mother of Abd Allah), co-opting the defeated house of Haïl in the reign of Al Saud.

EXCURSUS 2. SON OF THE KING VS. BROTHER OF THE KING

In a society that favors lineal succession, it is expected that a contestant to the throne would express his close familial ties to the ruler, and in a society with strictly enforced primogeniture, the heir would hold a title such as crown-prince. But would a competitor call himself brother of the (ruling) king in a society where fratrilineal succession exists together with patrilineal succession? In the following brief excursus I will list and discuss all the examples of the kinship terms "brother"and "sister" used by persons claiming a close affiliation with the ruling clans of Sumer, as found in the extant texts from the Ur III period.

Only one person used the kinship term "brother" in relation to the king. This person is otherwise unknown and the affiliation is expressed in only two texts.

Text ID	date	
Nisaba 8, 44 (BM 103420), obv. 9	AS 8 ix 24	ur-^{d}en-lil$_2$-la$_2$ šeš lugal
MVN 8, 129, obv. 12	AS 4 iv 5	ur-^{d}en-lil$_2$-la$_2$ šeš lugal

Table 5: "brother of the king"

Only four persons specified their familial affiliation with the second most important person of the empire, the *sukkalmah*, in terms of brotherhood.

Text ID	date	
JCS 10, 30 9, obv. 2	ŠS 8 ii 05	ur-^{d}nanna sukkal šeš ARAD$_2$-^{d}nanna sukkal-mah
MVN 17, 12, rev. 14	X ii 16	lu$_2$-^{d}šara$_2$ šeš sukkal-mah
TCTI 2, 3711, obv. 3	X iv 21	a-hu-ni šeš sukkal-mah
TCTI 2, 4161, obv. 2	X x 21	šu-i$_3$-li$_2$ šeš sukkal-mah

Table 6: "brother of the *sukkalmah*"

A few persons called themselves "brother of the governor" to specify their affiliation with the head of an important family:

Text ID	date	
BPOA 2, 2641 (BM 105554), obv. 3	Š 34 ii	ARAD$_2$ šeš ensi$_2$ umma^{ki}
ASJ 19, 226 72, rev. iv 7	(no date)	ARAD$_2$ šeš ur-^{d}li$_9$-si$_4$
JCS 28, 215 26, obv. 4	Š 43	a-kal-la šeš ensi$_2$ (Umma)
OrSP 47-49, 500, obv. ii 15	(no date)	a-kal-la šeš ensi$_2$ (Umma)
SAT 2, 1078, rev. 1	AS 8	lu$_2$-^{d}utu šeš ensi$_2$ adab^{ki}
AUCT 3, 31, obv. 2	ŠS 7 x	lu$_2$-^{d}utu šeš ensi$_2$ adab^{ki}
ITT 2, 4090, rev. 2	Š 42	lu$_2$-^{d}nin-šubur šeš ensi$_2$ (Girsu)
LB 610 (unpubl.), obv. ii 26	(no date)	ur-ba-gara$_2$ šeš ensi$_2$ (Girsu)
NATN 123, obv. 6-7	Š 40	ur-x-[x] šeš 坂ensi$_2$販(Nippur)

Table 7: “brother of the governor”

Babati, the brother of queen Abī-simtī, whose seal was copied in the Babylonian school, was an important person in the empire (see p. 21). Strangely, however, only one text includes the information, known from his seal inscription, that Babati was the brother of the queen. Aside from Babati, we know of only two persons who mention their relationships to a named royal consort.

Text ID	date	
BCT 1, 126, obv. 4	AS 3 iii 19	ba-ba-ti šeš *坂nin販
CT 3, 35 (BM 21335), obv. col. i 12	(no date)	ARAD$_2$-mu šeš nin$_9$-kal-la
OIP 115, 199, obv. 5	Š 46 iii 19	i-TI-e$_2$-a šeš e$_2$-a-ni-ša

Table 8: “brother of the queen”

Some persons in texts from Girsu were referred to as “brother or sister of the *ereš-dingir*-priestess.” The *ereš-dingir*-priestess is presumably identical with the wife of the governor of Girsu, an office held by the *sukkalmah* after AS 6.

Text ID	date	
UNT 26, obv. 2	Š 47 xii	ki-mah dam ur-sa_6-ga šeš ereš-dingir-ra
Amherst 27, rev. 1	Š 37	ugula ur-sa_6-ga šeš ereš-dingir
MVN 2, 283, obv. col 1', 7'-8'	(no date)	[x] ur-sa_6-ga / šeš ereš-dingir
BAOM 2, 28 45, obv. 2	Š 48 xi	ab_2-la-la-a nin_9 ereš-dingir-ra-ke_4
TUT 112, obv. col. 1, 8'-9'	(no date)	x ab_2-la-la-a / nin_9 ereš-dingir-ra-ke_4 mu dumu-ni ba-$uš_2$-$še_3$
MVN 22, 180, obv. 15	Š 43	Lu_2-AB.DI šeš ereš-dingir
BAOM 2, 24 14, obv. 2	Š 39 vi	Lu_2-AB.DI šeš ereš-dingir

Table 9: "brother / sister of the *ereš-dingir*-priestess"

Only one person used the kinship term "sister of the queen," Bizua; she is only rarely attested:

Text ID	date	
ASJ 3, 74, obv. 5	AS 4 viii 16	bi_2-zu-a nin_9 nin
Fs. Jones 68, rev. i 18	ŠS 6 i 04 to xii 30	bi_2-zu-a nin_9 nin
TCL 2, 5484, obv. 7	AS 5 viii 20	bi_2-zu-a nin_9 nin

Table 10: "sister of the queen"

Only two texts mention someone who claimed fraternal affiliation with a general:

Text ID	date	
SNAT 333, obv. 10	AS 2 xi	ur-lugal šeš šagina
RTC 331, obv. 2	Š 35 vii	da-da-a šeš lu_2-^{d}utu šagina

Table 11: "brother of the general"

Apart from the examples we have seen here, there are few references to unnamed wives, brothers, and sisters of high-level officials of the empire (see for example, OIP 115, 74 [Š 43 ix 22], which mentions both the sister of Ṣelluš-Dagan (obv. 7; nin_9 ze_2-lu-uš-^{d}da-gan) and the wife of Šarakam (obv. 5; dam ^{d}šara_2-kam), among others).

The single most numerous group of people claiming affiliation with the royal clan through brotherhood is a group of approximately forty persons, each of whom claimed to be the brother of a (royal) concubine. This group of people, who can only be associated with the royal concubines through circumstantial evidence, are all mentioned in texts similar to the simple messenger texts. They all appear together with military envoys traveling to and from the eastern provinces. The texts are all written records of the provisions for these persons.

Text ID	date	
HLC 132 (pl. 99), rev. 15	month iii	[a]-mur-dutu šeš lukur
OMRO 66, 55 20, rev. 10	month v	a-bu-ni šeš lukur
MCS 5, 27 (= HSM 6367), obv. 4	month xii	a-hu-a šeš lukur
MVN 9, 135, obv. 11	month vii	a-na-ti šeš lukur [a]
OMRO 66, 55 20, obv. 8	month v	a$_2$-bi$_2$-li$_2$-a šeš lukur
RA 59, 145 (= FM 56), rev. 3	month iii	ba-ba-a šeš lukur
RTC 349, obv. 4	month viii	ba-lu$_5$-a šeš lukur
MVN 7, 377, rev. 1	month viii	da-gu šeš lukur
RTC 347, obv. 2	month xi	e-la-<ak?>-nu-id šeš lukur [b]
BM Messenger 171 (=BM 020148), obv. 11	month x	e$_2$-ni-bi šeš lukur [c]
ABTR 13, rev. 4	month vii	⌜er$_3$⌝ -ra-LUGAL šeš lukur
BM Messenger 157 (= BM 020239), rev. 2	month vi	ha-ti šeš lukur
HSS 4, 66, obv. 6	month x	i-din-dutu šeš lukur [d]
MVN 9, 136, obv. 8	month viii	i-din-e$_3$-a šeš lukur [e]

a) Perhaps the same person who is mentioned without title or familial relation in PDT 1, 434, together with Ninkala (spelled *nin-kal-la*), Šulgi-simti, and other important figures from the empire as recipients of pairs of boots of *dušia* leather (*^{kuš}šu?ub$_2$ du$_8$-ši-a e$_2$-ba-an*). The text also mentions the father of Šulgi-simti; *DIB$_2$-ib-si-na-at*. The personal name Iṭib-sinat is mentioned in seven Ur III texts altogether. In all seven texts he appears as a high official together with other high-ranking officials and members of the clan of Ur-Nammu (see BCT 1, 38 [Š 48 viii 19]; BIN 3, 603 [IS 2 xii 1]; OIP 115, 293 [Š day 7]; Princeton 1, 81 [AS 4 ix 26]; SAT 2, 774 [AS 4 ix 25]; TBM 1, 451 [Š 46 ximin]; and PDT 1, 434 discussed here).

b) Only the personal name *e-la-ak-nu-id* is known to me.

c) Perhaps the same as the military person mentioned in MVN 6, 215 (Š 34 vii), with the title "police officer" (*aga$_3$-us$_2$*) and captain (*nu-banda$_3$*).

d) Includes the provisions for the daughter of the king (*dumu munus lugal*).

e) Perhaps identical with the Iddin-Ea (spelled *i-DI-e$_2$-a*) who was a known brother of Ea-niša mentioned above fn. 61.

Text ID	date	
SAT 1, 122, obv. 3	month viii	iš-me-a šeš lukur
SAT 1, 157 (= BM 21022), rev. 4	month vi	ku-da-num$_2$ šeš lukur
SNAT 333, obv. 10	AS 2 xi	ur-lugal šeš šagina
SNAT 333, obv. 10	xxx	ur-lugal šeš šagina
SAT 1, 112, rev. 1	month i	la-bi-ru-um ki šeš lukur mu ha-gar^{ki} gibil-še$_3$
SET 212, line 16	(no date)	la-la-a <šeš> lukur [f]
TUT 211, rev. 4'	(no date)	la-la-a šeš lukur
SAT 1, 122, rev. 2	month viii	la-ni šeš lukur
TBM 1, 138, rev. 5	month iv	lu$_2$-^{d}nanna šeš lukur
ABTR 13, rev. 12	month vii	lu$_2$-gu-la šeš lukur
HLC 168 (pl. 104), rev. 14	month iii	nig$_2$-e$_2$-ša-šu šeš lukur
SAT 1, 145, obv. 3	month i	nu-a-a-ti šeš lukur
A 824 (unpubl.), rev. 8	month i	nu-ur$_2$-i$_3$-li$_2$ šeš lukur
TUT 211,obv. 7	(no date)	puzur$_4$-⸢eš⸣-[dar] [šeš lukur]
SET 212, obv. 7	(no date)	puzur$_4$-eš$_4$-dar šeš lukur
SAT 1, 106, rev. 3	month vii	a-da-lal$_3$ šeš lukur
RA 19, 42 89, rev. 4	month iv	puzur$_4$-šu šeš [lukur]
HLC 106 (pl. 94), rev. 10	month iii	puzur$_4$-šu šeš lukur

f) The reconstruction is suggested by the following reference combined with the circumstantial evidence that only men appear as recipients of rations in these texts.

Text ID	date	
SAT 1, 161, rev. 2	month vii	šu-^{d}utu šeš lukur
MVN 9, 136, rev. 11	month viii	šu-e$_3$-a šeš lukur
TUT 212, rev. 7	month viii	šu-eš-dar šeš lukur
RTC 355, obv. 5	month i	šu-eš-dar šeš lukur
RA 19, 40 21, obv. 3	day 19	šu-i$_3$-li$_2$ šeš [lukur(?)]
HLC 161 (pl. 103), rev. 7	month v	šu-i$_3$-li$_2$ šeš lukur
SAT 1, 148, obv. 2	month vii	ud-du-ša šeš lukur

Table 12: "brother of the concubine"

All of the texts quoted in the table above mention deliveries for persons traveling to and from cities in the eastern provinces. Some of these people are called "couriers" (*lu$_2$ kas$_4$*) or "messengers" (*sukkal*), but others have military titles such as captain (*nu-banda$_3$*), chief of police (*aga$_3$-us$_2$ gal*, literally "chief follower of the crown"), or simply knight (*lu$_2$ ^{geš}tukul*). See, for example, SAT 1, 157 (= BM 21022) (no year, month 6):

Obverse	
1. 1(ban$_2$) kaš DU lugal	1 *ban$_2$* of regular standard quality beer,
u$_4$ 2(diš)-kam ša$_3$ uru	for two days while in the city,
2. 1(diš) dug dida kaskal-še$_3$ ze$_2$-la-a	1 jar of *dida* (beer) for the road: Ṣelaya,
aga$_3$-us$_2$ gal sa-bu-um^{ki}-še$_3$ DU-ni	police chief, traveling to Sabum.
3. 2(ban$_2$) kaš 2(diš) dug dida kaskal-še$_3$	2 *ban$_2$* of beer, 2 jars of *dida* (beer) for the road,
lu$_2$-^{d}en-ki u$_3$-kul u$_3$ nu-ur$_2$-NE	Lu-Enki, *ukul*, and Nur-NE, captain
nu-banda$_3$ dumu nu-banda$_3$	son of the captain,
a-dam-dun^{ki}-še$_3$ DU-ni	travelling to Adamdun.
4. 3(diš) sila$_3$ kaš iš-me-a lu$_2$-kas$_4$	3 *sila$_3$* of beer. Išme-Ea, the runner,
Reverse	
1. šušin^{ki}-ta DU-ni	travelling from Susa.
2. 5(diš) sila$_3$ kaš dan-i$_3$-li$_2$ sukkal	5 *sila$_3$* of beer, Dan-ili, messenger,
3. 3(diš) sila$_3$ kaš a-a-kal-la lu$_2$-kas$_4$	3 *sila$_3$* of beer, A(ya)kala, runner,

sa-bu-um^{ki}-ta DU-ni	travelling from Sabum.
4. 2(ban$_2$) kaš 2(diš) dug dida kaskal-še$_3$	2 *ban$_2$* of beer, and 2 jars of *dida* (beer) for the road,
ku-da-num$_2$ šeš lukur u$_3$ i-din-^{d}suen	Kudanum brother of the concubine, and Iddin-Suen,
sukkal a-dam-dun^{ki}-še$_3$ DU-ni	messenger, travelling to Adamdun.
5. 1(ban$_2$) kaš da-da-a aga$_3$-us$_2$ gal	1 *ban$_2$* of beer, Dadaya, police chief,
u$_3$ šu-i$_3$-li$_2$ sukkal šušin^{ki}-ta DU-ni	and Šū-ili, messenger, travelling from Susa.
6. iti šu-numun	Month "Seeding."

The other people mentioned in this and similar texts all seem to belong to two different social strata. The elite group of military staff and "diplomats," on the one hand, and the mid-level group of couriers and messengers, on the other.

The first person, Ṣelaya, has the title police-chief (*aga$_3$-us$_2$ gal*). Nothing is known about this person other than this reference. Sabum, the destination of his travel, was located on the route to Susa, east of Sumer.

The next entry is for two persons, both travelling to Adamdun, an area south of Sabum, southeast of Sumer.[497] The title of Lu-Enki, *u$_3$-kul*, is presumably related to the military since it appears exclusively within this group of texts. The title of Nur-NE, Lu-Enki's companion, is usually understood as a military title comparable to a captain (*nu-banda$_3$*). Lu-Enki is not otherwise attested with the title *u$_3$-kul*. A messenger by the name of Lu-Enki is attested frequently as a member of the diplomatic corps; see, for example, MVN 1, 142 (AS 5 viii 24), obv. 7 - 10: 1(diš) gu$_4$ 5(diš) udu šimaški(LU$_2$.SU) / 5(diš) maš$_2$ gal šimaški / li-ba-an-aš-gu-bi lu$_2$ kin-gi$_4$-a li-ba-nu-uk-ša-ba-aš lu$_2$ mar-ha-ši^{ki} / giri$_3$ lu$_2$-^{d}en-ki sukkal, "1 ox and 5 *šimaški* sheep, 5 large *šimaški* goats; Libanaš-Gubi, the envoy of Libanuk-Šabaš, the man of Marhaši,[498] via Lu-Enki, the messenger." See also CT 10, 30 (= BM 014612) (Š 43), where a certain Lu-Enki, son of the captain (*nu-banda$_3$*), is mentioned. A police chief is called Nur-NE in TBM 1, 122 (no year, month 8), traveling from Urua (*^{u2}urua$^{a\ ki}$*).

---

497 See W. Sallaberger 1999: plate 4, p. 157.

498 Libanuk-Šabaš is called governor (*ensi$_2$*) of Marhaši in TCL 2, 5508 (AS 4 i 6). Although it is likely that */libana/* was a Marhaši PN theophoric element, the two names recorded here are the only known names of persons from Marhaši where such an element is detectable, except for persons with names such as Hašib-Atal (BIN 3, 12 [Š 46 ix 12]), who probably was not a native of Marhaši, and Amur-DINGIR, an envoy of Libanuk-Šabaš (see, for example, AUCT 2, 278 [AS 4 ii 25]). Other names of persons from Marhaši are: Aršik-u (see, for example, CST 235 [AS 1 viii 17]); Banana (see, for example, CST 436 [ŠS 6 iii 29]); Arbi-mašbi (MVN 1, 124 [AS 1 viii 17]); Marhuni (see, for example, MVN 13, 636 [AS 8 i]); PN the envoy of Aršik-ug(u)bi (see, for example, MVN 15, 194 [AS 1 v 29]); Bariašum (see, for example, OrSP 47-49, 24 [AS 3 vi 2 to 30]); and PN the envoy of Arwil-ug(u)bi (see, for example ASJ 19, 204 13 [AS 1 vi 21]).

The next persons subsequently mentioned, Išme-Ea,[499] Dan-ili, and A(ya)kala, were all lower-level officials. Their rations were considerably smaller than those of the first group.

Kudanum, the brother of the concubine, is only mentioned in this text and in TBM 1, 112. The last two persons, Dadaya and Šū-ili, are recorded as coming from Susa. Šū-ili, the messenger, is recorded frequently in the published record. Dadaya travels to Susa with Apilanum in HSS 4, 67 (no year, month 8), and to Adamdun together with Iddin-Ea in MVN 9, 136 (no year, month 8).

The term *lukur* qualifies two groups of women, one being the prosperous group of royal consorts and to a lesser extent consorts of other high-ranking officials, the other being a group of temple staff. The group of men with some affiliation to the military or the diplomatic corps discussed in this excursus is the only closed group distinguishing their status through a laterally defined genealogical association. Whether this relation was with either of the two groups of concubines, outlined above, is less important than the sociological conclusions that can be drawn from this observation. We can conclude that in a patriarchial society a person's rank was presumably defined through his patrilineal descent only, but persons without any relation to the ruling group except the marital link of their sister were forced to use this as their claim of affiliation.

---

499 See, for example, SET 212, which mentions a person called Išme-Ea, son of the captain traveling from Sabum, obv. 15-16: iš-me<-e$_2$>-a dumu nu-banda$_3$ / sa-bu-um^{ki}-ta DU-ni.

BIBLIOGRAPHY

W. Andrae

1902-03 "Aus einem Berichte W. Andrae's über seine Exkursion von Fara nach den südbabylonischen Ruinenstätten," *Mitteilungen der Deutschen Orientgesellschaft* (*MDOG)* 16, 16–24.

J. Bauer

1998 "Der vorsargonische Abschnitt der mesopotamischen Geschichte," in P. Attinger et al. (eds.), Mesopotamien, Späturuk-Zeit und Frühdynastische Zeit (*Orbis Biblicus et Orientalis* (*OBO)* 160/1; Freiburg).

R. H. Beal

1992 "Is KUŠ$_7$ the Reading of IŠ = kizû ?," *Nouvelles Assyriologiques Bréves et Utilitaires* (*NABU*) 1992:48.

A. Bligh

1984 *From Prince to King, Royal Succession in the House of Saud in the Twentieth Century* (New York and London).

J. Boese and W. Sallaberger

1996 "Apil-Kin von Mari und die Könige der III. Dynastie von Ur," *Altorientalische Forschungen* (*AoF*) 23, 24–39.

R. Burling

1974 *The Passage of Power, Studies in Political Succession* (New York & London).

D. Charpin

2004 "Histoire politique du Proche-Orient amorrite (2002–1595)," in Charpin, D.; Stol, M. and Edzard, D. O., Mesopotamien: die altbabylonische Zeit (*OBO* 160/4; Göttingen/Fribourg).

M. Cohen

1996 "The Gods of Suburban Umma," Fs. Limet (*Tablettes et images aus pays de Sumer et d'Akkad: Melanges offert a Monsieur H. Limet*) (Liege) 27–36.

G. Contenau

1915 *Contribution a l'histoire économique d'Umma* (Paris).

J. L. Dahl

2002 "Land Allotments During the Third Dynasty of Ur, Some Observations," *AoF* 29, 330–338.

2006 "Early Swine Herding," in: B. Lion et C. Michel, éds., *De la domestication au tabou : Le cas des suidés dans le Proche-Orient ancien, Travaux de la Maison René-Ginouvès 1* (Paris) 31–38.

nd. *Neo-Sumerian Texts in the Schøyen Collection* (= *NSTSC*; ...).

R. H. C. Davis

1980 "William of Jumieges, Robert Curthose and the Norman Succession," *The English Historical Review*, Vol. 95, Issue 376, 597–606.

D. Edzard

1957 *Die "Zweiten Zwischenzeit" Babyloniens* (Wiesbaden).

1959 "Königsinschriften Des Iraq Museums II," *Sumer (Journal of Archaeology and History in Iraq)* 15, 19–28.

1960 "Sumerer und Semiten in der Frühen Geschichte Mesopotamiens," *Bulletin du Musée d'Arts et d'Histoire de Genève (Genava) NS* 8 (= *Rencontre 9*; Geneva) 241–258.

T. El-Hibri

1962 "Harun al-Rashid and the Mecca Protocol of 802: A Plan for Division or Succession?" *International Journal of Middle East Studies*, Volume 24, Issue 3 (1992), 461–480.

R. K. Englund

1990 *Organisation und Verwaltung der Ur III-Fischerei* (*Berliner Beiträge zum Vorderer Orient* 10; Berlin).

1995 "Regulating Dairy Productivity in the Ur III Period," *Orientalia, Nova Series* (*OrNS)* 64, 377–429.

2003 " Worcester Slaughterhouse Account," *Cuneiform Digital Library Bulletin (CDLB)* 2003:1.

B. Foster

1982 *Umma in the Sargonic Period* (*Memoirs of the Connecticut Academy of Arts and Science*, Vol. 20; Connecticut 1982).

1993 "Management and Administration in the Sargonic Period," in M. Liverani (ed.), *Akkad, the First World Empire. Structure, Ideology, Traditions* (Padua), 25–40.

E. Flückiger-Hawker

1999 *Urnamma of Ur in Sumerian Literary Tradition* (*OBO* 166; Freiburg).

D. Frayne

1997 *Ur III period (2112 - 2004 BC)* (*The Royal Inscriptions of Mesopotamia, Early Periods* 3/2; Toronto).

M. Gallery

1975 *The Office of the šatammu in the Old Babylonian Period* (unpublished dissertation; Yale)

1980 "The Office of the šatammu in the Old Babylonian Period" *Archiv für Orientforschung* (*AfO)* 27, 1–36.

I. Gelb

1960 "Sumerians and Akkadians in their Ethno-Linguistic Relationship," *Genava NS* 8 (= *Rencontre 9*; Geneva) 258–271.

1971 "On the Alleged Temple and State Economies in Ancient Mesopotamia," *Studi in Onore di Edoardo Volterra*, Vol. 6, 138–154.

T. Gomi

1976 "Shulgi-Simti and her Libation Place (ki-a-nag)," *Orient. Report of the Society for Near Eastern Studies in Japan* 12, 1–14.

1984 "On the Critical Economic Situation at Ur Early in the Reign of Ibbisin," *Journal of Cuneiform Studies (JCS)* 36, 211–242.

J.-P. Grégoire
1970 *Archives Administratives Sumériennes* (Paris).

W. Hallo
1956 "Zariqum," *Journal of Near Eastern Studies (JNES)* 15, 220–225.
1966 "The Coronation of Ur-Nammu," *JCS* 20, 133–141.
1969 "The Cultic Setting of Sumerian Poetry," in A. Finet (ed.), *Actes de la XVIIe Rencontre Assyriologique Internationale* (= *Rencontre* 17; Brussels) 115–134.
1972 "The House of Ur-Meme," JNES 31, 87–95.

W. Heimpel
1994 "Towards an Understanding of the term siKKum," *Revue d'Assyriologie et d'Archéologie Orientale (RA)* 88, 5–31.
1997 "Disposition of Households in Ur III and Mari," *Acta Sumerologica (ASJ)* 19, 63–82.

D. Henige
1986 "Comparative Chronology and the Ancient Near East: A Case for Symbiosis," *Bulletin of the American Schools of Oriental Research (BASOR)* 261, 57–68.

Th. Hobbes
1957 *Leviathan, or the Matter, Forme and Power of a Commonwealth, Ecclesiastical and Civil* (Oxford).

D. Holden and R. Johns
1981 *The House of Saud* (London).

F. Hrozny
1912 "Die ältesten Dynastien Babyloniens," *Wiener Zeitschrift für die Kunde des Morgenlandes* (*WZKM*) 26, 1–20.

P. Huber
1999-2000 "Astronomical Dating of Ur III and akkad, *AfO* 46–47, 50–79.

Th. Jacobsen
1939 *The Sumerian King List* (*Assyriological Studies* 11; Chicago).
1957 "The Reign of Ibbisin," *JCS* 7, 36–47.
1991 "The Term Ensí," *Aula Orientalis* 9, 113–121.

T. Jones and J. Snyder
1961 *Sumerian Economic Texts from the Third Ur Dynasty* (Minneapolis).

J. Kechechian
2001 *Succession in Saudi Arabia* (New York).

J. Klein

1981 *Three Šulgi Hymns* (Ramat-Gan).

1990 "Shelepputum a Hitherto Unknown Ur III Princess," *Zeitschrift für Assyriologie* (*ZA)* 80 (1990) 20–39.

F. W. König

1964 "Geschwisterehe in Elam" *Reallexikon der Assyriologie und vorderasiatischen Archaologie* (*RLA)* 3, 224–231.

M. Krebernik

1984 *Die Beschwörungen aus Fara und Ebla* (Hildesheim).

M. T. Larsen

1976 *The Old Assyrian City-State and its Colonies* (*Mesopotamia* 4; Copenhagen).

M. Liverani

1995 "The Medes at Esarhaddon's Court," *JCS* 47, 57–62.

J. Le Patourel

1971 "The Norman Succession, 996-1135," *The English Historical Review*, Vol. 86, No. 339. 225–250.

T. Maeda

1990 "Father of Akala and Dadaga, governors of Umma," *ASJ* 12, 71–78.

1996 "Ruler's Family of Umma and Control over the Circulation of Silver," *ASJ* 18, 254–260.

K. Maekawa

1974 "Agricultural Production in Ancient Sumer," *Zinbun. Memoirs of the Research Institute for Humanistic Studies* 13, 1–60.

1987 "The Management of Domain Land in Ur III Umma: A Study of BM 110116," *Zinbun* 22, 25–82.

1989 "Rations, Wages and Economic Trends in the Ur III Period," *AoF* 16, 42–50.

1996 "Confiscation of Private Properties in the Ur III period: A study of é-dul-la and níg-GA," *ASJ* 18, 102–168.

?1996 "The Governor's family and the 'temple households' in Ur III Girsu," in K. Veenhof, ed., *Houses and Households in Ancient Mesopotamia* (*Compte rendu de la Rencontre Assyriologique lnternationale* 40; Leiden) 171–179.

1999 "The "Temples" and the "Temple Personnel" of Ur III Girsu-Lagash," in K. Watanabe ed., *Papers of the Second Colloquium on the Ancient Near East - The City and its Life held at the Middle Eastern Culture Center in Japan (Mitaka, Tokyo), Sonderdruck* (Heidelberg) 61–95.

R. Mayr

1997 *The Seal Impressions of Ur III Umma* (unpublished dissertation; Leiden).

D. McGuiness

1982 "Ur III Prosopography: Some Methodological Considerations," *Archív Orientální* 50, 324–342.

P. Michalowski

1975 "The Bride of Simanum," *Journal of the American Oriental Society (JAOS)* 95, 716–719.

1977 "Durum and Uruk during the Ur III Period," *Mesopotamia. Revista di archeologia a cure del Centro Ricerche Archeologiche e Scavi di Turno per il Medio Oriente e l'Asia* 12, 83–96.

1977 "Amar-Su'ena and the Historical Tradition," in: M. de J. Ellis, ed., *Essays on the ancient Near East in memory of Jacob Joel Finkelstein* (Hamden) 155–157.

1983 "History as Charter," *JAOS* 103, 237–248.

1993 *Letters from Early Mesopotamia* (Atlanta).

2004 "The Ideological Foundations of the Ur III State" in J.-W. Meyer et. al. eds., *2000 v. Chr. Politische, Wirtschaftliche und Kulturelle Entwicklung im Zeichen einer Jahrtausendwende; Colloquien der Deutschen Orient-Gesselschaft (CDOG), Band 3* (Saarbrücken), 219–235.

P. Moorey

1978 *Kish Excavations 1923–1933* (Oxford).

A. L. Oppenheim

1964 *Ancient Mesopotamia; Portrait of a Dead civilization* (Chicago)

D. Owen

1993 "The Ensis of Gudua," *ASJ* 15, 131–152.

2001a "The Household of Princess Simat-Ištaran, Sister of Šu-Suen" unpublished paper read at the RAI 47 (2001).

2001b "On the Patronymy of Šu-Suen." *NABU* 2001/17.

T. Ozaki

2004 " A New Reading of En-DU$_8$-DU in Ur III Umma Texts," in: H. Waetzoldt, ed., *Von Sumer nach Ebla und zurück: Festschrift; Giovanni Pettinato zum 27. September 1999 gewidmet von Freunden, Kollegen und Schülern* (Heidelberg) 221–222.

S. Parpola and K. Watanabe

1988 *Neo-Assyrian Treaties and Loyalty Oaths* (*State Archives of Assyria* II; Helsinki).

P. A. Parr

1974 "Ninhilia: Wife of Ayakala, Governor of Umma," *JCS* 26, 90–111.

J. N. Postgate

1992 *Early Mesopotamia, Society and Economy at the Dawn of History* (London).

1995 "Royal Ideology and State administration in Sumer and Akkad" in J. Sasson, ed., *Civilization of the Ancient Near East* (New York) 395–411.

W. Powell

1982 *Saudi Arabia and its Royal Family* (Secaucus).

F. Pomponio

1992 "Lukalla of Umma," *ZA* 82, 169–179.

J. Reade

2001 "Assyrian King-Lists, the Royal Tombs of Ur, and Indus Origins," *JNES* 60, 1–29.

J. Renger

1976 "The Daughters of Urbaba: Some thoughts on the Succession to the Throne during the 2. Dynasty of Lagash," in B. L. Eichler, ed., *Cuneiform Studies in Honor of Samuel Noah Kramer* (*AOAT* 25: Neukirchener-Vluyn), 367–369.

W. Sallaberger

1993 *Der Kultische Kalender der Ur III-Zeit, Teil 1 & 2* (*Untersuchtungen zur Assyriologie und Vorderasiatischen Archäologie* 7/1 & 7/2; Berlin/New York).

1996 *Der Babylonische Töpfer* (Ghent).

1999 "Ur III-Zeit," in P. Attinger et al., eds., *Mesopotamien, Akkade-Zeit und Ur III Zeit* (*OBO* 160/3; Freiburg 1999).

A. Schneider

1920 *Die Anfänge der Kulturwirtschaft. Die Sumerische Tempelstadt* (Essen).

M. Sigrist

1992 *Drehem* (Bethesda 1992).

D. Snell

1982 *Ledgers and Prices* (*Yale Near Eastern Researches* 8; Yale).

1997 *Life in the Ancient Near East* (New Haven).

W. von Soden

1952 *Grundriss der Akkadischen Grammatik* (*Analecta Orientalia* 33; Rome).

E. Sollberger

1954-56 "Sur la chronologie des rois d'Ur et quelques problemes connexes" *AfO* 17, 10–48.

L. Speleers

1917 *Catalogue des intailles et empreintes orientales des Musées Royaux du Cinquantenaire* (Bruxelles).

P. Steinkeller

1981 "The Renting of Fields in Early Mesopotamia and the development of the concept of "Interest" in Sumerian," *Journal of the Economic and Social History of the Orient* (*JESHO)* 24, 113–145.

1982 "On the Reading and Meaning of igi-kár and gúrum (IGI.GAR)," *ASJ* 4, 149–151.

1987 "The Administration and Economic Organization of the Ur III State: The Core and the Periphery," in McG. Gibson & R. Biggs, eds., *The Organization of Power* (*Studies in Ancient Oriental Civilization* 46; Chicago)

1987 "The Foresters of Umma: Toward a Definition of Ur III Labor," *American Oriental Series (AOS)* 68, 73–115.

1988 "The date of Gudea and his dynasty," *JCS* 40, 47–53.

1993 "Early Political Development in Mesopotamia, and the Origins of the Sargonic Empire," in M. Liverani, ed., *Akkad. The First World Empire. Structure, Ideology, Traditions* (Padua) 107–129.

1996 "The Organisation of Crafts in third Millennium Babylonia: The Case of Potters," *AoF* 23, 232–253.

2001 "New Light on the Hydrology and Topography of Southern Babylonia in the Third Millennium," *ZA* 91, 22–84.

2003 "An Ur III Manuscript of the Sumerian King List," in W. Sallaberger, K. Volk, A. Zgoll, eds., *Literatur, Politik und Recht in Mesopotamien. Festschrift für Claus Wilcke* (Wiesbaden) 267–292.

M. Stepien

1996 *Animal Husbandry in the Ancient Near East* (Bethesda).

M. Stolper

1982 "On the Dynasty of Šimaški and the Early sukkalmaḫ's," *ZA* 72, 42–67.

M. P. Streck

2001 "Das Onomastikon der Beamten am neubabylonischen Ebabbar-Tempel in Sippar," *ZA* 91, 110–119.

V. V. Struve

1969 "Some new data on the organization of Labour and on Social structure in Sumer during the reign of the third dynasty of Ur," (originally written in Russian in 1949), in I. Diakonoff, ed., *Ancient Mesopotamia: Socio-Economic History, A Collection of Studies by Soviet Scholars* (Moscow) 127–172.

M. Such-Guitiérrez

2001 "Die Prinzessin Meištarān," *Aula Orientalis* 19, 87–108.

C. Suter

2000 *Gudea's Temple Building* (Groningen).

F. Thureau-Dangin

1910 "Notes assyriologiques, I: La tablette S. 3; II: La duree du regne de Dun-gi; III: Gu-de-a, gendre d'Ur-Ba-u; IV: Zag-úa; V: La trouvaille de Drehem," *RA* 7, 179–191.

M. Touzalin

1982 *L'administration palatiale à l'époque de la troisième dynastie d'Ur. Textes inédits du Musée d'Alep*. Thèse de doctorat de troisième cycle, soutenue à l'université de Tours, Sous la direction d'Olivier Rouault (15 décembre 1982)

P. Van Den Berghe and G. Mesher

1980 "Royal Incest and Inclusive Fitness," *American Ethnologist*, Vol. 7, Issue 2, 300–317.

G. van Driel

1999/2000 "The Size of Institutional Umma," *AfO* 46-47, 80–91.

M. van de Mieroop

1999/2000 "An Accountant's Nightmare: the Drafting of a Year's Summary," *AfO* 46-47, 111–129.

C.-A. Vincente

1995 "The Tall Leilan Recension of the Sumerian King List," *ZA* 85, 234–270.

H. Waetzoldt

1972 *Untersuchungen zur Neusumerischen Textilindustrie* (Rome).

1975 Review of "Gertrud Faber-Flügge, Der Mythos ,Inanna und Enki"..." in Bibliotheca Orientalis 32, 382 - 384.

1995 "Änderung von Siegellegenden als Reflex der 'großen Politik'," in U. Finkbeiner, ed., *Boehmer Fs* (Mainz) 659–664.

Aa. Westenholz

1999 "The Old Akkadian Period, History and Culture," in P. Attinger et al., eds., *Mesopotamien, Akkade-Zeit und Ur III Zeit* (*OBO* 160/3; Freiburg).

M. Weber

1968 *On Charisma and Institution Building, Selected Papers, Edited and with an Introduction by S. N. Eisenstadt* (Chicago & London).

R. Whiting

1976 "Tiš-Atal of Nineveh and Babati, Uncle of Šu-Sin," *JCS* 28, 173–182.

C. Wilcke

1971/75 "Zum Königtum in der Ur III-Zeit," in P. Garelli ed., *Le palais et la royautée* (= *Rencontre* 19: Paris) 177–232.

1988 "Die sumerische Königsliste und erzählte Vergangenheit," in, J. Von Ungern-Sternberg, ed., *Vergangenheit in mündlicher Überlieferung* (Stuttgart) 113–140.

1989 "Genealogical and Geographical Thought in the Sumerian King List," in: H. Behrens et al., ed., *DUMU-É-DUB-BA-A* (= *Fs. Sjöberg*; Philadelphia) 557–571.

Wu Yuhong

1995 "High-ranking "Scribes" and Intellectual Governors during the Akkadian and Ur III Periods," *Journal of Ancient Civilizations* 10, 123

Yu. Yusifov

1976 "The Problem of the Order of Succession in Elam again," *Wirtschaft und Gesellschaft im alten Vorderasien* (Budapest) 321–331.

R. Zettler

1987 "Administration of the Temple of Inanna at Nippur under the Third Dynasty of Ur," in McG. Gibson & R. Biggs, eds., *The Organization of Power* (*SAOC* 46; Chicago) 101–114.

INDEXES

Members of the royal family and the imperial elite:

Umma personal names:

Geographical names:

Index of terms:

Texts cited in full

Texts referenced